Literature, Religion, and Postsecular Studies
Lori Branch, Series Editor

Conspicuous Bodies

Provincial Belief and the
Making of Joyce and Rushdie

Jean Kane

THE OHIO STATE UNIVERSITY PRESS
COLUMBUS

Copyright © 2014 by The Ohio State University.
All rights reserved.

Library of Congress Cataloging-in-Publication Data
Kane, Jean, 1955–
  Conspicuous bodies : provincial belief and the making of Joyce and Rushdie / Jean Kane. — First edition.
     pages cm. — (Literature, religion, and postsecular studies)
  Includes bibliographical references and index.
  ISBN 978-0-8142-1260-8 (hardback) — ISBN 0-8142-1260-3 (cloth) — ISBN 978-0-8142-9364-5 (cd-rom)
 1. Joyce, James, 1882–1941—Criticism and interpretation. 2. Joyce, James, 1882–1941—Religion. 3. Rushdie, Salman, 1947—Criticism and interpretation. 4. Rushdie, Salman, 1947—Religion. 5. Faith in literature. 6. Human body in literature. 7. Human body—Religious aspects. 8. Identity (Psychology) in literature. I. Title. II. Title: Provincial belief and the making of Joyce and Rushdie. PR6019.O9Z66958 2014
  823'.912—dc23
                              2013047490

Cover design by Laurence J. Nozik
Text design by Juliet Williams
Type set in Adobe Minion Pro

∞ The paper used in this publication meets the minimum requirements of the American National Standard for Information Sciences—Permanence of Paper for Printed Library Materials. ANSI Z39.49–1992.

9 8 7 6 5 4 3 2 1

For Raymond

Contents

Acknowledgments ix

Introduction 1

Chapter 1 Joyce's Conversion and the Counterdiscipline of Drink 8

Chapter 2 The Canonization of Salman Rushdie:
Mythic *Midnight's Children* and Hindu-Muslim Embodiment 41

Chapter 3 Spirits Discipline *Ulysses* 69

Chapter 4 Muslim Simulation and the Limits of the "Star Text" 97

Chapter 5 Embodied Panic: Modernist "Religion" in the
Controversies over *Ulysses* and *The Satanic Verses* 120

Chapter 6 The Religion of Celebrity 141

Notes 159
Bibliography 184
Index 201

Acknowledgments

Writing feels like a solitary, concentrated enterprise, but is actually a noisy conversation conducted over many years. The work of imaginative writers and their interpreters joined with teachers, mentors, and colleagues in the making of this book. C. Clifford Flanigan, of the Comparative Literature Department of Indiana University, plunged me into *Ulysses* during my freshman year of college, and I would like to remember him, a teacher of passionate intensity, for sparking my interest in Joyce. Michael Levenson, Stephen Arata, and Teju Olaniyan shepherded this project through its first stages, Karen Robertson its later ones. I am immensely grateful to these luminous intellects and generous people for their help with the conception and execution of the manuscript. My thanks go as well to my past and present colleagues in the English Department at Vassar College, particularly to Tomo Hattori, Laura Yow, Julie Park, Heesok Chang, and Robert DeMaria, and to colleagues elsewhere, Helene Meyers, Guy Raffia, and Elisabeth Frost. William Germano gave me insightful advice about shaping the project. Sandy Crooms of The Ohio State University Press has been a spirited and humane guide, an editor among editors. I thank her deeply for her work with me. The colleagues and associates working with me have also been adept and generous. My thanks go to editors Eugene O'Connor, Lindsay Martin, and Taralee Cyphers as well as to Rebecca Bender and Scott Smiley.

My parents, Joan A. Williams Kane and Raymond F. Kane, as well as my siblings, Raymond J. Kane, James C. Kane, Joan A. Kane, and Christopher G.

Kane, deserve recognition here, as does Jim Kimsey. Judy Nichols, Bill Nichols, Nancy Nichols, and Jannay Morrow have nourished and supported me. Thomas P. Lukas also helped me to produce this book.

Finally, I would like to thank the Sisters of Providence of St. Mary of the Woods College for their role in bringing this manuscript to publication.

Introduction

In a 2009 story on National Public Radio's *All Things Considered*, psychotherapist Jim Cates spoke about treating Amish adolescents. Cates adapted his techniques to help youth whose identity formation differs "fundamentally" from that of his typical clients, who strive for independence based on their accomplishments. "What [Amish youth] are going to do is some kind of manual labor, which doesn't really identify who they are; it's just something they do to make money," Cates said. "If they're going to be Amish, they're going to get married and stay married for the rest of their lives. So they're not individuating. It's not about 'who am I going to bloom into,' it's about becoming part of a larger group." His Amish clients feel awkward focusing on themselves, as they belong to a culture that regards "self-disclosure as prideful." He often meets them with their families, at home, and encourages them to talk about others as a route to articulating their emotional difficulties.[1]

Cates's work with a contemporary American subculture illuminates my focus on persons who differ in striking ways from the "individual," just as his viewpoint highlights the problems in describing them. His characterization of Amish adolescents shares with many theories of the contemporary an assumption of the "individual" as a normative base even as deviations from the subject position are being articulated. In Anglo-American literary criticism, religion acts as a locus classicus of such foundationalism: the contemporary worshipping subject is understood through the somatic, psychic, and cognitive premises of the individual who emerged in concert with liberal

Christianity in the late nineteenth century. Persons formed by other modes of belief are routinely erased or distorted by the premises of the Christian formation buried in the universalism of "religion." This book distinguishes such subjects, and the practices that generate them, from what Certeau calls the "strategy" of individualism.[2] In disinterring disciplined spiritual agents from the hermeneutic "religion," I aim to show the crucial role of minority spiritual practices in modelling the bodies devised by cosmopolitan modernists and their successors. Disciplinary belief, long understood as aesthetically generative but physically and intellectually repressive, in fact also *produces* the somatic knowledge that centrally informs modernist representation. I trace the genealogy of anthropological religion in the twentieth century through the careers of James Joyce and Salman Rushdie, paradigmatic "masters" of modern and postmodern experiment. Joyce and Rushdie use their insider experience of spiritual techniques to reimagine bodily epistemes, yet they read these productions from an external vantage based on theological, "religious" premises. Under the sign of oppression, spiritual regimes enhance and enlarge the capacities of the free "individual" in the texts as well as in the public profiles of the writers. The entrenched opposition between a gothic religion and a liberatory art actually reveals the challenges that performative agency has posed to Western understandings of subject formation—depictions that elicit panic over the imagined dissolution of physical and psychic boundaries.

While the anthropological borrowings of modernists—Eliot, Lawrence, Forster, and Joyce premier among them—have been amply explored,[3] critics have until recently paid little attention to the historical premises of religion as an analytical category. In recent decades work on modernist literary production has focused, after Andreas Huyssen[4] and exemplified by Lawrence Rainey,[5] on the professional and commercial strategies and material practices that generated the seemingly autonomous art object and its creator.[6] Critics such as James Buzard, John Marx, Jed Esty, and Ian Baucom[7] have textured the criticism of the last twenty years in examining the finer transactions among the British imperium, English nationality, and colonial formations. I follow a different but related plot through a modernism that moves between auto-ethnographic and ethnographic positions, cosmopolitan and provincial identifications, insider knowledge and outsider display of identity. Rather than understanding religion as an analogue—for language, for commodity,[8] or for other symbolic systems—I focus on the meanings of belief that are assumed in such comparisons. Joyce and Rushdie claim spiritually disciplined bodies that authenticate and animate colonial and postcolonial identities in the act of surpassing and objectifying them. These formal and professional maneuvers would not be possible without the framework of a "religion" that sits comfortably with the sedimented structures of modern and contemporary individualism, and that continues to freeze and misread other modes of belief and techniques of embodiment, as well as the epistemic premises with which they interact.

"Belief's transformation into pastness is, in fundamental respects, the narrative of Western culture's birth into the modern," signifying both quaintness and authenticity, says Jenny Franchot.[9] Modes of disciplinary belief have exemplified not just anachronism, but archaism. The association of regulated practice and countermodernity arose in part from modal differences between Christianity and orthopractic systems such Judaism and Islam. As a dominantly "orthodox" religion, Christianity has from its origins placed doctrine and theology, rather than somatic moral techniques, at the core of belief.[10] But these differences were greatly amplified by changes within institutional Christianity itself. Beginning in the eighteenth century, Christian theology began to move the basis of belief away from the metaphysical and epistemological. According to Claude Welch, this shift "meant a new kind of self-conscious and systematic recognition of the involvement of the religious subject—his point of view, his cognitive act, his interest, his willing and his choosing, with which theological reflection has to begin. Consciousness of the truth of the religious object was peculiarly one with self-consciousness."[11] By the last third of the nineteenth century the emphasis on sentiment accompanied political developments in Europe and America that privileged the subject's civil relation to the state over a religious identity: rather than worldly and public, belief became a secondary affiliation, a content assigned to an interior space of the individual citizen.[12] Liberal Christianity retreated from a distinct, formative role in the worldly sphere. John Corrigan elaborates: "The nineteenth-century Protestant mythology of the autonomous human feeling and thinking subject in fact rested on an assumption about the complementarity of body and soul, of an inner subjective world and a mechanical, objective outer world somehow conjoined." As a result, the "self" was understood to fit both models, whose relations were largely undefined and ambiguous, as is reflected in formulations such as Emerson's "double-consciousness."[13]

The discipline of *Religionwissenschaft*, or comparative religion, emerged during this period,[14] bearing with it the premises of the new dominant form of Christianity. Judaism and Islam proceed from different premises: in their "orthopractic" mode, disciplinary practice is integral to the disposition and episteme of moral formation.[15] Orthopraxy does not strongly separate emotion from knowledge, thought from act, or particular from communal flesh; practice generates knowledge as a moral, somatic, and affective totality.[16] Just as, in Judith Butler's analysis, acts *produce* rather than merely express sex,[17] spiritual regimes aim to produce physicality as an "ability," a "potentiality," or a "power," Talal Asad explains.[18]

Asad persuasively argues that these changes fundamentally shaped the anthropological category of "religion" in ways that obscure other cultural histories and modes of spirituality.[19] Joyce and Rushdie accordingly read performative techniques through the lens of theology, ritual, and symbol, the characteristics of anthropological "religion." But unlike other European modernists, who revitalized metropolitan conventions by turning to the "pre-modern" materials of non-Western cultures, or even American expatriates, who shaped cosmopolitan aesthetics after their provincial roots,[20] Joyce and Rushdie claimed the archaic through their own nativist beliefs, calling on the disciplinary modes of nineteenth-century Irish Catholic and contemporary subcontinental Muslim practice, and later drew them into relation with Judaism or Hinduism. Both writers could operate as indigenes of their national and religious cultures—themselves to varying degrees saturated with Protestant British influence—and as cosmopolitan Europeans. The "secondary" capitals of Dublin and Bombay assert the urban over the pastoral in the writers' national identities, at the same time that these locales function as provincial literary terrain from the perspective of European capitals. The "provincial" spiritual bodies of Irish Catholicism and Indian Islam similarly act as pivots in the authors' public images as insider-outsiders. Rushdie, raised as an upper-class Muslim in a newly independent India, lived primarily in England from the age of fourteen. As has been well established, Joyce lies on the cusp of the imperial and the colonial, born into an Ireland politically and linguistically incorporated into Britain. Often less precisely articulated is his historical position in relation to the particularities of the Christian formation in Ireland. Turn-of-the-century Irish Catholicism was characterized not only by its primacy in political identity formation, but also by modal differences. Though Christian, and therefore formed by the orthodox and increasingly expressive religious formation that I have described, Irish-Catholic belief was from the mid-nineteenth century more strongly embedded in both the disciplined practice and the worldly identity that European Christianity had largely abstracted or shed. So often represented as archaic residue, the epistemic and somatic character of belief resulted from the unique status and trajectory of Ireland as a European, Christian colony and from the specific historical trauma of the famine. Ireland's "disciplining" also occurred in concert with, and as a result of, the Catholic hierarchy's "ultramontane," or absolutist turn in reaction to democratic and liberal movements of the mid-century, as Geert Lernout shows.[21]

This book follows the plot of Joyce's use of Irish-Catholic orthopraxy from its proto-genesis in *Dubliners* (1914) and its representation in *Ulysses* (1922) to its revision and final baffling in the Muslim praxis depicted by Rushdie. The aporia between cosmopolitan postmodernism and Indian transcendence that appears in *The Satanic Verses* (1988) resolves in the exchange of spirituality for celebrity in *The Ground beneath Her Feet* (1999). Initially received as cosmopolitan, both authors pushed their religious and national ties to the forefront of their fiction and its reception. I set these profiles against the bodily discourses of intertwined spiritual and organic distress that their fiction employs. *Dubliners* and *Midnight's Children* (1980) recode the "individual" as a presumed somatic and subjective structure. In *Dubliners*, habitual intemperance renders the spiritual conversion narrative concrete, as drinkers "fall" into a mere embodiment and out of agency. The habit is depicted as deeply tied to the sensual repression of Irish-Catholic men, but *Dubliners* ultimately colludes with this repression, even as the counterdisciplinary agency of liquor models communal mobility. *Midnight's Children* privileges a Vedic body that negotiates the clinical "European" and the traditional "Indian" models of experience through a sustained conceit of their opposition. This spiritual-medical conception of the subject as tenuously tied to a porous, communal body differs structurally from the relations presumed by Western individualism, the ground of "postmodern" and "magic realist" as well as "exoticist" readings of the novel.

Ulysses (1922) and *The Satanic Verses* (1988) move fully into somatic representations based on the orthopractic spiritual model. Both novels realize experimental depictions of the person through the explicit protocols of spiritual practice, which generates epistemology and collective agency from actions. These somatic and epistemic technologies join with machinic ones to open and exhibit provincial bodies. In the third chapter I argue that the orthopractic symbolic of Judaism allows for the imagination of generative Irish-Catholic embodiment. The novel embraces the productive capacities of disciplinary practice and casts chronic drink as the auratic and degenerate "blood" of the Irish-Catholic father, who, animated by material "spirits," realizes the capacity for aesthetic generation. In the succeeding chapter, I present *The Satanic Verses* as the culmination of orthopractic technique and religious appropriation of it, through the occupation of the master signifier of Islam. Vedic medicine gives way to visual technology as the medium of somatic incorporation. The "technical" production of *Verses*' Muslim migrants by spiritually saturated Indian popular film supplies a corporate, fluid, and mobile embodiment that remains tied to an "Indian" bodily syntax and allows for the staging of the disciplined Muslim body as physically merged with Muhammad's.

Ulysses and *The Satanic Verses* signify more extravagant responses to the metropolitan literary appetite for exposure of minority religious bodies. Chapter five demonstrates that the controversies engendered by the novels turn not on "religion" against "art," but rather on distinct models of personhood. The controversies that the novels provoked set bodies depicted as externally governed productions against "the" body as an autonomous, self-governed space. Regulated agency, connected to the somatic and psychic disciplines of "archaic" religion (as well as of machinic technology in the debate over *Ulysses*), was experienced as an assault on sovereign individualism. I examine *Ulysses'* early popular reception to demonstrate that the novel created panic by threatening the "strategy" of individualism. Through the somatic technologies that he employs, Joyce "subjects" readers to their own bodies, canceling an agency felt to depend on an oscillating relationship between merging with and mastering physical embodiment. The terms established by the *Ulysses* controversy remained virtually unchanged in debate over *The Satanic Verses*, though the assignation of positions is diametrically opposite, as the individual, produced by the civil body of Anglo-England, panicked before its violent subjection to a totalized, repressive Islam. In both cases, minority religions functioned as frozen signifiers of dictatorial authority, whose display elicited panic over the loss of personhood, understood solely as the embodied individual of the West.

In the wake of these "scandals," popular celebrity relieved Joyce and Rushdie of the need to represent the minority religious body as entirely coincident with a particular geographic territory. The writers themselves became signifiers not only of literary prestige but also of the surpassing of disciplinary oppression. Censorship, accompanied in Rushdie's case by a very real threat to his life, acted as the repressive force against which the authors more widely asserted their artistic freedom from embodiment itself. If, as Jaffe argues, the substitution of texts for bodies is characteristic of modernist discourse, the texts come to function as the authors' material vehicles.[22] The "technopoetics" of *Finnegans Wake* dramatize modernity as a similarly diffuse, mobile production of the writer's body and the writer's body as a production of contemporary media. In Rushdie's formulation of this nexus, celebrity becomes indistinguishable from migrancy. In *The Ground beneath Her Feet*, the representational barrage acts as a particular characteristic of metropolitan celebrity, which is entirely dispersed and uncontrollable. The contrast in the significations of Joyce's and Rushdie's celebrity underscores the threat of virtual simulation and the "feedback loop" of mass communication to the Joycean legacy claimed by Rushdie. While Joyce remained—and to this day, as I would argue, to large extent still remains—in control of his public representation, *The Ground beneath her Feet* registers the impossibility of maintaining such direction when the writer himself has become a simulacrum.

Modernism in this reading describes a set of strategies practiced throughout the twentieth century, a view forwarded by critics such Aaron Jaffe[23] and Rebecca Walkowitz.[24] But I focus on an anthropological strategy that persists, largely undisturbed, in contemporary Western criticism. The reading of orthopraxy through the "orthodox" and expressive lens of (liberal, Christian) religion finally brackets embodiment as a source of epistemic knowledge and performative mobility, insisting instead on understanding worshipping bodies as symbolic, mimetic vehicles of affect and adherents as abjected by behavioral and intellectual constraints. Religion remains crucial to modernist practice as the sine qua non of countermodernity. While Anglo-American critics have embraced the emerging minority literatures of the last decades—particularly transnational and postcolonial authors whose work enters into the metropolitan marketplace—we also continue to cling to old habits of reception and critical practice. As Gauri Viswanathan observes, the construction of "religion" as a practice of reading cultural repression, productive only in the aesthetic recapture of theological figures,[25] empowers the (metropolitan) author function at the expense of more nuanced responses to literary representations. Minority literary productions, as well as our public discourse, call for more considered responses to other formations of the "person" and other productions of knowledge, for a genuine encounter with the difficult and compelling issues of difference that they pose.

1

Joyce's Conversion and the Counterdiscipline of Drink

"While religion remains largely the incarnation of an atemporal notion or indestructible essence, it is, more prosaically put, only the result of a discriminatory act performed in the West and there alone," Daniel Dubuisson contends.[1] The philosopher radically dismantles "religion" as an autonomous sphere of experience and a universal domain of knowledge, locating its roots in classical concepts revised by Paul and Augustine. I open with Dubuisson's critique because it starkly illuminates the formation of religion as an anthropological category, itself "the historical product of discursive processes."[2] Critics of twentieth-century literature have been slow to attend to religion's foundationalism, in spite of the explosion of "postcolonial," "transnational," and other minority works that foreground spirituality in diverse modes.[3] Discarded as a preoccupation of New Critical aesthetics and structuralist master codes, belief appears as a topic of interest in relation to institutional-political histories, magic realist myth, or economic analogue when it bears upon literary production at all. This book follows a major plot of religion by recalling the bodies that it has misrepresented or ignored. I illuminate the use and eclipse of nondominant (Western) practices in modernism and its late-century descendants, concentrating on writers who depict spirituality as essential to their aesthetic, inherent in their subject matter, and crucial to their cultural identities. The careers of James Joyce and Salman Rushdie turn on the hermeneutic religion and its associated binaries, even as their texts produce bodies formed after other modes of belief. Unlike their cosmopolitan peers, Joyce and Rushdie represent the worshipping "other" from the inside, their depictions informed by direct experiential knowledge, while they also occupy the more conventional ethnographic observer position. As Robert Crawford persuasively argues, modernism is a "provincial phenomenon" and manipulation of the outsider position "a quintessential provincial strategy" deployed by Scottish and American writers.[4] Crawford, like James Buzard and others, characterizes such a posture as the "insider's outsideness" and connects it to the authorizing procedures of anthropology.[5] I argue that the provincial spiritual body acts as a significant pivot of the insider-outside position. Joyce and Rushdie generate bodies modelled on their past spiritual practices while they simultaneously read these forms externally.[6] The inside-outside vantage allows them to surpass the dictates of religious practice while using its agency to enrich the individuals that they exemplify. The author gains power by perpetually rising from a spiritual, provincial body to which he must remain tethered. Joyce and the "sub-Joycean"[7] Rushdie depict provincial agents by orchestrating a dual matrix: that of the individual, based on the "strategy" of individualism and its given bodily organization, and that of the person, devised after the model of disciplined practice. The urge toward bodily reformulation adapts spiritual techniques that make an epistemology from the regulated practices of a community. I show that countermodern religion—cast as an intellectual and somatic pedagogy and set against an aesthetic of innovative performativity—characterizes the modernism that continues to structure contemporary cosmopolitan fiction.

If this technique suggests an anthropological apprehension of "native" colonial or ex-colonial bodies as signs or performances of cultural totality,[8] religion defines it. "The boundary line of religion and culture at the turn of the twenty-first century is a major site of intellectual action and interaction," proclaims Susan Mizruchi in her introduction to the 2001 collection *Religion and Cultural Studies*.[9] She marks the end of an era in which "historians and literary critics interested in 'culture' in the modern sense—as an intellectual category with a history—tended to shy away from religion as a field of inquiry."[10] While it is true that "religion" has in recent years enjoyed more theoretical attention through "postsecular" and "posthumanist" studies, the very categories that the Mizruchi collection uses show the continued need for deep historical investigation of the premises of religion, secularism, and culture. "Only through historical analysis can one deconstruct the commonplace dichotomy of a supposedly secular and modern West and a religious and backward Rest," state Peter van der Veer and Hartmut Lehmann, who, like Gauri Viswanathan in literary studies, attribute the universalized conceptualization of "nation" and "religion" to Western expansion. Highlighting the idea's roots in eighteenth-century Christian theism and European philosophy,[11] Talal Asad, Russell McCutcheon, Tomoko Masuzawa, Jonathan Z. Smith, Michel Despland, and Richard King, among others, have forwarded controversial critiques of religious studies as a discipline.[12] Its founding premises bear upon the self-definition of Western culture, which understands "religion" as synonymous with doctrine, and the "individual" as coincident with the person who accepts or rejects it. "We seem to be living in a world mapped—though not very neatly—in terms of so many varieties of religion, which sometimes overlap, converge and syncretize, and often conflict with one another," says Masuzawa. "It is presumed, moreover, that religion is one of the most significant . . . factors characterizing each individual society, and that this is particularly true in 'premodern' or otherwise non-Western societies."[13]

The mode and development of Christianity permeates such assumptions. A dominantly "orthodox" religion, Christianity has from its institutional origins placed doctrine and theology, rather than somatic moral techniques, at the core of belief.[14] Post-Enlightenment Christianity moved its basis further toward sentiment and experience[15] to compensate for its loss of epistemological privilege, metaphysical authority, and institutional power, "shift[ing] . . . the weight of religion more and more onto the moods and motivations of the individual believer," Asad notes.[16] Friedrich Schleiermacher (1768–1834) stands as an exemplary figure in this genealogy, for his influence on mainstream Christian thought in the nineteenth century and for his *Glaubenslehre* as a formulation of knowledge about it. Like Coleridge, Schleiermacher emphasized the self as the ground of epistemic truth in (German) Protestant theology, so that, in Welch's description, "consciousness of the truth was particularly one with self-consciousness."[17] Schleiermacher posited an independent basis for religion and theology, at the same time that he sought to include them in the structure of *Wissenschaft*:[18] *Gefühl*, or intuition and feeling, in contrast to "thinking or acting," constitutes the "essence" of religion, which, he asserts, "maintains its own sphere and its own character only by completely removing itself from the sphere and character of speculation as well as from that of praxis."[19] Andrew Dole corrects misreadings of Schleiermacher in the Anglo-American academy, which present religion as an "abstract and ahistorical condition of human subjectivity" devoid of its context in social life and practical cultural embodiment.[20] In this, Corrigan contends, Schleiermacher's "complex notion of the 'feeling of absolute dependence' in the 'embodied self' was an attempt to locate the self precisely on the border of organic existence and the thinking and feeling 'I.'"[21] Nonetheless, Schleiermacher forwarded a dominant tendency in Anglo-American Christianity to locate spirituality in the interior and to reorient theological knowledge to the affective sphere. Politically and experientially, the private domain came to encompass "a variety of religious distinctions that had no place in political society," according to Viswanathan, who focuses on nineteenth-century England. Disarticulated from legal structures, religious belief became an adjunct to rather than a foundation of identity, enabling minorities to form a primary bond to the state. Secularization split identity "on the axis of citizenship and subjecthood" by treating belief as private and appropriating to the state "reason, logic, and evidence."[22] Thus both Western law and Christian institutions moved religious identity and religious knowledge to a space in the formal structure of the private, affective "individual" produced by secular social and political processes. As Viswanathan establishes in her groundbreaking study, this change contrasted with British imperial practices, which intensified rather than loosened the imbrications of political, communal, and sectarian identities in colonies such as India, where converts to Hinduism or Christianity were still classified legally according to their religion of origin.[23]

Unlike liberal Christianity, Islam, Judaism, and some forms of Catholic monasticism base belief on disciplinary practice, which is understood as integral to the disposition and episteme of moral formation.[24] "Orthopractic" or "instrumental" modes of belief do not strongly separate emotion from knowledge, thought from act, or particular from communal flesh; rather practice generates knowledge as a moral, somatic, and affective totality, training the adherent in concert with the community. The "orthodox"—that is, doctrinally oriented—and affective formation of secularist Christianity assumes a corporeality, through which sentiment and belief are expressed in relation to an accepted theology. Praxis instead creates a totality of corporeality, knowledge, and belief through acts performed in the context of the community as a means of regulation.[25] Just as, in Judith Butler's analysis, acts *produce* rather than merely express sex,[26] disciplined practice aims to produce physicality as an "ability," a "potentiality," or a "power," Asad explains.[27] He cites the *umma* of Islam as an example of praxis and the model of personhood that it creates: while members are "self-governing" as agents, they are not "autonomous."[28]

The *modal* difference indicated by the contrast between "orthodoxy" and "orthopraxy" is somewhat confusing, because it runs counter to the more common understanding of "orthodox" as a strict or originary version of a belief. Here, in relation to belief mode, however, the distinction refers to the primary *type* or *medium* of belief—that is, crudely put, whether it is grounded in doctrine or in physical practice.

Turn-of-the-century Irish Catholicism sits on the cusp of this modal contrast. Though Christian, and therefore formed by the orthodox and increasingly expressive religious formation that I have described, Irish-Catholic belief was from the mid-nineteenth century more strongly embedded in both the disciplined practice and the worldly identity that European Christianity had largely abstracted or shed. In 1908, Michael J. F. McCarthy declared that alone among European countries, Ireland had not undergone secularization.[29] So often represented as archaic residue, this religious formation resulted from the unique status and trajectory of Ireland as a European, Christian colony, from the specific historical trauma of the famine, and from the Roman hierarchy's increasing centralization and hardening anti-liberalism.[30] Though critics have often stressed post-famine *British* attempts to "rationalize" folk practices associated with Roman Catholicism,[31] similar efforts *within* the ultramontane Church significantly re-formed the bodily habitus of Irish Catholics. S. J. Connolly observes that the policy of the Church in post-famine Ireland contributed to the intensification rather than the weakening of Catholicism's power during the latter half of the nineteenth century, when an "effective social discipline" began to take hold.[32] David Lloyd similarly states that the social, sensory, and spiritual "disciplines" of this posttraumatic period produced "a new physical economy of the Irish body."[33] Writing in the 1970s, Lawrence J. Taylor still notes, "Bodily control is, from the earliest days, an absolutely central feature of any Irish-Catholic's life and the conceptual, discursive realms of religion are encountered in the context of that very physical experience."[34] Somatic regulation formed what Marcel Mauss calls a "bodily habitus," made by corporeal and social techniques.[35]

Joyce directly represents spiritual praxis in *A Portrait* when the adolescent Stephen privately undertakes a program of sensory, affective, and intellectual reform. The narrator reports: "Each of his senses was brought under a rigorous discipline. In order to mortify the sense of sight he made it his rule to walk in the street with downcast eyes, glancing neither to right nor left and never behind him. His eyes shunned every encounter with the eyes of women." The narrative proceeds to chronicle the ways in which Stephen "mortifie[s]" each sense in his daily routine.[36] These physical disciplines are accompanied by devotional activities and meditations: "Every part of his day, divided by what he regarded now as the duties of his station in life, circled about its own centre of spiritual energy."[37] Joyce emphasizes the repressive function of these practices through his very means of representation—a list rather than a dramatization—as well as through their failure to produce emotional control. Katherine Mullin reads the scene as inflected by purity movements' "emphasis upon the self-regulation of the wayward body through Catholic ritual" as Stephen's "self-discipline substitutes and tropes for masturbation";[38] Christine van Boheemen understands his "education" in corporeal suffering as a narrative project of "desensitization of the body ... to shift the locus of reality from physical selfhood to language."[39] Yet Stephen's self-imposed regime of intricate masochisms more explicitly represents the mechanism of orthopraxis in its aim to recast moral disposition through a program of physical acts. That is, Stephen trains not only his libido, but also his complete sensory energies, to cultivate his spiritual capacity.

Sullivan contends that Clongowes Wood "immersed" Joyce in a "religious atmosphere" that was "almost monastic in its intensity"; its "discipline" and "psychological impact" permanently shaped him.[40] The orthopraxy of late nineteenth-century Irish Catholicism suggested in *A Portrait* centrally informs the bodily technologies that *Ulysses* registers in the symbolic of Judaism, as I discuss in chapter three. But Joyce's reformulation of the individual associated with the dominant, liberal Christian formation begins with *Dubliners,* which anticipates such techniques through the representation of alcohol's counterdisciplinary agency. The collection displays its distance from repressed provincial Irish-Catholic men through a self-conscious scrutiny associated with anthropology and, in Joyce's characterization, with a medical diagnosis of native spiritual distress. Chronic drunkenness deeply circumscribes the power of the individual subject as well as his community, which participates in a dynamic of willed dispossession through evasion and denial. But in his portraits of chronic intemperance Joyce also imagines a material-spiritual substance that dissolves the particularity of individual subjects while acquiring somatic and psychological power. Here I build on Garry Leonard's contention that Joyce's revision of subjectivity begins in *Dubliners,*[41] as well as on Kershner's view of the collection as discursively performative[42]: I contend that the stories start to recast the individual through their anticipation of *bodily* performativity. The organic and political reading of the Dublin figures as merely oppressed accords with the image of Joyce as a writer hovering, like his character James Duffy, at "a little distance" from the provincial bodies that he diagnoses, more "outside" than "inside" in his perspective. His medical gaze acts analogously to a theological reading, as both methods externally represent a subject rendered in important ways invisible. A sardonic mirror of prescribed physical practice, the habit of intemperance finally effects a resistance to theological reading, shown through a somatic vocabulary that encodes moral and psychic disorganization. Or perhaps it would be more precise to say that these emblematic Dubliners submit to symbolic readings of their habits—the kind of reading performed by the narrative gaze as well as by later critics—but the observed would rather destroy themselves than reveal who they are or what they know.

Dubliners at Birth and Christening

Taking issue with both New Critical and poststructuralist assumptions, John Nash observes: "Joyce consistently characterises an audience as a 'body' divided by the very act of reading; to imply a cultural 'fit' between Joyce, Paris, and his 'demanded' audience is highly dubious. It is disconcertingly close to the colonialist position to imply that Joyce's 'appropriate audience' would somehow later be 'achieved' in Europe . . . and that an Irish reading public was necessarily forsaken or nonexistent."[43] I extend Nash's argument by attending to representations of the divided body as a performative *spiritual* one that affords different interpretations based on the appropriate mode of belief. Given that "reading is implicated in bodily needs," and the specific conditions of reading "resonate with somatic effects,"[44] Joyce struggles to reconcile the divisions within his own depictions of provincial embodiment. Spiritual practices supply an important route for establishing his postures in relation to Irish-Catholic bodies. The perception of a provincial audience began with the stories of *Dubliners*, but the depiction of this audience as incommensurate with Joyce's artistry did not, for the simple reason that early notices did not treat an Irish audience as distinct. Depicted as realistic or naturalistic prose in keeping with the metropolitan literature of the previous century, *Dubliners* did not in fact register as a dominantly Irish, much less a Catholic, volume with its first readers, in spite of the initial reception of some individual stories.[45] The author's profile changed dramatically in this regard when *Ulysses* appeared. In 1925 the Irish literary scholar Ernest Boyd complained about the accuracy of Joyce's strong characterization as a cosmopolitan European writer. While Boyd was not alone in claiming Joyce for Ireland, he did so unconventionally, by interrogating the binary of "provincial" and "cosmopolitan" so important to the "the process of making Joyce a coterie author." An older generation of Irish writers, including Yeats, had also been vilified by popular Irish publications such as the *Catholic Bulletin* and the *Irish World* for being "bestial, filthy-minded, and blasphemous," but, Boyd asserts, Joyce was often distinguished from them as uniquely repudiated by his country and church.[46] In his 1923 revision of *Irish Literary Renaissance* (1916), the scholar similarly complains that "the syllogism seems to be that J. M. Synge and James Stephens and W. B. Yeats are Irish writers, therefore James Joyce is not."[47]

Boyd's comments—directed primarily against Valéry Larbaud[48] but equally accurate depictions of the views promoted by Ezra Pound,[49] Jane Heap, and Joyce himself—point to the careful shaping of Joyce's reputation through insistence on Irish parochialism. Joyce and his circle deployed the category of the "provincial"[50] ethnologically in order to establish the author's international literary profile, and an anthropological conception of "religion" played a critical role in enhancing his prestige. While displaying the intimacies of Irish-Catholic bodies to a wider, English-speaking audience, the author persistently denigrated the native and attenuated his connection to it. At the same time, he and his supporters kept alive an image of other Irish writers as doctrinaire, hobbled by narrow nationalistic concerns and folkloric preoccupations. Perhaps surprisingly, given the endurance of this profile, the first Joyceans were the ones to push the Catholic context of his work to the forefront of his public image. In the late teens, Joyce and members of his circle stressed the significance of disciplinary training to his sensual imagination as well as to his rigorous intellect, justifying his explorations of bodily intimacies on the grounds of an orthopractic understanding of belief, in which mind and body form a unity as a result of regulated communal practice. Catholicism's emotional and mental strictures underwrote the scrupulous depiction of anatomy, habit, and practice.

Returning to the reception history of *Dubliners*, partly embedded in responses to *A Portrait of the Artist as a Young Man*, shows the degree to which Joyce shaped his image by displaying provincial bodies generated by minority religious praxis. My reading of *Dubliners*, like Boyd's, contests the prolific binaries suggested by ideas of the cosmopolitan and provincial in literary modernism, but also attempts to show the ways in which the contrast constituted modernism. Both Boyd and Larbaud would seem to accept the equation of the cosmopolitan with an aesthetic elite marked by "privileged ... detachment" from political agency.[51] The detachment not only from a particular origin, but from "earthly" matters altogether, bears on anthropological religion in two, opposed ways: it offers a model of transcendence as well as an intractable grounding in given materialities and identities. Both of these relations, publically seized on by modernist cosmopolitans, overshadow practice as a route to transcendence *through* particular acts. Joyce in fact employed techniques modelled on spiritual practice to reformulate quite earthly persons and tie them to the register of transcendence. Under erasure, minority "religion" describes the limit of modernist critique and forges its strongest link to a postmodern or metropolitan art insufficiently attentive to imperial legacies.

Dubliners stands as Joyce's first attempt to portray a body made by religious praxis. Chronic drunkenness epitomizes Irish stasis by rendering material an abstracted spiritual decline. The drinkers' fall "into" a mere body reverses the aims of the spiritual discipline that represses the lower middle-class men of Catholic Dublin, the Anglo-Irish "metrocolonials" of a "nominally self-consistent metropolitan nation-state contrived to aggrandize itself by simultaneously absorbing and othering the proximate area of the Celtic fringe," in Valente's description.[52] The stories that centrally feature intemperance—"Counterparts," "Grace," and "A Painful Case"—rely on the medical and moral vocabularies that Joyce uses to describe the collection as a whole, in order to depict the syndrome of drink. In doing so, the narratives invoke the emergent medical understanding of chronic drinking as an organic disease as well as the older interpretation of excessive drink as a vice. Yet Joyce also surpasses these conceptions by using intemperance to depict what Arthur Kleinman calls a "somatopsychic" or indiscriminately physical and psychic "illness" that characterizes not only the drinker but also his community. In the somatopsychic model, according to Kleinman, "'feeling' [is] expressed and interpreted more subtly, indirectly, globally, superficially, and above all somatically" than is typical of contemporary Western typologies, which distinguish organic "disease" from psychic distress.[53] The drunkards' descent into an anonymous, mere embodiment associated with dependence and vulnerability reverses the bodily disciplines of religion, as well as those of Victorian masculinity, and parodies the naked soul, stripped of particularity. Such religious programs aim to reshape the adherent's interior through repeated, strictly proscribed acts. Drinking in *Dubliners* instead somatizes the interior through a compulsive disorder. In these "conversion" narratives, the habitual "practice" of drinking strips the intemperate of an individual social identity, of the limited degree of autonomy that he formerly possessed. *Dubliners*' male inebriates lose their names and their power of speech as their mouths become sites of consumption and injury alone. Furthermore, the drunkard's loss of a privileged "self"—a property of the expressive and interiorized characters of the collection—prompts the immediate community's attempt to reinscribe a particular identity on the mere body of the drinker. The drunken body, subject to evasion, collusion, and the palliative exercise of a moribund religion, epitomizes communal immobility.

In producing the drunkard, *Dubliners* illustrates the operation of the Žižekian symptom that characterizes the double-bind of metrocolonial manhood, by locating the covert dynamics of the system in its primary disruption.[54] Valente explains: "[T]he chief external barrier to Irish self-possession and self-command, British domination, translated into an inner psychosocial impediment as well." While "manliness named the sublimation of internal heteronomy—the sway of animal passion—into self-coincident, self-directed agency, metrocolonial subjectivity incurred the conversion of imposed subordination into an internal heteronomy, an unmastered division of cultural investments, political loyalties, and ethnic and class attachments."[55] Liquor, I am contending, brings to the forefront the conflict of the animal spirits of the brute and the self-restraint of the Victorian gentleman, the twin faces of the stereotypes of the Celtic male "subject of freedom."[56] Metrocolonial men, "*dispossessed of their dispossession*,"[57] vividly display this state in the microeconomy of chronic drunkenness.

Joyce's clinical-ethnographic detachment from his subjects acts as a narrative synonym of his public attempts to write from outside the Irish bodies that he diagnoses and displays. The privileged gaze onto and into drunkards, who evince a native "typicality,"[58] finally intensifies the narrative discipline exercised over them. In treating repression as oppression alone, the stories ultimately reinforce the stasis that they seek to animate. *Dubliners* replicates institutional Catholicism's suspicion of sensual pleasure by offering the desire for global, synthetic integration as a pathological effect alone, and by depicting intemperance solely through its fragmenting and destructive effects. Here Joyce does his most radical thinking about Irish-Catholic embodiment by representing liquor itself as a powerful somatic and linguistic agent. Alcohol's potential for generating a mobile somatic style, for registering the productive capacities of spiritual discipline, appear most explicitly in the female drunkard of "A Painful Case," when the instability of female sympathies combines with the signifying power of liquor. The subaltern-sexual politics that Valente describes certainly govern the story, as the mark of Mrs. Sinico's impurity slides from romantic passion to passionate inebriation. Yet "A Painful Case" violates the sex binary that portrays Dublin women's dependency as religion and men's as drink. Though spirits disable the female drunkard just as they do the male—indeed Mrs. Sinico is the only featured Dubliner to die from the affliction—the congeries of Victorian feminine embodiment and alcohol's spiritual-linguistic capacities adumbrate the new productive power of liquor in Joyce's later work. Mrs. Sinico first generates the conjunction of "spirit" and "spirits"[59] that mark *Ulysses'* masculine model of totalized embodiment, in which drunkenness produces a positive as well as a destructive dynamic of movement and incorporation, a potential resolution of the contradictory stereotypes of Celtic men.

•

Upon its initial publication in 1914, *Dubliners* attracted little attention from the literary press. The book was reviewed less widely than *Chamber Music* (1907), Joyce's verse collection, had been. Yet *Dubliners* continued to elicit comment after the publication of *A Portrait* by the American house Huebsch in December 1916—often in overviews of Joyce's work that appeared when *Ulysses* began to emerge in serial. Readers attempted to grasp and relate what must have appeared as rapid and radical change: because of *Dubliners'* delayed publication, the serialization of *A Portrait* in *The Egoist* introduced the novel in the same year, and *Ulysses* began to appear in the *Little Review* just a year after *A Portrait*'s book publication. By the late teens, many critics were treating *Dubliners* as a mere prelude to or platform for the evolutionary leaps of Joyce's prose.

To a remarkable degree given the initial paucity of comment, however, the first reactions to *Dubliners* anticipated major elements of Joyce's reception through the mid-thirties. Yet, as I have said, reviewers made no mention of Catholicism and paid only passing attention to the collection's Irish provenance, major elements of Joyce's later profile. The earliest reviews complain of the author's limited view of life while they praise his mimetic fidelity to it; admire his realism while regretting its thoroughness and formlessness; note his technical skill and even genius while deploring his attraction to the sordid and the "unmentionable," euphemisms for bodily representations. Complaints about sensory representation become direct in reactions to *A Portrait* and dominate the popular reception of *Ulysses*. Emphasis on Irish character and on Catholicism, introduced by Pound and Joyce during the mid- to late teens, functions in 1922 and after to blunt the frequent revulsion toward the novel's investigation and display of bodies. The success of this formula can be measured by the disappearance of bodies as a concern in the emerging academic criticism in the forties.[60] In the 1950s and 1960s, when scholars returned in numbers to the neglected early work, they seized upon religious motifs with an almost fanatical intensity. Rereading the collection through the techniques devised by the encounter with *Ulysses*, critics underscored the Catholicism of the earlier prose as a source of elaborate schema, unifying design, and aesthetic metaphor. The essentially allegorical interpretations of Joyce's theological tropes and Christian allusions, epitomized by the "epiphany," became a hallmark of New Critical scholarship—one reason, perhaps, that the rubric has not been subjected to more vigorous recent scrutiny, as have many other touchstones of mid-century criticism.

The first notices about *Dubliners* place the collection in continental as well as Irish literary contexts. Joyce is compared to French naturalists and Russian realists such as Maxim Gorky as well as to Irish writers George Moore and Cunninghame Graham.[61] *Dubliners*, according to the 1914 *Everyman*, possesses "the power of genius . . . in every line, but it is a genius that, blind to the blue of the heavens, seeks inspiration in the hell of despair."[62] The *Athenaeum* similarly chastises Joyce for his insistence on treating "[the] more sordid and baser aspects" of life, given its beauties and his own "great skill both of observation and of technique."[63] The author's realism or naturalism flattens the arc of plot by focusing on "mood" or "atmosphere" rather than "episode," on character rather than action, according to some critics.[64] Remarks about the nature of these characters, seen as marginal and base, serve to convey readers' discomfort with Joyce's representation of physicality. None of the early comments mentions specific sensory emphases or physical depictions, and comments tend to connect characters' unsavory traits to class rather than to race or ethnicity. *Academy* praises the vividness of the setting: "[W]e feel Dublin about us as we read," the reviewer notes.[65] Even the *Irish Book Lover* fails to regard the collection as a general national or religious allegory. The reviewer "cannot deny the existence of [the] prototypes" of these stories in Dublin, but, like other readers, wishes "that the author had directed his undoubted talents in other and pleasanter directions."[66]

Ezra Pound, in his 1914 review of the collection in *The Egoist*, supplied the first emphatic characterization of *Dubliners* as an Irish work. This Irishness arises largely from Joyce's rejection of Irish literature and politics, in Pound's inestimable logic. Pound's vehement tone suggests that he is reacting to a reductive or narrow characterization of *Dubliners* as provincial, and yet none of other major reviews that appeared previously had depicted the collection in this way. Pound is not responding to a popular or critical climate that is pigeonholing Joyce as a peripheral minority writer, or even as a quintessentially Irish or Catholic one. Rather the literary impresario is forcefully shaping a position for Joyce among "continental" and "English contemporary prose writers" by opposing these terms to the literature of the revival. "It is surprising that Mr. Joyce is Irish," Pound writes. "One is so tired of the Irish or 'Celtic' imagination (or 'phantasy' as I think they now call it') flopping about. Mr. Joyce does not flop about. He defines. He is not an institution for the promotion of Irish peasant industries. He accepts an international standard of prose writing and he lives up to it." Like other reviewers, Pound focuses on *Dubliners*' realism, but unlike them, he does so by portraying Irish literature as general, feminine, sentimental, and fantastic, against Joyce's "rigorous selection" of detail and his masculine "clear hard prose." Rather than "bank[ing] on 'Irish character'" as older Irish works do, *Dubliners* uses local detail to convey the "universal element." Pound's depiction of the Irish resembles that of the feminized and capricious Arnoldian Celt, against which Joyce is set as an English or European writer who transforms Irish materials through (objectifying, male) Kantian form.[67] With hyperbolic and strategic aplomb, then, Pound deftly establishes Joyce's profile as decidedly Irish through an ethnologic characterization of other Irish writers, whose identity overdetermines their productions formally. Joyce disciplines and elevates the raw material of his provincial forerunners.

Richard Kelly argues that with this review, Pound commenced to change Joyce's reputation from that of "an Irish writer bitterly attacking certain institutions in Dublin with the weapons of realism and satire" to that of "an international writer exploring the human psyche for the benefit of a tiny number of like-minded literari."[68] I would argue that this shift was not as radical or uniform as Kelly suggests. More importantly, it is precisely the relationship *between* these images that came to characterize the Joycean formulation, which was significantly influenced by the treatment of Joyce as a *Catholic* Irish writer. Pound's interpretation of *Dubliners* reveals the contours of Joyce's cosmopolitan Irishness, solidified in the reception of *Ulysses*. But later reviews of the stories do not register this change immediately. Instead, in becoming more disturbed by "sordid" aspects of Joyce's prose, critics manifest a latent discomfort with the congeries of class, ethnicity, and religion that circulate around the image of the Irish Catholic. Readers increasingly object not only to issues of moral character, but also to the sensory and perceptual representation of bodies in *Dubliners*, as in Joyce's subsequent work. Detached naturalism comes to signify disgust for humanity and scorn for the reader, instead of a merely limited or distanced perspective. At the same time, reviewers continue to praise the author's technical skill. Scofield Thayer, in a 1918 comment in the *Dial*, calls Joyce's plots "the hunchbacks of fiction" from an Aristotelian point of view, but then adds that when "rightly taken for what they are—media for the expression of character"—the stories are "uncannily indicative, even ratiocinative" depictions of the lives that they describe. The comment also introduces perhaps the most popular metaphor for negative assessments of Joyce, by using fluids to epitomize his characters' aimlessness, his authorial inclusiveness, and his unsavory attention to the full range of the senses. The cast of *Dubliners*, "[m]ore obviously flotsam than even the majority of mankind, . . . are yet almost at home on the shifting, contradictory currents of their life." Thayer continues:

> They sidle through the stale streets, they wear yachting caps . . . . They are not markedly discontented in their element, and like fishes in the yellow waters of an ill-kept aquarium, they gravely drift before us. They exhibit now on one side, now the other, and with a sad shamelessness, they keep back nothing. At the last we are reminded that they are not fishes: we are aware of their body smells.[69]

During this period Joyce's attention to smell becomes a staple of reviews that object to *A Portrait*'s engagement with corporeal sensation, though taste and tactility are also featured; drains, sewers, and excrement, which became ubiquitous metaphors for *Ulysses*, also make their first appearances in reviews of the novel. J. C. Squire complains of Joyce's "preoccupation with the olfactory,"[70] and H. G. Wells, after observing Joyce's "cloacal obsession," speculates about the author's own possibly abnormal body: "He tells at several points how his hero Stephen is swayed and shocked and disgusted by harsh and loud *sounds* and how he is stirred to intense emotion in the music and rhythm of beautiful words. But no sort of smell offends him like that . . . . We shall do Mr. Joyce an injustice if we attribute a normal sensory basis to him and then accuse him of deliberate offense."[71]

The issue of national or racial type emerges in combination with complaints about the full range of sensory representations, as reviewers also begin to worry the issue of Joyce's (or Stephen's) typicality as an Irishman. Now associated with a Wellsian strain of criticism,[72] ethnologic and political assumptions enter into these remarks in predictable ways. Significantly, the stereotypes employed accord with Pound's depiction of the revival but fail to distinguish Joyce and his characters from provincial "phantasists." A. Clutton Brock of the London *Times Literary Supplement* calls Stephen "one of many Irishmen who cannot reconcile themselves to things; above all, he cannot reconcile himself to himself. He has at times a disgust for himself, a kind of mental queasiness, in which the whole universe seems nauseating as it is presented to him through the medium of his own disgusting self"; as a result, "thoughts pass through his mind like good or bad smells."[73] The *Freeman's Journal* of April 7, 1917, observes of *A Portrait*'s tea table: "Had it been a description of the desolation of No Man's Land on the Somme or the Yser, the horror could hardly have been laid on more thickly, and all through the book food is scarcely mentioned without the same shudder of disgust." Yet the same comment, responding to views such as the ones I cite above, frets that "English critics . . . are already hailing the author as a typical Irishman, and his book as a faithful picture of Irish life," though "[i]t would be just as accurate to declare that DeQuincey's *Opium Eater* embodied the experience of an average English youth."[74] Bearing out these fears, an unsigned review in the *New Age* describes the novel as "a portrait of young Ireland, Catholic Ireland," full of men "who have no souls."[75]

In spite of the ethnographic cast of such comments, Stephen's "typicality" is more directly connected to his process of maturation than it is to either his Irishness or his Catholicism, and when the issue of religion—completely absent from the early reviews of *Dubliners*—appears in some of the popular literary commentary on *A Portrait*, it is treated as a manifestation of the protagonist's personal intensity, as evidence of the author's attunement to "spiritual nuance," often absent in English prose,[76] or to the nature of Ireland's modernity. Rather than focusing on Catholic repression, much less on the morbidity and perversity that they may produce, critics discuss religion in relation to formal effects, noting the work's representational fidelity to the subject and readers' identification with the protagonist. John Macy, in the *Dial*, says that he cannot judge the accuracy of the novel's depiction of "the emotional conflicts of the Catholic religion" but that Stephen's "wrestlings with his sins and his faith are so movingly human that they hold the sympathy even of one who is indifferent to the religious arguments."[77] A few reviewers go as far as to characterize Irish Catholicism as "medieval" or "atavistic," yet call the protagonist and the narrative "modern" as well. In *Vanity Fair*, John Quinn observes that Stephen's conversations with his fellow students, which are "saturated with their religion in spite of their free-thinking, with the boy-Latin they talk," are "medieval and yet quite modern."[78] In a more broadly ethnographic and national vein, Van Wyck Brooks in *Seven Arts* calls the novel "atavistic" and suggests that it comes out of "the strange reality" of "the black chieftains and [the] subterranean sympathies of Catholic Ireland and Catholic Spain." Nonetheless, he continues, "it is a living society that Joyce pictures, one that conforms to the twentieth century in its worldly apparel but reveals in its table-talk and its more intimate educational and religious recesses a mediaevalism utterly untouched by that industrial experience that has made the world kin, for good or for ill."[79]

Much as Pound foregrounds Irish writers in order to distinguish Joyce from them, Joyce strongly asserts *A Portrait*'s Catholic context to separate himself from it. Again, this identity is asserted through rejection, though one not as denigrating as Pound's characterization of the revival. But the Pound-Joyce formulation of the non-Irish Irishman and the non-Catholic Catholic that came to dominate the scholarly treatment of *Dubliners* were minor or disguised features of the initial reception, as I have shown. Joyce promoted the Catholic foundation of *A Portrait* through his translation of a review by Diego Angeli, which had initially appeared in an August 1917 issue of *Il Marzocco*. Joyce's version of "Un Ramanzo di Gesuiti" [One Jesuit novel] appeared in the February 1918 *Egoist*. Angeli argues that Joyce must be understood as a worldly atheist "in revolt" against his religion and country; the reviewer simultaneously insists that Protestants cannot properly appreciate *A Portrait*. English and American readers find "immorality, impiety, naturalism and exaggeration" in the novel "[p]ossibly" because "their own Protestant upbringing renders the moral development of the central character incomprehensible to them." Equating Joyce with Stephen, Angeli continues: "For Mr. Joyce is a Catholic, and more than that, a Catholic brought up in a Jesuit college .... No writer, so far as I know, has penetrated deeper in the examination of the influence, sensual rather than spiritual, of the society's exercises."[80]

The appearance of this review in the *Egoist* was quickly followed by an overview of Joyce's work that similarly emphasized Catholicism. Written by Joyce's acquaintance, Padraic Colum, "Joyce's Dublin" appeared in the May 1918 *Pearson's*. Robert Deming calls Colum's emphasis on religion "curious"[81]—presumably because of the absence of this topic from earlier commentary, for Colum clearly points in the direction that the author desired. Pitching the article to his relationship with Joyce, Colum emphasizes the significance of Dublin and of Catholicism to the writer's identity and creations. The "sordidness" and "misery" of the characters featured in *Dubliners* result from a city "thwarted on the side of culture" and "low on material circumstances." Colum continues: "Against this background of economic decay and incomplete culture and shut-in sin . . . [,] Stephen makes his spiritual assertion," as if to redeem the characters of the stories. The protagonist triumphs over his first "spiritual morass" through the "virtue of a power of spiritual vision backed by the discipline of the Catholic Church"; having rejected this orthodoxy, Stephen at the end of the novel "will strive . . . to give a soul to his people." Like Angeli, Colum insists that American and English readers encounter an unfamiliar environment in *A Portrait*, "a life that has been shaped by Catholic culture and tradition." The reviewer elaborates: "James Joyce's book is profoundly Catholic," not doctrinally but culturally, and Stephen's "ideal of beauty is the ideal that has been attained to [sic] in the masterpieces of Catholic art."[82]

These articles reveal the not quite invisible hand of Joyce in establishing his image as an Irish and Catholic artist who knows, exposes, and transcends Irish-Catholic bodies. Like Pound, Joyce calls attention to this profile not as a defense against a metropolitan reception that would pigeonhole or dismiss him as a minority, sectarian, or provincial writer, but rather as a method of highlighting the Irish body's generation by Catholic discipline. If Pound frames *Dubliners* as Irish because it transcends Irishness, Joyce frames Catholic embodiment through his rejection of Catholicism as a faith. He instead highlights the religion as productive of knowledge that is somatic as well as intellectual and cultural. While crafting his image by emphasizing these rejected affinities, in his prose the writer displays the Irish-Catholic bodies of Dublin with striking intimacy. Through this strategy, the first Joyceans began to transform the revulsion, shock, or confusion that reviewers express over his bodily portrayals into signs of the reviewers' own philistine, priggish, or rigidly bourgeois perspectives, attitudes linked to doctrinaire religion and colonial hypocrisy.

Critical attention to the deep scrutiny of minority religious bodies, so important to Joyce's notoriety in the twenties, drops away by the late 1930s, as does attention to *Dubliners*. Armed with the classical and theological schematics of *Ulysses*, scholars revisit the collection in the 1950s and 1960s. Rather than approaching the stories teleologically, as so many reviewers came to—even Pound, by 1918, is stating that *Dubliners* merely "contained several well-constructed stories, several sketches rather lacking in form" and asserting that "[t]here is very little to be said in praise of it which would not apply with greater force to *A Portrait*"[83]—the New Critics reread Joyce's early work proleptically. Homeric and Catholic theological patterns became almost obsessive concerns of *Dubliners'* exegetes. In 1944 Levin and Shattuck argue that the collection follows a design of Homeric correspondences, though not as systematically as *Ulysses* does. More typical by the 1960s is an emphasis on theology: critics read the stories as religious allegories overlaid with the arcana of Dublin and of scholasticism. These hidden designs unite *Dubliners* into novelistic coherence and elevate the collection to the status of the later work. In a 1958 essay in *Modern Fiction Studies*, for instance, Julian Kaye notes, "It is now time to take another look at *Dubliners*. Recent textual studies of *Ulysses* and *Finnegans Wake* have tended to make *Dubliners* look thin."[84] Brewster Ghiselin had already established that "so narrow an understanding of *Dubliners* [was] no longer possible," because "[r]ecent and steadily increasing appreciation of the fact that there is much symbolism in the book has dispelled the notion that it is radically different from Joyce's later fiction." According to Ghiselin, *Dubliners* is both "a group of short stories and a novel, the separate histories . . . composing one essential history, that of the soul of the people which has confused and weakened its relation to the source of spiritual life and cannot restore it. The 'symbolic paralysis' results from a deficiency of impulse and power" even though "moral paralysis" may be physically expressed, as in "The Sisters."[85]

Scholars' reduction of belief formations and practices to the vocabulary of abstraction and intellection demonstrates an essentially anthropological understanding of "religion" in the criticism of this era, one that coincides with critics' ethnographic relationship to the object constructed as the Joycean text, and finally to "'Joyceness'"—a merging of the writer and his work, in Buzard's characterization, and the authorial "imprimatur" in Jaffe's.[86] "Religion" is assumed as the rubric appropriate to the coherent object of the writer's work. A given, it affords external reading of doctrine and rite, defined as the essence of belief, better to secure its analogue with aesthetic language. The bodies of *Dubliners*, even in "paralysis," are virtually ignored in favor of the focus on the symbolic meanings that they bear. Interestingly, this critical framework allows John Hagopian to pursue the "'true scholastic stink'" of "Counterparts" while barely mentioning Farrington's drunkenness; the critic drives instead toward an allegory of wrath and prayer.[87] Carl Niemeyer similarly discusses the Dantean parallels in "Grace" in some detail before mentioning that inebriation caused the protagonist's fall.[88] While the excesses of this critical method may seem obvious today, we have little challenged the conception of "religion" from which it proceeds and which Joyce promoted even as he generated religiously inflected bodies from much fuller premises. Instead of questioning the assumptions that inform "religion" in Joyce's modernism, we learned to ignore it.[89]

The Habit of Drink and Irish-Catholic Counterdiscipline

Reviewers' strong reaction to what Jane Heap calls "the geography of the body"[90] resolved in two stages, both of them shaped by Joyce and his circle. Angeli and Colum highlight the religious production of these bodies through the generative as well as the repressive aspects of Catholic practice: Colum speaks of the "power" that religious discipline grants Stephen and Angeli of the sensuality of Jesuit training—both indications of an orthopractic orientation. The somatic potential of Catholic discipline nonetheless disappears in the resolution of the *Ulysses* controversy, where "religion" becomes entirely repressive of bodies and intellects, and spiritual power moves completely into an art freed from belief's mental and physical strictures. The mid-century criticism of *Dubliners* replicates this movement as "religion" becomes a ritualistic and symbolic phenomenon largely divorced from physicality. The ethnographic and historical discourses that the author deploys also fall away from notice. The drunken Paddy stumbles everywhere through *Dubliners,* but critics, like the sober Dubliners, do their best to avoid naming him. This resistance is related to what Manganaro describes as a long academic reluctance to read Joyce's subjects ethnographically—to regard his procedures as cultural mapping rather than as aesthetic fidelity to detail.[91]

While Joyce acknowledges only the Church's domination of embodiment, alcohol supplies him with a latent surrogate for the productive capacities of spiritual discipline. Crucially, the author draws upon a mode of belief oriented toward physical practice rather than doctrine in this formulation. Both chronic drinking and religious discipline are performative practices that generate bodies as epistemes; liquor, the stereotypical Irish cure, seems to exercise the agency that the drinker and his would-be rescuers lack. Chronic drunkenness provides a model of mind-body totalization generated by repetitive, regulated action in a communal context, and of the collective power that they can create. The inebriate offers Joyce an arena for disrupting and revising the oppositions that structure and ultimately immobilize the metrocolonial. Yet he also uses the disciplinary protocols that somatize repression to represent drink as a compulsive practice. It disorganizes the structures of individuals and communities, bodies and minds. Alcohol's implicit promise of liberation from constraint instead produces corporeal and psychic fragmentation. As an anonymous "type" governed by a physical compulsion, the drunkard becomes a site of confusion and exchange between the psychic and the corporeal, as well as among distinct subjectivities, and dramatizes the ennui that economic constraint shares with surplus.[92]

The boredom that Nash associates with violence in Joyce's projection of an audience for and in *Dubliners* manifests in the stories through the anxious dynamics of compulsion, injury, and denial.[93] Most immediately, the spiritual-medical nexus of *Dubliners* represents chronic drinking as a somatic compulsion, in which affect is experienced as pain, treated through the antidote of liquor, and compounded by physical injury. The lineaments of the intemperates are shaped by the reassessment of chronic drinking during the nineteenth century, in which medical conceptions replaced religious and moral ones, as Foucault describes in other spheres of experience. Middle-class reform movements reflected intense interest in controlling and classifying drinkers and drinking practices. As Katherine Mullin demonstrates in detail, these efforts belonged to broad, international "social purity" movements in America and the UK.[94] Temperance movements put into wide circulation the conception of heavy drinking as a disease and the chronic drinker as an "alcoholic," transforming a practice into an identity. Rather than supplanting previous interpretations even within the new paradigm, however, this model absorbed the negative pole of the traditional view—in which drinking figured as a vice or sin—while occluding its positive associations with celebration, ritual, tradition, and health. The chronic drinker became both a moral and a physical casualty, both a degenerate and a patient, within this framework. In such constructions, drinking is at once a symptom and a cause of disease, a vice and a cause of vice. Thus the vice model overtly, or more surreptitiously, inflected the medical reappraisal of intemperance, just as traditional understandings began to absorb elements of the new paradigm. The chronic drinker was rarely regarded as a neutral subject, but rather as a defective one, whose appearance was constantly connected with certain classes and ethnicities.[95]

In the Irish context, the temperance movement that grew from drinking's medicalization took a particular course, heavily influenced by sectarianism.

As Elizabeth Malcolm reports, the first, American temperance campaign was received from 1829 in Ireland as an "almost wholly" evangelical and Protestant, middle-class movement. It took hold most vigorously in the north and aimed in large part at regulating the work force. The presence of brewing and distilling industries in the south,⁹⁶ as well as the association of temperance with Protestant evangelicalism, may have contributed to the comparatively slow growth of Catholic interest until the advent of Father Theobald Mathew's society in 1839. Mathew's campaign, enormously successful in rural areas in a period coincident with partial crop failure, drew heavily on Catholic ritual, as adherents "took the pledge" not to drink and could purchase a medal, presumably to show to employers.⁹⁷ The Irish Catholic hierarchy, like Home Rule advocates of the later century, remained tepid toward the issue of abstinence until the emphasis on individual reform, promoted by nationalist organizations after the death of Parnell, encouraged a more negative attitude toward alcohol. "Ireland Sober Is Ireland Free," a slogan taken up by temperance groups, equated sobriety with health and self-management and resonated with a challenge to the stereotype of the drunken Paddy, based on the tacit synonymity of somatic, psychic, and political dependency.⁹⁸ By the late century, Valente notes, "the achievement of national independence came to be *predicated* upon the cultivation of a manly *acesis*, of which teetotalism was all but the official seal." The antitreating movement became a specific target of such temperance efforts, "fram[ing] heavy drinking as a matter of ethnically inflected group membership."⁹⁹

In Ireland at the turn of the century, drink constituted a particular resistance to the Irish nationalist and modernizing projects, according to David Lloyd. Though "render[ed] within nationalism as a problem of intemperance," Irish drinking practices in fact stood as "an element of unincorporated difference" that was "transformed and reconstituted in relation to an emergent modernity." Irish temperance movements came to forward a modernizing project aimed at articulating and regulating sex differences and their spheres as well as disciplining public spaces of labor. Temperance nationalism, Lloyd contends, "is not so much about the repression of an evil, drunkenness, as it is about the reconstitution of the social formation and the establishment of the domestic sphere as the counterpart to an invigorated masculine public sphere of economic and political labor."¹⁰⁰

The historical development that I have been describing prompted a field of discourse about drink, the drinker, and drinking practices that *Dubliners* engages to describe the illness of masculine colonial subjects and the compromised status of their agency. "Counterparts," the only story in the collection to occupy the drinker's perspective, depicts the reverse conversion narrative as a transfer of affect to sensation and of oppression to domination. Here the drinker experiences his negative emotions as somatic conditions and seeks a cure in the medicine of liquor. The suggestion of illness is reinforced through pub slang, such as "g. p."—or general physician—for a glass of porter and "poisons" for drinks.[101] Joyce contrasts Farrington's somatization, the aches and pains that he suffers, with the drama of his compulsion as an "illness" and a communal "sickness," rather than a "disease," in Kleinman's terms.[102] As in "Grace," the drinker's tongue, throat, and mouth attain particular significance as the locus of articulation, one that constantly compounds his abjection. Joyce's representation of drinking as an act of compulsive mimicry ultimately functions to interrogate the "counterpart" in relation to nationalist as well as masculinist imagery: Torchiana notes that the term "counterpart" initially referred to the copy of a legal document, and Lloyd observes that "the copy is torn off from the original in such a way that, when the two are brought together, the copy authenticates the original."[103] "Counterparts" pursues the alienation of signifier and signified through the sign of the drinker's body.

As Lloyd, Valente, and others have shown, "Counterparts" engages with the historical reorganization of masculine labor, leisure, and domesticity and illustrates the impasse of internalized masculine stereotypes. Building on their insights, I focus on alcohol's power to evacuate or dissolve social categories and ideals, even as the drinker's body is increasingly alienated. Farrington promises at the beginning of the story to represent an oppressed colonial worker. Though pre-industrial, his labor as a legal copyist is portrayed as machinic, the demand for precision coupled with mindlessness; his namelessness suggests his exchangeability. But the narrative proceeds to depict his body as a labor of drink as much as it is of institutional oppression: the story's relentless twinnings draw the alienation of Farrington's job into close parallel with the alienation produced by his habit. At the same time the story initially offers a British reading of the Irish clerk as an imperfect or incomplete version of the industrious Saxon and a perfect fulfillment of the Celtic stereotype—a hulking, angry, idle, and improvident drunk. As Margot Norris points out, Farrington in his physicality also stands in opposition to the literary scriveners that he evokes, such as Melville's Bartleby or Gogol's Akaky Akakievich.[104]

Rather than employing the thematic of mimicry to challenge or menace imperial, economic, or literary paradigms, "Counterparts" vigorously directs our attention to the predictable failure of Farrington's imitations and rebellions. Suggestive of the Fenian revolutionary, through his "savage" resentment and his resemblance to an "emotional barometer . . . set for a spell of riot," the clerk also evokes the rural peasant through emblems such as his "shepherd's plaid cap" and the creative author through the act of writing, his wandering imagination, and his staged tale-telling (80, 79, 77). The story uses such allusions subtly to refuse any romantic or straightforward rationale for the clerk's compulsion: he is as poor a copy of these types as he is of the Saxon. Lloyd's reading suggests that "Counterparts" may destabilize the relations of the model to the copy, for Farrington's poor imitation might also imply the problematic status of the models he fails to embody: the narrative may menace the nationalist and pastoral original by suggesting their own reactive will to power and impotence. The clerk's response to the voice of authority or the body of power—associated twice in the story with Protestant Irish or British men who perform for female audiences—shows the conversion of rage into repression and protest into theatrical gesture. Indeed, the story's dramatization of Farrington's three "tests of manliness" interlink the always already defeated expression of masculine strength, in Valente's reading.[105]

These resonances find their chief dynamic in Farrington's constant conversion of discomfort—whether rage, boredom, or tension—into a physical pain to be eased by drink. When he is chastised for making a mistake at the office, the clerk's posture of repentance masks his anger, which quickly recedes into a desire to repeat the behavior that produced his poor performance. "A spasm of rage gripped his throat for a few moments and then passed, leaving after it a sharp sensation of thirst," the narrator reports. Farrington decides that he must "slake" his thirst before he can accomplish any work (76–77). Back at the office after he has done so, "his body ache[s] to do something, to rush out and revel in violence" as his "inflamed face," which is "the colour of dark wine or dark meat" (79, 77), conflates the heat of rage and drink. But his mounting aggression leads to the loosening of his tongue when his boss upbraids him again:

—I know nothing about any other two letters [Farrington] said stupidly.

—*You—know—nothing*. Of course you know nothing, said Mr Alleyne. Tell me, he added, glancing first for approval to the lady beside him, do you take me for a fool? Do you think me an utter fool?

The man glanced from the lady's face to the little eggshaped head and back again: and almost before he was aware of it his tongue had found a felicitous moment:

—I don't think, sir, he said, that that's a fair question to put to me.

There was a pause in the very breathing of the clerks. Everyone was astounded (the author of the witticism no less than his neighbours) and Miss Delacours, who was a stout amiable person, began to smile broadly. (79–80)

Though the narrator begins to call Farrington by his name only when he leaves work,[106] suggesting that his conditions of labor erase his particular identity, events in the pub undermine the promise of a restored authenticity. At the same time, as Valente observes, Farrington as a name derives from the Irish *fer,* or "man," and so infuses this shift with ethnic particularity. "Manhood" is in this way bestowed on the protagonist just when he has "forfeited that status, irretrievably, through the hypermasculine manner of his assertion."[107] At the pub, the clerk transforms the incident into a tale of triumph for the amusement and admiration of his cronies: the "author" of a tale of insubordination, the copyist momentarily experiences oral pleasure through his imaginary revision of the power dynamic, a positive valuation of the "loosened" tongue, in Lloyd's view.[108] But even this experience of pleasure, an act of communication and creativity, registers ambivalently, as it fits with Farrington's self-aggrandizing desire to appear as a "strong man" (85) and dissipates through the stoking of new resentment that ends in another theatrical display—an arm-wrestling contest with the English Weathers—and another defeat. Not only through his failures but also through his means of understanding conflict, Farrington illustrates the alienation of protest from any legitimate platform, exemplified in the repetitive labor of producing rage and the conversion of rage to somatized "illness." He finds relief only when he returns home to beat his son for not completing his domestic chores. The arm that fails Farrington against Weathers finds its strength in actual violence. Aggression, no longer merely rhetorical or performative, is directed at a boy rather than other men. The "free play" of the father's arm (86) finally gratifies his urge to violence and domination at the same time that it functions as the terminus of his physical alienation, the point of generational transmission of abuse. The drinker's "fall" into the body, as the analogue of spiritualized narrative of sin, is taken by the son.

If "Counterparts" illustrates the dynamics of the drinker's psyche, "Grace" depicts habitual drinking as a communal illness and the mobility of alcohol as a quasi autonomous agent, with powers analogous to those generated by disciplinary spiritual practice. In contrast to spiritual praxis, however, liquor appears to influence subjects without their conscious knowledge or apparent volition, much as it loosens Farrington's tongue "almost before he [is] aware of it" (80). This influence extends to the sober community around the drinker, whose tongues are constrained by the blunt fact of his fall into a stigmatized identity, associated with violence and loss of self-control.

But "Grace" also emphatically demonstrates the agency of liquor itself as a materialized "spirit" that possesses all the somatic and linguistic mobility that the drinker and the community around him or her lack. In this, alcohol adumbrates the operation of the orthopractic-linguistic spirit of *Ulysses*, where drink finally achieves a positive valence and religious practice models the totalized episteme of the minority religious body. Here, however, the syndrome also produces an opacity that might be read as a resistance to theological reading generated by the practice of drunkenness. The narrator, no less than the provincials who populate the story, finds mystification at the site of enunciation of chronic drink. Though critics such as Norris, Leonard, and Vesala-Varttala[109] have pointed out the unstable allegiances of the various narrators of the stories, they share—regardless of their silences, evasions, alliances, and challenges to the reader—a baffling at the scene of drunkenness. In the eyes of nationalist reformers, "alcoholic excess induces emotional excess" at once "preclud[ing] or revers[ing] the integrated dynamics of manly sublimation," Valente contends.[110] The microeconomy of the family and community serves up a compensatory hypersublimation in their refusal to address the problem directly. R. B. Kershner observes that here "alcohol is an emblem of the unmentionable central subject, everywhere present and nowhere acknowledged."[111] Institutional religion supports and intensifies this denial. The incitement to classification stimulated by intemperance signifies the larger refusal to acknowledge it. As a somatic and social practice, chronic drinking prompts display of the daily economies of replication that maintain the political status quo: the intemperate enacts not only his own pathology, but also that of his community. At the same time the narratives about drunkards constantly thwart the desire to locate the problem in the drinker, to restore his individual identity, and to fix his injury without addressing the syndrome that produced it. In this, the stories present an anatomy of temperance nationalism's denial of stereotypes without addressing their actual mechanisms, as Lloyd describes.[112] As the rhetoric of pain and injury, sin and vice circulates around the inebriates of the collection, the stories refuse to endorse either medical or institutionalized moral vocabularies.

The first scene of "Grace" highlights a sober gaze onto the still form and the panicked, laborious attempts to identify it. The terms attached to the unconscious body trace a descent, from the "gentleman" who could pay for a drink to "the man" lying in filth. Such nuances do not reveal who he "is." The anonymity of the drunkard as a social type appears as a literal fact, for the narrator, like the characters in the pub, knows the unconscious man only as a dead weight:

> Two gentlemen who were in the lavatory at the time tried to lift him up: but he was quite helpless. He lay curled up at the foot of the stairs down which he had fallen. They succeeded in turning him over. His hat had rolled a

few yards away and his clothes were smeared with the filth and ooze of the floor on which he had lain, face downwards. His eyes were closed and he breathed with a grunting noise. A thin stream of blood trickled from the corner of his mouth. (136)

"Grace" anatomizes the intemperate in the shadow of an older, celebratory drinker who represents festivity, renewal, and community. In his low position and his filth, as well as the excess consumption that caused them, the man recalls the grotesque body that Mikhail Bakhtin describes. But unlike the Rabelaisian figure, the drinker of "Grace" regenerates and ascends only parodically. The pub bystanders' seemingly perverse preoccupation with naming the body, which they move and turn as if to locate it materially in an identity, highlights their avoidance of the obvious surmise: the man "is" an intemperate. According to the dynamic that "Grace" pursues, his anonymity signifies the erasure of his name as a marker of individual subjectivity and agency, as well as the transformation of his practice into an identity. Kernan's name cannot be found because it would designate him a subject, and therefore not a drunkard.[113] At the same time, the reluctance to speak Kernan's cultural label draws a parallel between the voicelessness of the chronic drinker and that of his sober compatriots.[114]

The narrator is equally cautious in surmounting this impasse, finally resolved when the body is moved to the main floor of the pub and designated an "injured" man (137). The equivocal epithet neatly avoids the rhetoric of vice or a description of etiology, its ambiguity preserved when the unconscious form is finally revived:

> The constable asked:
> —Where do you live?
> The man, without answering, began to twirl the ends of his mustache. He made light of his accident. It was nothing, he said: only a little accident. He spoke very thickly.
> —Where do you live? repeated the constable. (138)

Kernan's desire to diminish or erase his fall through the vaguely medical or legal designation corresponds to the "nothingness" of his identity as a drunkard, an anonymity that he is eager to preserve in the act of denying its cause. In fact, Kernan is not merely reluctant to speak, he is to some extent physically unable to do so. When Jack Power emerges from the back of the bar to take charge of Kernan and escort him home, the friend fails to learn the nature of the "accident" but does inspect the "injury": "—I 'an't, 'an, [Kernan] answer[s], 'y 'ongue is hurt." Kernan submits when Power replies, "—Show."

> The other leaned over the well of the car and peered into Mr Kernan's mouth but he could not see. He struck a match and, sheltering it in the shell of his hands, peered again into the mouth which Kernan opened obediently. The swaying movement of the car brought the match to and from the open mouth. The lower teeth and gums were covered with clotted blood and a minute piece of the tongue seemed to have been bitten off. The match was blown out.
> —That's ugly, said Mr Power. (139)

The examination of Kernan's mouth is an important moment in *Dubliners* because it exemplifies the distanced technique of the narratives, which search for a somatic cause of chronic drinking and find only the injury that results from it. Kernan's mouth initially appears as an opaque, mystified appetite that cannot be seen, but becomes illuminated as a grotesque injury, a bloodied void.[115] The precise description of this orifice substitutes for an explanation of the man's condition, a condition of which everyone is aware and yet no one will recognize. In opening the grotesque mouth for official inspection—Powers works for the Royal Irish Constabulatory Office in Dublin Castle, an armed police force whose primary political aim was the suppression of Irish dissent[116]—"Grace" encapsulates the transformation of the celebratory drinker into the medical anatomy of the alcoholic and the spiritual fall into a somatic state that collapses the physical and moral, individual and communal, decline into a "mere" embodiment. The language of injury and accident evades as much as describes Kernan's condition, and the intimate description of his "ugly" mouth conflates his inability with his refusal to articulate himself, merging the site of his compulsive consumption with the nullification of his specific identity.

The visual and auditory evidence displays and obfuscates the meaning of Kernan's practice. Only after Power has peered into the "the mouth" does the narrative answer the questions posed about Kernan's identity. His drinking is habitual, and his injury will also impair his ability to work, for he is an agent and taster for a London tea company. "The mouth" is a tool of his trade, just as visual surveillance is a tool of Power's. The scene staged in Kernan's bedroom two days later echoes the tableau in the bar, for the men arranged around the "invalid" (143, 144, 148) revise the vocabulary of organic injury in a spiritual register. The broad outline of the story thus resolves into a conventional narrative of redemption: the men hope to persuade the "fallen" Kernan to attend a Catholic retreat. His habit is now understood as a moral failing. Entirely spiritualized, the rhetoric of physical distress slides easily away from corporeal appetites and into familiar abstractions. Kernan's physical injury, transmuted into a moral vice, will be cured not by any self-examination, or even by abstinence, but rather by masculine fellowship in an institutional religious setting—a retreat "for business men" (149), devoted to economic rather than physical consumption. Though during the scene in the bedroom Cunningham twice challenges Kernan by insisting that the "boose" caused his injuries while he was "peeloothered" (144, 145), the subject is quickly derailed. "Grace" colludes with the community's reading of Kernan as damaged physically or spiritually, at the same time that it satirizes misreadings of his condition through focus on bodily damage rather than compulsion and on a perverted institutional Catholicism rather than on deeper psychic or larger spiritual issues. His policing by functionaries of the state and Church, enacted through interrogation and inspection, depict the drunkard as a dominated body, exemplified by the medical metonymy of "the" bloody mouth. But just as Farrington fails to represent an oppressed body of labor, Kernan fails to represent a victim of institutional surveillance. The "boys" who function as Farrington's counterparts in the pub reappear in "Grace" as male crowds who collude with the silence about his injury's real cause and the putative adults who come to his social and moral rescue. Kernan emerges as a production of communal "illness," a body fallen into a medical-moral anonymity that must be reintegrated into a particular, available identity—one that does not test the contradictions of its predicates.

The "spiritual agencies"[117] (148) of alcohol in "Grace" trace a continuity between the compulsions of the subject and those of the community, both of which work to disavow their power over the habit. On the one hand, the narrative presumes that Kernan acts as an autonomous individual, responsible for and capable of controlling his consumption; on the other hand, the story depicts him first as a mere body and then as an agent capable of speaking his damage alone. Finally evasion characterizes the male community around him. Liquor accrues power in this plot, as it dominates not only the drunkard's sentience and physical control, but also the acceptable speech of the community of rescuers. Much like the doctrinal definition of "grace," alcohol exercises transformative somatic and linguistic powers that exceed the subjects'. The plot of conversion suggests that the Dubliners' agency is compromised at the same time that the narrative judges their actions harshly. In this capacity alcohol brings to mind "Plato's Pharmakon," in which Jacques Derrida claims that the representation of liquor enacts the instability of language itself. The play of significations within *pharmakon* resembles the inscription of "liquor." Like *pharmakon*, alcohol, "even while it means *remedy*, cites, recites, and makes legible that which in the same word signifies, in another spot and on a different level of the stage, poison."[118] *Dubliners* effects this movement corporeally as well as linguistically. While the stories suppress the remedial effects of excessive alcohol, they stage the mobility of its effects, and therefore its signification, on subjects and on communities. At the same time that the drunkard is stigmatized and classified, he acts as an emblem of the polis. The "conversion" of Kernan to a sober individual is as shallow as his "conversion" to Catholicism, and through the paralleling of these categories illustrates a performative practice that embodies the community.

In the production of the intemperate physically, as illustrated in "Counterparts," and communally, as dramatized in "Grace," *Dubliners* suggests the model of religious praxis in a negative but productive performative capacity. *Dubliners* anticipates *Ulysses*' realization of the corporeal generativity of both religious discipline and of chronic drink. *Ulysses* actually occupies the experience of drunkenness as a model of somatopsychic integration, aesthetic generation, and positive dissolution of the individual as the formulation of the person. The most explicit expression of this movement in *Dubliners* is the female intemperate, whose given characteristics differ significantly from those of male drinkers. As the sole female chronic drinker in the collection, and one of the few in Joyce's *oeuvre*, Emily Sinico illustrates the equation of "spirit" and "spirits" represented in *Ulysses* and *Finnegans Wake*. The fluidity of the normative woman combines in Mrs. Sinico with that of the drunkard, and her depiction as a restorative agent for the repressed man anticipates the new, remedial effects of liquor in Joyce's later work.

Ardent Female Spirits and Alcohol's Agency

Like "Grace" and "Counterparts," "A Painful Case" dramatizes the problem of finding an episteme for the drunkard. Emily Sinico undergoes the same loss of particular identity that her male counterparts do. Yet the different determinants of female subjectivity and embodiment alter both the effect and the significance of her fall. While the male intemperates experience their emotions as somatic conditions, signalling their divorce from affect, Emily Sinico is depicted as emotional, sensual, and somatically expressive before she turns to drink.

Her compulsion does not signify an attempt to surmount a physical and psychic split; rather it results precisely from their intimate relations. Notably, not her mouth but her entire form acts as the chief physical signifier of her drunkenness. Sober or drunk, Sinico figures a totality governed by female psychosomatic sympathies. The medical interpretation of her drinking as a sordid disease is set against a spiritual thematic that portrays her as a curing elixir for the repressed male protagonist. Using an associative, linguistic logic, "A Painful Case" grants the habitual drinker a positive value—though at the expense of her life. When the angel in the house indulges in liquor, she gains an afterlife in spirits not easily contained.

Mrs. Sinico is a victim of her own constitution insofar as her intemperance is continuous with the psychosomatic sympathies of the female organism. But "A Painful Case" portrays her as the victim of James Duffy, the man who provokes her grief by rejecting her romantically. In his critique of Irish masculinity, Joyce casts her drinking as an epiphenomenon of Duffy's emotional stasis. Here, however, the repressed man is a sober intellectual who "live[s] at a little distance from his body" (96) as from Dublin, and the drunkard's voicelessness merges with the sober woman's. Emily Sinico loses her voice long before she becomes an intemperate: as Kershner notes, she has only one line of direct discourse in the story.[119] Told from Duffy's point of view, the narrative represents her through a somatic language of expressive totality, in comparison with the physical description of Duffy's head alone. When the two meet, the narrator relates:

> Her face, which must have been handsome, had remained intelligent. It was an oval face with strongly marked features. The eyes were very dark blue and steady. Their gaze began with a defiant note but was confused by what seemed a deliberate swoon of the pupil into the iris, revealing for an instant a temperament of great sensibility. The pupil reasserted itself quickly, this half disclosed nature fell again under the reign of prudence, and her astrakhan jacket, moulding a bosom of certain fulness, struck the note of defiance more definitely. (97)

Mrs. Sinico is from the first connected with emotional excess through her form, which immediately reveals her character. As a number of critics have observed, nineteenth-century medicine postulated the "sensitivities" or "sympathies" of the female organism, which merged psyche and corpus. Foucault asserts in this regard, "The entire female body . . . is always in immediate complicity with itself, to the point of forming a kind of absolutely privileged site for the sympathies; from one extremity of its organic space to another, it encloses a perpetual possibility of hysteria."[120] Significantly, Mrs. Sinico gazes back at the man who reads her, but her eye itself reveals a confusion of deliberation and swoon, sensuality and restraint, repeated even in the fit of her slightly exotic jacket to her breast.

The physical depiction of the female body as sensibility becomes abstracted as Duffy and Sinico become companions; Duffy's poetic images of their relationship supplant her direct portrayal. Ignoring the sensuality that his initial reading of her registered, the bachelor experiences her as a detached sensuousness, as if his mind were an organ being brought into "sympathetic" complicity with her warmth. "Thoughts" and "subjects" (98, 99) enact the movement of the pair's developing intimacy, and when conversation gives way to music, their eardrums act as displaced erogenous zones. If Mrs. Sinico initially appears as a fervent but restrained body, she quickly becomes an ardent phantasm, for Duffy increasingly regards her eyes as mirrors and her ears as sounding boards for his self-glorification. He "attache[s] the fervent nature of his companion more and more closely." Yet she soon "disillusion[s]" Duffy by actually touching him, asserting her own desire (99).

In what Norris reads as a narrative strategy of sadism in cancelling an adulterous romance—perhaps because Duffy is homosexual—Mrs. Sinico is nonetheless multiply a victim of her embodiment as a woman.[121] The movement of physical to spiritual rhetoric in first half of "A Painful Case" models the literal movement of Mrs. Sinico's body in the second half of the story, where she is rendered as a disembodied spirit. Echoing her near-faint when Duffy dismisses her, Mrs. Sinico four years later falls in front of a tram. Duffy learns of her death from a newspaper article that suggests drink played a role in the accident, in either event a kind of suicide. At this point the narrative presents *Dubliners'* conventional troping of the drinker's conversion, a loss of identity caused by a fall into embodiment. But Mrs. Sinico's tumble differs in important respects from those of the male drunkards. Alcohol merely exaggerates the somatic compliance that characterizes the female organism because the drunkard's fall is continuous with the woman's swoon. Moreover, while "Grace" and "Counterparts" focus on the larger communal dynamics of their protagonists' habits, "A Painful Case" restricts the symbolic function of the drunkard, reducing the affected community to one. The female case, the private case, illuminates the pathology of the drinker in relation to one other person, rather than exploring any wider significance for the female intemperate.

It is precisely the ideology of privacy that the newspaper report of the inquest into her death disturbs. The news story threatens genteel anonymity with mere embodiment, which can be forensically inspected. Though Mrs. Sinico's fractures and contusion are clinically recounted, they fail to explain her death: "The injuries were not sufficient to have caused death in a normal person," Dr. Halpin concludes. "Death, in his opinion, had been probably due to shock and sudden failure of the heart's action" (101). Visual scrutiny of the drunkard once again fails to add up, to reveal who the drunkard "is." But the etiology of the female drunkard constantly collapses back into tautology, as the broken heart, the train, and the liquor that Mrs. Sinico is revealed to have consumed habitually all code her anatomy as an emotional text. Similarly, the medical and forensic language of the journalist, the police, and the physician consists of empty axioms: the meaning of this accident is trauma, the shame of its publicity is exposure. As mere spirit and mere body, Mrs. Sinico remains a mirror of her male examiners. But the newspaper article reporting her death points to a crux of *Dubliners'* own representation, for in this embedded report Joyce parodies the diagnostic language and clinical posture that he assumes in relation to the drunkards of the collection. As the stern judge of the intemperate's meaning, Duffy takes on a function assigned to the narrators of "Grace" and "Counterparts," even as he represents a caricature of their nuanced ironies. Duffy readily accedes to the newspaper's portrayal of Emily Sinico and vigorously articulates its implication of moral and criminal vice, which are redoubled for an already spiritualized femininity: "Evidently she had been unfit to live, without any strength of purpose, an easy prey to habits, one of the wrecks on which civilization has been reared," he reflects (103). Yet Mrs. Sinico's spirit refuses to remain fixed in the vocabulary of impurity or reversion. Feminine sympathies, narratively released from a particular body, move rapidly through forms that realize Duffy's former projections. He experiences her touch, drinks her "spirits," and hears her name in a departing train. The mix of alcohol and female sympathies seems to allow for the dead woman's materialization, filling the "little distance" between Duffy's intellect and body, his censure and affection. Poisoned by the drink that she attempted to use to cure her broken heart, Sinico in death becomes the elixir that cures Duffy, effecting his somatopsychic unification, regardless of his sexual proclivities. In this sense, liquor becomes a privileged site for the embodiment and transmission of female emotion, affording a reading of Duffy himself as a physical manifestation of her spirit. The indeterminacies of drinking as a symptom—and in particular as a female symptom—open another possibility for the "conversion" of male repression, while the female subject remains obscure, her inaccessibility overdetermined by the collapse of femininity into intemperance. Just as her annihilation leads to his conversion, her private, female meaning exposes the larger contours of masculine inertia.

•

Duffy's initial posture toward Mrs. Sinico's intemperance also points to the problematic of chronic drinking in *Dubliners*. The protagonist acts as a figure for the author, his gaze trained from a little distance on the ambiguous and resistant flesh of the drunkard. This gaze, as Cheryl Herr notes, "stills" its object, a body understood as already paralyzed.[122] As his letters attest, Joyce aims to cure rather than further disable his subjects: "[I]n composing my chapter of moral history in exactly the way I have composed it I have taken the first step towards the spiritual liberation of my country," he informed Grant Richards on May 20, 1906, in the midst of their editorial disputes.[123] Joyce describes Irish-Catholic illness with Aquinian clarity in order to shock it into motion again. Yet if the desire for drink is rendered as compulsive in *Dubliners*, the desire to inspect drinkers in search of a master etiology is equally dogged. This detached visual inspection constitutes Joyce's principal use of the techniques of both medicine and anthropology, a representational mode allied with a modernizing and objective reading of bodily symptoms that congeals into the sign of a specific organic disease, or an objective reading of bodily practices that resolves into manifestations of cultural totality. Whether patient or native, the insider's account is of little relevance to this scrutiny, for the body under inspection acts as the signifying text. The narrators of *Dubliners*, with a "scrupulous" and terse style of description and a focus on immediate events, display little interest in exploring the impalpable, and their subjects are rendered as resistant to or incapable of speech because of the very nature of their condition.

The power gained by Joyce's diagnostic rigor, and the dictates of the gaze, ultimately cancel this agenda. In submitting to inspection, the intemperates of *Dubliners* challenge the narrative's power to define them, to say precisely who they "are," to find a language or an image that can capture definitively the meaning of their stilled forms. At the same time, the narrative stance that *Dubliners'* early readers found so harsh reflects the literary posture that Joyce cultivated during the reception of his early prose works. "Joyce's writing of his reception was bound up with his long-distance specular relationship with Ireland," Nash observes in discussing the imagination of an Irish readership for *Dubliners*.[124] Narratively, too, the author stands at a distance from the Irish-Catholic body whose intimacies he displays, extracting knowledge from the forms in which he is vitally invested. Joyce, like Duffy, repudiates the drinkers with whom he conducts intimate relations. It might not be too much of an exaggeration to say that they repudiate him as well, through the compulsive performance of a "spiritual" counterdiscipline that submits to symbolic, theological, or diagnostic reading but will not yield its episteme through it. The power of alcohol to generate an epistemology from the body, after the model of orthopraxy, portends the positive valuation of chronic drinking in *Ulysses,* in which the gaze is demoted and the Irish-Catholic body is produced as well as dissolved by the material-spiritual operations of drink. But *Dubliners* also illuminates the practice of "reading" bodies produced by orthopraxy through the theological and allegorical "symbol" of mainstream Christian orthodoxy, a technique that allows the author to display bodies shaped by belief at the same time that he disguises the centrality of religious practice to his literary method. Though the collection anatomizes the paralyzed, lumpish, and inebriated body to compel movement, the attempt to know the drunkard through an external, theological or clinical, reading of his anatomy finally compounds its domination. The Dubliners' only mode of resistance is indistinguishable from capitulation.

2

The Canonization of Salman Rushdie

Mythic *Midnight's Children* and
Hindu-Muslim Embodiment

*L*ike *Dubliners*, *Midnight's Children* uses nativist illness to reimagine a national-spiritual body as the basis of a minority personhood. But while Joyce, through his narrative point of view, detaches from "the" Irish-Catholic subject, Rushdie incorporates himself into an absorptive and fissiparous Hindu-Muslim subcontinent. If Joyce aimed to show his cosmopolitan credentials by scrutinizing the Irish-Catholic body from an outsider vantage, Rushdie asserted his insider status as a provincial—his authority to speak not only about, but also *for* India. The British author relied less on religion than on the modern concept of traditional "Indian myth" to guarantee his nativist credentials. Protagonist Saleem Sinai's Vedic embodiment allows for an authorial locus within the national body, depicted as quintessentially corporate and permeable. Pitting Indian spirituality against imperial empiricism, *Midnight's Children* artfully and comically dismantles the authority of European hermeneutics while using Vedic protocols to disrupt a singular religious, regional, or even subcontinental identity for the traumatized nation-state. Yet this version of the subaltern subject also enforces its inevitable, actual dissolution. Rushdie's strategy obscured the author's distance from older national Indian literatures while privileging an "imaginary" textual and spiritual India.

Midnight's Children imitates the construction of "Indian myth" as a national project as well as an Orientalist one, and uses spiritual identity to continue a modernist project as well as to initiate a postcolonial disruption. In contrast to the central evocation of religion, myth can establish a transcendental realm without the burden of worship or doctrinal assent. Located outside the time, and often the space, of a fragmented or evacuated modernity, myth often signifies cultural totality, particularly an aesthetic one. This approach "takes for granted that nations, 'cultures,' and or *Völker* are primordial, bounded, unproblematic entities and that myth is the equally primordial voice, essence, and heritage of the group," Bruce Lincoln observes.[1] Romantic, Herderian myth, which Asad calls "a secular discourse of Enlightenment," negotiated the shift away from sensuous and bodily engagement with the sacred in Christianity and thus contributed to the assumption of an a priori, modern "secular self."[2] "Mystical" texts, formerly understood to contain obscured spiritual and eschatological content, similarly came to denote a literary genre and style; interpretive emphasis moved from an interest in miracles to a focus on subjective states disconnected from regulated practices or belief.[3] *Midnight's Children*, like many subsequent "postcolonial" and "transnational" novels, partakes of Herderian romanticism: the narrative lumps together various genres and disciplines of Sanskrit texts as a *Nationalliteratur*[4] at times indistinguishable from an Orientalist imaginary. Notably, the novel's consolidation of disparate identities through myth has roots in Indian nationalism as well as in Western stereotype. The formulation of a common basis of mystical-spiritual texts was deeply influential in the anticolonial and religious nationalism that developed in nineteenth-century India. Figures such as Rammohan Roy (1772–1833) and Vivekānada (1863–1902) embraced the British equation of India with spirituality as a means of opposing Christian imperial power, much as the Irish used Celtic myth and sectarian allegiance. Attempting to solidify an Indian identity, anticolonialists aimed to integrate disparate Hindu regional and performative oral traditions and to incorporate empirical epistemologies into a political program.[5] "Rational religion," which in certain respects paralleled the move toward liberal Christianity in the West, sought to reconcile belief with a scientific epistemology thought to be contained within Hinduism as well as in the bodily discipline of yoga. Built in part on the construction of a Hindu canon, these movements accepted critical editions of the *Mahabharata* and the *Ramayana* as the center of a classical Bharat, the ideal Hindu state,[6] and privileged in particular the ancient Vedas.[7] Gandhi later drew upon this social construction, which elevated a textual spirituality.[8] *Midnight's Children* uses an analogous strategy of consolidation. Instead of forwarding a unified Hindu identity, however, Rushdie coordinates Hindu corporeality with other religious and national identities and texts, prominently the Qu'ran and *A Thousand and One Nights*.

"The way I've always written has been shaped by the everyday fact of religious belief in India," Rushdie said in a 1983 interview.[9] His first two novels highlight this interest through their use of myth and mysticism as ciphers for metaphysical belief. "The structures and metaphors of religion (Hinduism and Christianity as much as Islam) shaped his irreligious mind, and the concerns of these religions with the great questions of existence . . . were also his," Rushdie writes of himself in *Joseph Anton* (2012).[10] Yet the treatment of myth as a syncretic vehicle for different religions and older narratives registered quite differently in the author's first novel. Rushdie's use of "Indian myth" to insert himself into the corpus of the subcontinent changed him from the Oxbridge-associated author of the fantasy *Grimus* (1975) into the premier Indian author of the 1980s. At the beginning of *Midnight's Children*'s public career, Rushdie's relationship to the subcontinent was hesitant and attenuated, according to his own report. By 1983, with the publication of *Shame*, he was declaring in the Indian periodical *Celebrity*: "If you have to choose a nationality as a writer, I'd call myself an Indian writer."[11] But his claim on "insider" status as an Indian—a claim that contradicted earlier self-characterizations—vexes *Midnight's Children,* as well as Rushdie's subsequent work and eventually his reception. While *Shame* and later novels prominently feature a "migrant" cosmopolitan as a central figure, *Midnight's Children* attempts to absorb the author's "outsider" status into an indigenous protagonist.[12] Rushdie resolves the anxiety of identity through an "authentic," spiritually syncretic Indian agent, generated in part by the writer's own temporal, geographic, and literary distance from the subcontinent and enshrined as the index to his aesthetic.

In rendering its dynamic and yet impaired protagonist, *Midnight's Children* surmounts the problematic of *Dubliners,* in which distanced scrutiny and critique of the colonial corpus finally reinforce its stilling. Rushdie's method of representation registers an acute awareness of the provisional nature of the writer's claim to an authoritative Indian voice, a dilemma that Joyce did not share. Saleem encodes the transactions between the body of the cosmopolitan author and the body of the subcontinent, between *Midnight's Children* and Indian literary production by nationals in majority languages. The metonymic production of an India in fact lost[13] to the author through time and emigration produces the romance that gives birth to India as a nation-state and as a collective modern history. It is based on an eroticized lack and leads to an imaginary of wholeness satisfied in myth but not in politics. In the end, Rushdie's relation to the subcontinent overdetermines his protagonist's physical dissolution. Saleem's phallogocentric metaphor for his textual production acts as a competing analogy to the incorporative model of the Vedic body that constitutes the novel's primary conceit. The novel's final dissolution of an actual India—or the dream of nationalism, as Saleem would have it—is inevitable not only because of the national body's metonymic generation, but also because of the author's. As one romance of India fails, another thrives.

Rushdie's Rebirths

"The Empire is striking back," Rushdie proclaimed at a 1982 conference on Indian writing in English, held at London's Commonwealth Institute. "I suggest that the flowering of these new literatures may be the most important to occur in any language since the earlier incursions of Flann O'Brien, Beckett, and Joyce."[14] Rushdie spoke as a recent winner of the Booker Prize and as a rapidly emerging spokesman for minority writers in English. His remarks highlight his early and consistent identification with modernist Irish writers, and especially with Joyce, in part because of their rejection of national predecessors. In spite of the topic of the conference, Rushdie paid scant attention to other Indian writers in English, except for G. V. Desani, whose *All about H. Hatterr* (1947) modelled Indian appropriation of the imperial tongue. Rushdie observes that Desani "showed how English could be bent and kneaded until it spoke in an authentically Indian voice.... Desani's triumph was to take babu-English, chamcha-English, and turn it against itself: the instrument of subservience became a weapon of liberation. It was the first great stroke of the de-colonizing pen."[15] In his own moment, Rushdie saw such energies expressed not by other contemporary writers in India, but rather by Ngugi wa Thiong'o, Earl Lovelace, Toni Morrison, Andre Brink, and Derek Walcott, well-known metropolitan authors with other minority or postcolonial affiliations.[16]

The address is noteworthy for Rushdie's mention of an Indian literary history in English, though not for its neglect of Indian literatures in older subcontinental languages. As his career progressed, the writer rarely alluded to any national literary traditions, other than mythic and legendary ones, usually in orature. At times he denied that even Indian nationals writing in English bore any relationship to him at all.[17] The Indian-born British Rushdie identified, as Joyce did, with a cosmopolitan European literature. In describing the genesis of *Midnight's Children*, he explicitly set his work against "the literature that had been produced about India," which he found "dated," "dainty," and "delicate" while the country that he had revisited was in fact "massive" and "elephantine."[18] Rushdie said in another interview that he had wanted to write a "'big city novel,'" one that captured the sensuous materiality of contemporary life in Bombay.[19] In such remarks, the writer casts Indian literature as a subject matter rather than the product of a geographic location or its languages, an equation that bears centrally upon his metropolitan posture as an "Indian" writer who epitomized an emerging subgenre of postcolonial literature. In his 2012 memoir, Rushdie relates that his problem was one of "authenticity"; he "worried" as he conceived of the novel that "his Indian connection had weakened" or been "lost."[20] It is, finally, the English language that Rushdie claimed as his province and the Indian body, produced by spiritual practices and texts, that he needed as a major source of modernist transcendence.

This Rushdie emerged at a moment open for new directions—not in "the" Indian novel, but in those written in English, by both national and migrant authors. Meenakshi Mukherjee writes that the Indian novel in English was at a "low point" in 1980, as the generation of the 1930s, while still active, had "ceased to surprise." Though literatures in other Indian languages had been transformed by "young urban Indians of a certain class born after 1947," their work marked by playfulness, linguistic mixture, and popular vocabularies drawn from sources such as film magazines, Indian novels in English were "musty," overly earnest, and dualistic.[21] In a different vein, Amitava Kumar notes that the energies credited to *Midnight's Children* had long been evident in Indian popular culture, which the narrative highlights as a reference but which its popular and critical reception has left largely unexplored as a major hermeneutic. Kumar also questions the widespread equation of Rushdie with "Indianness, especially in light of the neglect of subcontinental literature in languages other than English."[22] None of these contexts registered in the quick Western recognition of the novel. The book's critical and popular success transformed Rushdie from an obscure writer of intellectual "fantasy" to an Indian-identified political writer fully engaged with cosmopolitan experiment. By the time of the 1983 publication of *Shame*, Rushdie was touted as a significant voice of the subcontinent and a father of the new Indian literature—and not necessarily just in "in English." At the time, Michael T. Kaufman of the *New York Times* asked Rushdie whether he was aware "in writing these India books that the clearing [he] was making was such virgin territory . . . [in] that no one had mined the myths of contemporary India." Rushdie replied, "Yes," and referred to his consciousness of the novelty of a "comic epic" that encompassed the reality of India.[23]

The status of Rushdie's Indian identity has been a consistent issue in his career since the success of *Midnight's Children*, even as the author's own statements about his relationship to his birthplace have varied. Initially his Indian profile seemed to stem from the subject matter of *Midnight's Children* rather than from the author's personal origins or minority status, neither of which registered in the (admittedly thin) reception of his first novel. *Grimus* is heavily indebted to mythic motifs that absorb religious content, including central references to the mystical Sufism of Islam, but it was received as British fantasy. Popular reviews of *Grimus* concentrated on questions of genre rather than any subcontinental or Muslim religious affinities. The novel features an eponymous European magician in conflict with the Native or "Red" American Flapping Eagle. Set in the imaginary geography of Axona, the narrative syncretizes a number of world mythologies and texts in a modernist allegory of mental colonization. Critics questioned its aims, as the novel combined high literary and "global" allusions with elements of genre fiction and barely mentioned any political allegory or spiritual content. The London *Times* grouped the book with two other first novels. Peter Tinniswood describes *Grimus* as an "adventure story by terms epic and comic."[24] In the *Times Literary Supplement,* David Wilson calls the work a "fable" aligned with but not solidly belonging to science fiction or political satire, the only genres in which its aspirations to "global metaphor" could be made fashionable.[25] Both readers question the ends to which these genres are put. Tinniswood cites *A Pilgrim's Progress* and the *Odyssey,* Wilson the film *2001: A Space Odyssey,* as touchstones. Neither review mentions any context for the novel other than a metropolitan one. Wilson in fact concludes by placing *Grimus* in a very specific British cultural location: "If one has doubts about the world Mr[.] Rushdie has created they don't concern his logic: the question is whether his dryly entertaining intellectual conceit is anything more than an elaborate statement of the obvious decked out in the mannerisms of Oxford philosophy."[26]

Grimus was not a critical or a commercial success. Rushdie has subsequently called it a failure,[27] from which he learned that "fantasy" must be grounded in an "observable reality" drawn from his own experience and recognizable to readers.[28] He has questioned the novel's classification as science fiction rather than literary fantasy, akin to works of Thomas Pynchon[29]—although elsewhere he has spoken of his interest in science fiction.[30] Brian Aldiss, "the godfather of British SF" and a fan of the work, later expressed relief that the book was withdrawn from consideration for the Gollancz Science Fiction Prize. "'Had it won . . . [Rushdie] would have been labeled a science fiction writer and nobody would have heard of him again,'" Aldiss stated in 2007.[31] Now back in print as part of a Random House series of Rushdie titles, it is housed in a "fantasy" niche linked to science fiction, its premier jacket blurb by Ursula LeGuin. Literary critics have recuperated the novel as "speculative fiction" and linked it more closely to *Midnight's Children.* Some have questioned the hard separation of science fiction from mythic modes of fantasy in Rushdie's work.[32]

As in the reviews of *Grimus,* the first notices for *Midnight's Children,* which appeared five years later, locate the novel primarily in a Western literary context and focus on the text. Rushdie's politics and background are treated explicitly not on newspaper book pages but in magazines, where a discussion of the text is more often combined with feature elements. *Newsweek* identifies the author as "a young Indian novelist living in London,"[33] the *New Yorker* calls him a "glittering" production of India,[34] and even *India West*—perhaps for different reasons—calls him "Salman Rushdie of Bombay."[35] Such references to the writer's national origin, his ethnicity, and occasionally his religion, became more frequent as the novel accrued renown. *Midnight's Children* won the Booker Prize in October 1981; *Shame,* set in Pakistan, appeared in 1983, and consolidated Rushdie's profile as an emerging cosmopolitan writer who could be fused unproblematically with his subcontinental past.

Like Joyce, then, Rushdie became more tightly linked to his national and religious origins as he achieved professional success. The first newspaper reviews of *Midnight's Children,* which appeared in February 1981, often characterize the author through his novel's subject matter and through comparison to other cosmopolitan writers who revise and critique their national histories—not through his biography. What Flaubert was to *Dubliners* and *A Portrait,* Marquez's *One Hundred Years of Solitude* (1967) was to *Midnight's Children.* Readers also frequently cite Günter Grass's *The Tin Drum* (1959) to indicate Rushdie's conflation of personal narrative and politically charged national epic in a self-conscious and highly literary experimental prose. Surprisingly, these comments rarely employ the term "magic realism"—Bill Buford in the *New Statesman* is a notable exception[36]—or focus unduly on the work's alternate reality as magical, but suggest such stylistic allegiances through references to Marquez, Grass, and Milan Kundera. Elements of the "fabulous" or the fable in this way become attached less to questions of popular genre than to modes of aesthetic-historical discourse and to Indian myth. John Leonard, in the *New York Times,* calls the novel an "epic" that, like those of Grass and Marquez, "gives us history, politics, myth, food, magic, wit and dung." Leonard later highlights political critique as intimately related to the narrative style, expressive of the "fragmentation" of Partition and its emotional effects.[37] Saleem's "alternative realities" are multiple, according to Elaine Feinstein in the London *Times,* and the novel full of "confusing superstitions" as well as "pungent dialogue and wit," but she leads her essay with a discussion of the novel's historical base.[38] *Newsweek*'s Charles Michener calls Rushdie an "aspirant to the ranks of V. S. Naipaul and Milan Kundera—private storytellers with public visions who cast contemporary nobodies into the whirlpool of current events."[39] The rarely mentioned Naipaul, paired with Kundera, suggests a synthesis of two different strands of contemporary writing. Though both are political and exilic, Naipaul betokens an older, more ambivalent and distanced "diasporan" Indian and minority identity, overtly political but less formally experimental, while Kundera signifies an exemplary postmodernist whose oppositional politics fully inform his aesthetic experiment.

Readily compared with novels composed in Spanish and German, *Midnight's Children* did not elicit much comparison to Indo-Anglian novels, much less to contemporary works in majority Indian languages such as Hindi or Bengali. Rather the rubric "writing about India," regardless of the writer's location, seemed to govern the paradigm that British and American literary journalists employed. Reviewers were just as likely to discuss Rushdie in relation to Paul Scott and E. M. Forster as they were to place him in the company of Marquez and Grass. Contrasting Rushdie's vulgarity and comedy to Anita Desai's gentility, Leonard opposes *Midnight's Children* to Anglo-British modernism and the "Raj" revival while at the same time using these writers to establish a context for narratives about India. Leonard states that *Midnight's Children* "is the shadow in Paul Scott's mirror or perhaps what E. M. Forster heard in the cave, with a lot of symbolic curry added."[40] In *TLS*, Valerie Cunningham locates *Midnight's Children* almost entirely within an impressive British literary tradition, but she is troubled by its combination with the object "India," in spite of her high praise. The novel's engagement with an ornate form seems a function of the exotic sublime in her estimation, as India is "fascinatingly particular and awingly representative of human variety." Rushdie's book possesses "fetching readability" as well as "literary importance": she notes Saleem's embodiment of Indian history and self-proclaimed obsession with correspondences while she praises the concrete sensory qualities of the narrative, its realization of the figure. But Cunningham also implies that the novel skillfully mimics its high literary predecessors, as if the "Indian text" were becoming jumped up with its pretensions. She says: "It's a remarkably dexterous performance. But if the granting of an Indian text so high a degree of self-consciousness were all, *Midnight's Children* might be dismissable as a smart refurbishing of bits of Sterne and James, of *Heart of Darkness* and *Finnegans Wake*, by courtesy of Deconstructionism and Wolfgang Iser." She continues, "That would, of course, be a harsh judgment, . . . its play of signifiers, of textualities, the drama of reading and writing of India is bolted firmly into its fierce political despairs and indignations."[41] Anita Desai herself, in a March 1981 review that appeared in the *Washington Post*, reflects a similar division between European masters and Indian material when she states that the novel is "not a national allegory or fable" but rather is "as universal as the works of Cervantes, Swift, Kafka, or

Grass."[42] She does lament that the novel, which is "of major interest to Indian readers," will probably not be "published, distributed or read" in India. She suggests that this situation obtains because of a national aversion to "the intolerable reality" of its circumstances and a preference for "maya, the shimmer of illusion" rather than because of the structures of the international literary marketplace.[43]

The earliest responses to Rushdie's work make a different, but related, distinction between a modernist fable, presumed "universal" temporally and geographically in spite of its generic affiliations, and the "Indian" fable, located in a specific political and literary history and intermixed with elements of Eastern myth and legend. Very few Western publications examined any more particular contexts for *Midnight's Children*, even though many reviews emphasized its engagement with political history and critique. The few pieces that explore such topics appeared in literary journals: these, like the comments in Indian publications, do not so much revise the dominant tropes of metropolitan journalism as they articulate the object "India" in at least some detail. Robert Towers, in the September 24, 1981, *New York Review of Books*, leads with Rushdie's "Muslim" background and orientation, which he contrasts with the "Hindu sensibility" of the novel.[44] Maria Couto, in "*Midnight's Children* and Parents: The Search for Indo-British Identity," an extended analysis that appeared in *Encounter*, places Rushdie in the context of J. G. Farrell's *The Siege of Krishnapur* (1973), Paul Scott's *Raj Quartet* (1966–77), and Ruth Prawer Jhabvala's *Heat and Dust* (1975).[45] After a substantial discussion of historical events, Couto analyzes Rushdie's affinities with G. V. Desani's *Hatterr*, noting the use of mixed languages and identities in both. Desani's work "is a kind of testament of the self questioning of a whole layer of Indian society in the post-colonial world," Couto observes, though *Hatterr* shows Desani's generational difference from Rushdie's in being "[t]he more Anglicized, the less 'Indo,' so to speak."[46]

Reviews in English-language Indian publications pay more attention to the religious and cultural content of the work but similarly concentrate on its technique in relation to an Indian subject matter rather than to any national literary milieu. Features and interviews do not treat Rushdie as a native author in any direct sense. "He does not feel like an 'Indian novelist,'" reports the *Times of India* in a November 1981 interview. The interviewer notes that the author does not write in his "mother tongue," Urdu, but praises the novel's "remarkable Indian-ness."[47] In a review that ran in the same paper a month later, N. J. Nanporia is made somewhat uneasy by the combination of metafictional techniques and subject matter, despite his overall praise of the novel. "The technique is the hero, but what is it in aid of?" Nanporia asks.

He questions whether the narrative's perceptual experiments "add up" to "the Indian reality," especially when they represent large historical events, "hardly truths that demand magical perception."[48] In its review feature, which, like Nanporia's, appeared after the novel had been lauded by the New York and the London *Times, India Today* labels *Midnight's Children* unique in "Indo-Anglian writing" and calls it "a sort of Bombay-based *World according to Garp*" (1978), a tragicomic novel by the American John Irving. More than many English and American reviewers, Sunil Sethi points to the "magic" that results from Saleem's mixture of "fact, fiction, and fantasy"; the protagonist is an "Indian Scheherazade" who tells stories with the same energy that he devotes to making pickles.[49] But Sethi also calls the novel's conclusion, in which India disintegrates in the wake of Indira Gandhi's 1977 declaration of Emergency, "one of the most ferocious indictments of India's evolution since Independence."[50] And a sidebar interview with Rushdie calls attention to the novel's "Muslim soul-searching," an affiliation rarely mentioned in any British and American articles.[51]

One of the few comments to place Rushdie in any sort of national literary context appeared in *India West*. This reviewer, like Sethi, responds to Western reactions to the novel. After acknowledging Rushdie's affinities with European writers such as Grass, Celine, and Kakfa, the reviewer takes issue with the *New York Times Review of Books*' [sic] proclamation that novel promises to "redraw the literary map of India." "This may be too far-fetched," the reviewer asserts:

> The fact remains that India's literary map has already been redrawn with masterful Indian strokes by the genius of R. K. Narayan and Raja Rao. Which is not to deny the strong streak of original genius that is clearly the hallmark of *Midnight's Children*. I am, of course, referring only to English language writers (otherwise known as Indo-Anglian writers) whose mirror reflects only a marginal section of India.[52]

Interestingly, the review also praises Rushdie's prose for opposing "literary and academic conventions" with a "fierce, sputtering, brawling" work that represents "a modern India." In doing so, the novelist aims to "burst out, to launch between the tired and tiring gestures of Indo-Anglian novelists such a[s] Balwant Gargi, Kamala Markandaya, Ruth Jhawala, and Anita Desai."[53]

The dominance of the British canon, leavened with some internationalism, is evident in Rushdie's own descriptions of the novel at the time of its publication. Interestingly, in the interview that accompanies Sethi's review in *India Today*, Rushdie himself places his book "in a very definite English tradition, that of Swift, Sterne and Dickens"; he also mentions as influences Latin American and German writers such as Grass and Thomas Mann. He refers to the novel's commonality with "Indian literature" not through any contemporary work in other languages, but rather through "[its] interest in myth and fable and story-telling."[54] When the interviewer asks whether *Midnight's Children* was aimed at this audience "exclusively," the author admits that he expected that it would be "more popular" in the West. He is surprised, he says, that subcontinental readers have been interested in a novel that he was afraid might seem "condescending" to them in its explanations of familiar references.[55]

The scholarship on *Midnight's Children* that emerged rapidly and voluminously in the 1980s focused on similar topics, such as the relationship of the public and private in the recording of history,[56] the reader response encoded in Padma's challenges to Saleem's story, and the narrative registers of truth. Critics were eager to put the novel in a cosmopolitan and European literary lineage as well as a mythic-legendary one, usually received as a generalized "Eastern" reference. The work's relation to *The Tin Drum* and *One Hundred Years of Solitude*, to *A Thousand and One Nights* and *Tristram Shandy* dominates the decade's scholarly reception. In the late 1980s and the 1990s, the transactions of fact and figure, history and legend, the use of national allegory, and the critique of realism become central concerns. But the formalist and political-historical emphasis of most of this criticism—particularly in the 1980s—favored European literary genealogy and cultural references even as scholars asserted the narrative's exemplary cross-cultural status, postcolonial critique of nationalism, emphasis on reader response, and use of distancing techniques. In contrast to this strain, early essays by Uma Parameswaran,[57] Wimal Dissanayake,[58] and John Stephens[59] insisted on Rushdie's links to Indian national writers in English such as Raja Rao and R. K. Narayan. Parameswaran emphasized the relationship of *Midnight's Children* to *Grimus* as well as to Rushdie's earlier stories.[60] Articles that treat myth and legend as a significant "Indian" or subcontinental connection assume this status without much acknowledgement of mediation. Nancy E. Batty, for instance, in the "The Art of Suspense: Rushdie's 1,001 (Mid-)Nights," concentrates on the links between the "desperate political acts" of Saleem and Scheherazade with reference to John Barth's use of the allusion in *Chimera* (1972), but gives no contextualization of *A Thousand and One Nights*, other than reference to the Burton translation, cited as a 1923 edition;[61] C. Kanaganayakam's "Myth and Fabulousity in *Midnight's Children*" draws a topical continuity between Rushdie and older Indian national writers in English while casting myth as a "backdrop of . . . timelessness" in diachronic relation to twentieth-century fragmentation, and the fabulous as the synchronic axis of "different modes of perception."[62] "Magic realism" as a vehicle for politicized myth appears in a 1985 essay by Jean-Pierre Durix.[63] In 1988, Stephen Slemon analyzes the term—coined in 1925 by Francis Roh[64] to describe postexpressionist painting, and applied beginning in the 1940s to Latin American narratives[65]—in relation to its then-recent use to describe literatures in English. "In none of its applications to literature has the concept of magic realism ever successfully differentiated between itself and neighboring genres such as fabulation, metafiction, the baroque, the fantastic, the uncanny or the marvelous," Slemon asserts. Still he argues for its usefulness in articulating a "post-colonial context," for "the magic realist narrative recapitulates a dialectical struggle within the culture's language" that is never resolved.[66]

The Somatopsychic Corpus and Āyurvedic Medicine

Midnight's Children soon came to be heralded for its Barthesian "openness" as a text. Rushdie himself has frequently noted that his subcontinental audiences tended to understand the novel as descriptive of history or reality while cosmopolitan readers responded to its technique as "fabulous."[67] Though the early reception does not suggest such a division, it does show that both Rushdie and his first audiences understood *Midnight's Children* primarily through an Anglo-British or cosmopolitan framework, not as a bellwether of expansive reader-response or a singular emblem of Indian literary identity. Such reactions emerged more gradually, as subcontinental readers enjoyed the confident exuberance with which Rushdie commandeered English to his own ends. Even in this identification audiences cast Rushdie in a Joycean cosmopolitan mode, in which a provincial content is worked over by a metropolitan aesthetic.

To establish the cultural credentials of the novel, Rushdie, like Joyce, calls on classical tradition and other media: oral epics, originating in legend, myth, and religious texts; visual media such as painting and popular film; culinary arts. Asked about the novel's use of the epics the *Ramayana*, the *Mahabarata*, and the Sanskrit animal fables and aphorisms that comprise the *Panchatandra* (100 BC–AD 500), Rushdie replies that the oral epic seemed the "inescapable" vehicle of the Indian novel because of its flexibility and cultural ubiquity.[68] Implicitly, these forms also accommodate "a reality in which the idea of the miraculous is all absolute truth" to the extent that "the miraculous and the everyday coexist."[69] Reviews as well as scholarly criticism noted or examined but infrequently questioned the installation of "Indianness" through these quintessential signifiers, embedded in a history teeming with particulars largely unfamiliar to Western readers: Aijaz Ahmad influentially asserted that Rushdie's captured "Indianness" through the multitudinous form of orature.[70] As scholarly attention moved from endorsement of *Midnight's Children* as the epitome of postcolonial literature and poststructural displacement to assertion of its "Third World cosmopolitanism,"[71] hybridity, or syncretism, and finally to condemnation of its easily consumed exoticism,[72] few critics paused to examine the more nuanced cultural and religious, rather than macro political and historical, contexts that inform the novel's central conceit.[73] Timothy Brennan's configuration of a self-aware, critical cosmopolitanism provides a starting point for such an analysis. I elaborate on it by grounding the novel's engagement with belief formations as a foundation of the novel's insider-outsider position. In this I disagree with Brennan's contention that Rushdie "superficial[ly] engage[s]" with "disposable genres" even as I elaborate on his observation that the author in his early fame "wrapped himself in the mantle of filiative authenticity."[74] Interpretations of *Midnight's Children*, even those that in recent years have articulated the novel's insider-outsider posture, have not treated the specific spiritual-somatic framework of Saleem's materialized agency. In this vein, Kumkum Sangari has noted Rushdie's quick appropriation by a metropolitan postmodernism: "From this decontextualizing vantage point various formal affinities can easily be abstracted from a different mode of cognition; the nonmimetic can be read as antimimetic, difference can easily be made the excuse for sameness," she observes.[75] Bishnupriya Ghosh has argued for Rushdie's inauguration of a "new kind of Indian vernacular" that must be situated in "contextual knowledges."[76]

I base my analysis on the situated practices that fund the text of *Midnight's Children*. Though many critics have examined the truth-status of Saleem's embodiment, its predicates have not often been questioned. Rather, they have been given, like both the postmodernity and the authenticity presumed early in the novel's popular and academic careers. Perhaps most significantly, the "self" that the novel is imagined to displace is an individual unquestionably equated with "the" subject-agent. Clifford Geertz illuminates the cultural specificity of the universalized "self" assumed as the ground of postmodern dislocation when he separates the concept of the "individual" from other formulations of the person: "The Western conception of the person as a bounded, unique, more or less integrated motivational and cognitive universe, a dynamic center of awareness, emotion, judgment, and action organized into a distinctive whole and set contrastively against other such wholes and against a social and natural background is, however incorrigible it may seem to us, a rather peculiar idea within the context of the world's cultures."[77] Rushdie in fact revises the individual as the axiomatic subject, agent, and bodily habitus—not merely through poststructuralist dissolution or fragmentation, but also, perhaps more fundamentally, through the techniques of materialization, porousness, and movement drawn from spiritualized medicine. *Midnight's Children* sets the clinical-ethnographic gaze against the speech of the indigenous patient who insists on the bodily reality of his spiritual distress. Resistance to clinical scrutiny, a consequence of the leaden opacity of Joyce's drunkards, is the active project of Rushdie's first-person narrator, who claims to be dissolving as a result of an illness that does not register as an organic disease. Saleem purports to embody a country born into an analogous dilemma: though India "has five thousand years of history" it is "nevertheless quite imaginary."[78]

The story begins with his putative grandfather, a Kashmiri Muslim recently returned from medical training in Germany. Through Aadam Aziz, the novel immediately installs medicine as the primary discourse of historiography and offers two hermeneutics of physical distress as competing epistemologies. They in fact dramatize a dynamic of contemporary Indian subjects. The objective standard of European history, aligned with a psychologized subject who must exhibit externally measurable signs of organic disease to qualify as sick, competes with the somatized experience of chronic distress, tacitly aligned with traditional medicine. Thus while *Dubliners* encapsulates communal Irish illness through a chronic drunkenness that resists the external reading that would classify it, *Midnight's Children* metafictionally plays with Indian illness as a possibly imagined condition, associated with mental rather than physical disease and contrasted comically with the superstitions of provincial characters. According to the Western clinical medicine that is part of Saleem's heritage, and to which he claims to ascribe, his "illness" must be judged as highly subjective, psychosomatic, or delusional. The narrator himself equates organic disease with fact, clinical anatomy, Western history, and literary realism, and illness with figure, "psychosomatic" pain, nativist tradition, and myth at the same time that he argues for the actual, material operation of his historical-spiritual plight.

Typically, Saleem maintains this rhetorical and epistemic binary by denying it—the "literal" is "not metaphorical" but "reality" can contain "metaphor" and still be "true." He articulates this hermeneutic when he describes the founding of the Midnight's Children Conference, shortly after his tenth birthday. Saleem uses his newly discovered telepathy to convene an ad hoc "parliament" that represents the utopian promise of a just, democratic, and cooperative government for the young nation-state. "Don't make the mistake," he warns the reader, "of dismissing what I've unveiled as mere delirium; or even as the insanely exaggerated fantasies of a lonely, ugly child." He continues:

> I have stated before that I am not speaking metaphorically; what I have just written . . . is nothing less than the literal, by-the-hairs-of-my-mother's-head truth. Reality can have a metaphorical content; that does not make it less real. A thousand and one children were born; there were a thousand and one possibilities which had never been present in one place at one time before; and there were a thousand and one dead ends. Midnight's children can be made to represent many things, according to your point of view; they can be seen as the last throw of everything antiquated and retrogressive in our myth-ridden nation, whose defeat was entirely desirable in the context of a modernizing, twentieth-century economy; or as the true hope of freedom, which is now forever extinguished; but what they must not become is the bizarre creation of a rambling, diseased mind. No, illness is neither here nor there. (197)

Midnight's Children supports the conflation of psychic and physical vocabularies by realizing the metaphor as substantial—a characteristic treatment of emotion in a Hindu devotional framework[79]—and by using somatization as a legitimate, culture-bound idiom of distress, as well as a source of comedy. When, in the present-tense narrative, Dr. Baligga is summoned, the story draws attention to the invisibility of Saleem's cracks as objectified signs rather than as narratable symptoms. Saleem calls him a "ju-ju man" and a "green-medicine wallah," but Dr. Baligga, like Saleem's putative grandfather, Aadam Aziz, is a clinical physician. "Believe this if you can: the fraud has pronounced me whole!" the protagonist recounts indignantly. "'I see no cracks,' [the doctor] intoned mournfully. . . . Blindly, he impugned my state of mind, cast doubts on my reliability as a witness, and Godknowswhat else: 'I see no cracks'" (66). Through the tendency to fuse what clinical medicine separates into organic and psychic distress, Vedic and other somatopsychic protocols act as the foundation of Saleem's semiotic. The protagonist's distress is not psychosomatic or figurative, according to these predicates. Through the conception of another epistemology of the body, his "illness" actually points to the ignored and suppressed metaphoric or culturally inflected content of an "objective" idiom of pain.

Rushdie repeatedly calls attention to the exchange of the "literal" and "metaphoric" in order to suggest their implication in one another, a relation that is transactional and catalytic. Between the stated registers of clinical and folkloric-mythic, objective and subjective, realistic and fantastic, *Midnight's Children* represents a substantial body in which psychic and physical states are intertwined and separations among subjects, as well as between bodies and their environments, are highly permeable. To establish this conceit, the novel draws on the conceptual framework of the Āyurveda, a traditional Hindu medicine connected to the spiritual philosophy of the Vendanta. Vedic medicine tends to understand "internal" states as substances that flow between objects and bodies.[80] Saleem's claims are not subjective in the individual sense, as they result from collective premises, and they are not merely psychic, as they totalize the emotional and the physical to express a chronic global distress. The "subtle" and the "gross," or physical, bodies posited by Vedic medicine constantly encapsulate reason and sentiment in each structure: the *manas*, the mind or heart, of the subtle body, for instance, is located in the heart, regarded as the seat of judgment as well as feeling.[81] Such vocabularies challenge not only the division of body and mind, individual and community, but also the formulation of "emotion" as a foundational category, representing events that are made rather than given and that vary culturally as much as any other phenomena.[82]

Midnight's Children parallels *Dubliners* in imagining the organic disease of the individual as the somatopsychic illness of the community, located in but not confined to the exemplary male corpus. According to Kleinman, in the somatopsychic mode, "'feeling' is expressed and interpreted more subtly, indirectly, globally, superficially and above all somatically" than is typical in cultures that strictly demarcate physical and mental distress.[83] In Saleem, Rushdie combines the grotesque Rabelaisian body of Western literature with transactional and somatopsychic bodies. The oscillation between these models realizes a distinctive "Indian" conception of the person, allied with Hindu understandings, traumatized and fathered by imperial history, and applied to a singular Muslim protagonist beset with a prophetic mission. The Āyurveda, like many traditional medicines, is embedded in a somatic psychology, in which sentiment is understood primarily as physical and fluid, and in a spiritual and moral philosophy that conceives of the body-self or person as highly interactive with its social and metaphysical contexts. Based on a doctrine of humors or energies, Āyurvedic theory presents disease as a disturbance of bodily balance, exemplified by *prana*, or the life force: physical, spiritual, and mental health are indivisible, and physical well-being impossible, without spiritual harmony. Given these premises, the "mental" disturbance that Saleem experiences appears as a humoral imbalance that equally affects his physical being. His belief is not merely expressive; it is constitutive.[84]

Unlike the autonomous, highly bounded individual that Geertz describes, the person posited in this hermeneutic is tenuously bounded and coterminal with multiple milieus. A body, which is as much a social and metaphysical as a private and organic domain, must consequently be protected through codes that govern hygiene, diet, and social interaction. McKim Marriott describes the premises of the individual, as contrasted with those of the Hindu formulation: "[Western] persons . . . are postulated as being normally self-reflexive ('individuals,' having identity with and being sufficient to themselves), and as symmetrical (equal), and transitive (consistent) in their relations with one another. 'Individuals' are indivisible, integrated, and self-developing units, not normally subject to disjunction or reconstitution. Given such units, interpersonal influences, inequalities, and changes have to be brought in as external factors or pathologies." In contrast, "[t]he Hindu postulations of mixing, unmarking and unmatching instead assert that persons are in various degrees nonreflexive (not necessarily identical with or otherwise related only to themselves), nonsymmetrical (not necessarily equal) and nontransitive (not necessarily consistent) in their relations. They emphasize that persons are composite and divisible (what one might better call 'dividuals') and that interpersonal relations in the world are generally irregular and fluid."[85] Intermediate processes, rather than dichotomous states, are "basic" to these experiential conceptions.[86]

In drawing attention to these different understandings, I do not suggest that Vedic philosophy, or the person that the novel represents through it, lacks a psychology, any more than I imply that somatization does not occur in Western contexts that assume an organic, measurable basis of a true "disease," in Kleinman's terms. Rather I point to the historical and cultural inflection of the Western epistemology of pain, in which psychology and affect are separated discursively and experientially, as they are not in somatopsychic expression or the spiritually embedded body of the "dividual" produced by Hindu understanding. As Kleinman observes, chronic pain syndromes are less prevalent in the Western hermeneutic than they were before the Victorian middle class began to elaborate a psychological conception of pain. He notes: "It is quite possible that this psychological idiom, one of Western culture's most powerful self-images, is the personal concomitant of the societal process of *rationalization* that Max Weber saw as modernism's leading edge . . . . From the Weberian perspective, the conception and experience of 'affect' among the middle classes is culturally shaped as 'deep' psychological experience and rationalized into discretely labeled emotions (depression, anxiety, anger) that were previously categorized and felt principally as bodily experiences."[87] Thus, for instance, when Saleem states that his Aunt Alia poisoned his family by serving food infused with her bitterness (395), his claim can be read as a concrete, "magical" representation of an abstracted, hostile affect, and such a reading accompanies the image. The juxtaposition calls attention to the psychological or social "climate" created by the aunt's hostility as an equally metaphoric understanding of mind-body and social relations, whose premises resemble the rationalization Kleinman describes. In similar instances, the boatman Tai's derisive remarks "infect" the young Aziz with "insidious venom," filling him "with insects" (22–23); years later, his wife's "invasion" of her daughter's dreams discloses secret affection for a man (60). Each description exemplifies the novel's tendency to render emotions conventionally regarded as psychic and abstract as concrete events. These depictions highlight the figurative quality of the "real" vocabulary of emotion as insubstantial and equally arbitrary. They also play upon the body's recapitulation of the cosmos and its metaphysical principles through symbolic correlations as well as actual materials. For instance, the three corporeal energies—*vayu* (air or wind), *pitha* (fire or bile), and *kapha* (water or phlegm)—correspond to those that animate the universe, as well as to the Hindu gods Brahma, Vishnu, and Shiva, who personify creation, preservation, and destruction. Tissues, which form the physiological system and correlate with various limbs and organs, must be balanced with the humors. Such correspondences link Alia's bitterness to bile, Tai's anger to venom, Saleem's body to universal matter and energy.[88]

Midnight's Children uses Vedic protocols not only to complement and converse with the "individual" and the realist codes for representing it, but also to synthesize allusions and contexts for a diverse corporate subject. The porous and recapitulative capacities of the Vedic corpus allow the narrative to open and recode Muslim patriarchy while positing Muslim Indian centrality. Rushdie thus renders concrete the allusive tissues of *Ulysses*, by taking the syncretic capacities of bodies inflected with spiritual significance to emplot a Muslim family: its originary "Aadam" spills three drops of blood, echoing the Qu'ran, when he attempts to pray and subsequently loses his belief. Later Saleem's telepathy, caused by the impacted phlegm that moistens his brain when he is startled by witnessing his mother's sexuality, allows for his association not only with the capacities of an omniscient, metafictional narrator, but also with Vedic fluids and tissues, with the receptivity of the prophet Muhammad to God's voice, and with the technological figure for linguistic transmission and exchange, All-India Radio. Midway through his chronicle, Saleem calls attention to the complex modes of interpretation that led him to see himself as a prophet-leader. "How, in what terms, may the career of a single individual be said to impinge on the fate of the nation?" he asks. He then responds: "I was linked to history both literally and metaphorically, both actively and passively . . . actively-literally, passively-metaphorically, actively-metaphorically and passively-literally, I was inextricably entwined with my world" (285–86). Each mode relates to an incident from his youth as Saleem endows metaphoric figure with concrete incident and bodily experience. His scientific "modes of connection" satirize the elaborate charts of Vedic medicine and cosmology, which replicate the multiple social and cosmic environments that comprise the discrete body, as well as his technological abilities.[89] The modes also justify Saleem's exegetical practice and support his understanding of leadership through the model of Muhammad.

The medical idiom for the spiritual-historical character of twentieth-century India thus attempts to encompass religious, ethnic, linguistic, and cultural plurality as the ultimate value of the nation-state while it points to a culturally particular depiction of the person. These ideas continue to inform representations of identity in popular culture. Christopher Pinney finds similar codes of embodiment in contemporary Indian regional photography, which shows "widespread . . . acceptance of the transience of the body and its status as a contingent receptacle for the soul."[90] Pinney attributes certain visual practices to the comparative weakness of cultural understandings of corporeality as expressive substance: "Because the visible is not deemed to be anchored—in most cases—by an invisible realm of character (for there is usually a distinction between the two), the external body is freed from the constraints with which it is shackled in the Western tradition of painted portraiture. What can be captured [according to the popular Indian aesthetic] is a person's general physiognomy rather than the face as a trace of the interior character."[91] In Western individualism, the discounted third term—Pinney calls it "character"—globally diffuses a particular, intimate ipseity that mediates between agent and vehicle and is elided from the topography of psychic-corporeal space that visibly expresses it. In *Midnight's Children,* which discounts the primacy of the visible symptom of illness, the corporate qualities of the protagonist allude to this "detachability" of the "self" from the "body" not through exchange, but rather through absorption of multiple subjectivities; not through visual, but rather through audible, registration.

Saleem absorbs others primarily as voices and as fluids, mechanisms that privilege Muslim prophecy and Vedic humors. McKim Marriott notes that Hinduism often characterizes the experiential world "as 'that which is moving' (jagat) and as a 'flowing together' (Samsāra)." As a "malleable substance," the environment is "constantly moving in and out" of the persons it also constitutes.[92] Rushdie's protagonist is accordingly a "swallower of lives" who "leaks history" (11, 4). Holes in bodies function as central images of injury and historical loss, as well as invitation and incorporation, throughout the novel. Orifices act as sites of interaction and heightened vulnerability in a form that Saleem repeatedly calls "grotesque" (57, 106, 335, 405, 431). Bodily apertures afford somatic exchange through failed sexual relations, through veiling, and through injury. In the same chapter that Aziz is begging Naseem to move during sex, a practice associated with discarding tradition, the fluid hole merges with the failure of clinical medicine to heal the wounds of imperial violence, represented by General Dyer's massacre of peaceful Indian protestors at Jallianwala Bagh in 1919. When Aadam Aziz returns to his lodgings in Amritsar on April 7, five days before the attack, he is covered in mercurochrome, or "red medicine," which his new wife mistakes for blood (35). The doctor has been treating victims of the unrest provoked by Gandhi's declaration of hartal, a day of mourning—traditionally over a death—as a protest against British rule. As Saleem recounts, when Aziz again returned home covered in red on April 12, "my grandmother[,] . . . trying hard to be a modern woman, to please him[,] . . . did not turn a hair at his appearance. 'I see you've been spilling the Mercurochrome again, clumsy,' she said, appeasingly. 'It's blood,' he replied, and she fainted" (37). In contrast to the "green medicine" that signifies fraudulent potions to Saleem, "red medicine" designates the authentic, clinical antidote as a "curative" for political protest as well: Aziz uses his bag of European medicine to treat the injuries that the Raj wantonly inflicts.

Alcohol serves as similarly unstable and particularly absorptive agent of history that also dissolves entities, as Ahmed Sinai's plot dramatizes. The required daily English cocktail hour at Methwold Estates continues after Independence, at the same time that Saleem's father invests in a land reclamation scheme. It recalls the East India Company's 1688 joining of the seven islands that compose Bombay, a repetition of the ancestral Methwold's "dream of a British Bombay." According to Saleem, Ahmed "fell . . . into the twin fantasies which were to be his undoing, into the unreal world of the djinns and of the land beneath the sea" (92). Both efforts to "reclaim" the nation through the new state result in his defeat, as liquor and water embody the emerging bourgeoisie's fantasy of mastering the past by compulsively repeating it. Though Saleem calls Ahmed's chronic drinking "alcoholism," his use of the device of the djinns emphasizes the practice as a "war" with externalized agents as well as a childhood interpretation of the "bottled spirits" contained in the glass that consumes the drinker (131). Set together, the figures show the metaphoricity of psychological struggle and conflict even as they represent the overwhelming physical grip of liquor on the drinker.

Metonymic Production and Mythic Authority

The "Indian myth" that served as an aesthetic and professional touchstone for Rushdie and as a critical one for his academic reception obscures the ingenious and complicated ways in which the novel negotiates subcontinental identity. By using bodily idioms embedded in spiritual understandings, the novel realizes a performative person from the sedimentary material of Western objectivity and the dynamism of Indian spirituality. Yet the Herderian notion of an essential myth, so deftly challenged in the depiction of the new nation-state, resists dismantling as a characterization of the author. Rushdie's own feelings of rootlessness or multiple roots, and his description of his "migrant" identity, chime in significant respects with his textual India: "The migrated self became, inevitably, heterogeneous rather than homogeneous, belonging to more than one place, multiple rather than singular, responding to more than one way of being. . . . Was it possible to be . . . not rootless, but multiply rooted?" he asks in his memoir.[93] Using similar terms, Saleem asserts that the body seems "[i]ndivisible, a one-piece suit, a sacred temple, if you will" and yet, he notes, "a human being inside himself is anything but a whole, anything but homogeneous; all kinds of everywhichthing are jumbled up inside him" (230–31). Saleem's heterogeneous corpus conflates a historical Indian subject with the psychological and physical situation of its migrant author, making his confusions substantial. *Midnight's Children* "works through" the authority of the "outsider" writer to inhabit the subcontinental body in such exchanges. Its modes of production and reproduction finally privilege a textual India over the spiritual embodiment connected to it. The holes that serve as conduits for the flow of substances and for the signification of neocolonial lack also open an insider position for the outsider author. These gaps manifest the "anxiety of Indianness" that marked Indian novels in English, according to Mukherjee, who contrasts their tone and focus to that of *bhasha* writers in older Indian languages.[94]

The multivalent opening acts as a crucial element in generation because Saleem's families are created through incorporation rather than through sex. Gaps in the "body" of history allow for these births and acquisitions. Though he recounts two generations of family history as if they composed his biological ancestry, Saleem eventually reveals that he was switched with another midnight's child just after his birth: "[W]hen we eventually discovered the crime of Mary Pereira, we all found out that it *made no difference!*" Saleem proclaims. "I was still their son: they remained my parents" (117). Such confusions allow Rushdie to claim British and Indian, rich and poor, as well as

Christian, Hindu, and Muslim "parents" for Saleem; the text imagines an affective community that does not rest on the bond of "blood" or on the phallus as the master signifier of community. Saleem's status as a masculine embodiment of the nation-state is also constantly lampooned and vitiated through his failure to fulfill the conventional functions of national paternity. The novel's subversion of an organic reproductive logic, like the conceit of an absorptive subject-agent, mitigates the obvious patriarchal cast of Rushdie's embodiment of India as male and recalls the feminine grotesque as opposed to the closed and classical Western form.

The romances that produce an affective family generate totality from the metonymic fragments. Both men and women project fantasies of fulfillment and emotional completion onto "parts" of others in order to fall in love. This dynamic plays a role in the attraction of Aadam Aziz to his wife Naseem, in their daughter Mumtaz's acceptance of her second husband, Ahmed (who renames her Amina, an allusion to the wife of Muhammad), and finally in Saleem's incestuous love for his sister Jamila, who comes to represent Pakistan. As the founding colonial romance, the relationship of Aziz and Naseem illustrates the interpenetration of national birth and future demise that characterizes the plot of all three pairings. Aziz falls in love with Naseem through a sheet with a hole cut in the middle, an opening that allows him to inspect the part of her body that is "ill" or pained. Her father's insistence on this modesty is belied by the constancy of his weekly summons for the doctor. Though she remains headless for most of the three years that he is treating her, "[t]his phantasm of a partitioned woman" haunts Aziz, who "come[s] to think of the perforated sheet as something sacred and magical because through it he had seen things which had filled up the hole inside him which had been created when he had been hit on the nose by a tussock and insulted by the boatman Tai" (26, 27–28). That is, the fantasy of Naseem replaces Aziz's lost faith and his severed connection to "traditional" Kashmir. The practice of purdah suggested by the sheet describes the ambivalent effects of this metonymic projection, as the beloved inevitably fails to fulfill the lover's desire for cohesion and wholeness.

Saleem's "fictional" genealogy repeats the metonymic movement of romantic desire through enabling misrecognitions. *Midnight's Children* treats this mode of production as the spur to literary and national genesis as well as the flaw that dooms Saleem to dismemberment and disintegration. Though the author unflaggingly champions Indian pluralism as a creative, ethical, and political value, he also relentlessly illustrates its fatal consequences. Plural absorption is an absolute value in the narrative, as any "immunity" is aligned with a rigid desire for purity, located in religious and ethnic nationalisms, and with monotheism. Not invasive disease, but rather any measure of self-protection, is cast as the true destroyer of the nation's character, through its alliance with essentialism, parochialism, dictatorship, and historical amnesia. Immunity can eradicate the idea of India, while the "illness" of decomposition obliterates only one body, one subject, in Rushdie's gloss. "The story of Saleem does indeed lead him to despair," Rushdie observes in "Imaginary Homelands." "But the story is told in a manner designed to echo . . . the Indian talent for non-stop self-regeneration. This is why the narrative constantly throws up new stories, why it 'teems.' The form—multitudinous, hinting at the infinite possibilities of the country—is the optimistic counterweight to Saleem's personal tragedy."[95] In this formulation the author suppresses Saleem's allegorical function and corporate capacities as a Vedic embodiment by separating and opposing terms that the narrative insistently joins: Saleem's personal tragedy is precisely India's political one. Yet here Rushdie instead relies on the vehicle of his chronicle to deliver the "optimistic counterweight" to the apocalypse suggested by the novel's conclusion. The fecundity of artistic form, in this gloss, and the perspective of mythic time, in the narrative, substitute for an embodiment of history, placeholders for reimagining India.

Midnight's Children departs from Vedic philosophy in refusing this permeable embodied subject any protection. Instead Rushdie portrays body-memory as the antidote to the nation's dissolution. The anatomical basis of memory informs his use of Vedic principles, which support a corpus compromised by historical trauma. In treating memory as the privileged antidote to an annihilating destruction, the narrative draws on nativist conceptions of remembrance as anatomically encoded and intimately connected to modes of perception and knowledge. According to Dieter Riemenschneider, recollection is "the central epistemological category of the novel," aligned with Hindu cosmology.[96] Certain Hindu and Buddhist philosophies portray perception itself as constituted in part by memory; for instance, attention, feeling, and volition, which are among the "universal" forms of consciousness, are informed by "particular" mental acts such as memory, concentration, and wisdom, according to Vasubandhu's Buddhist treatise, the *Vijñaptimātratāsiddhi*.[97] Not only learning in the general sense, but also self-knowledge, is connected to memory. But in spite of these somatic and cultural resonances, recollection suffers from the same split that the allegory of the somatopsychic corpus does: the author abandons this foundation as well when he allows the body-memory to survive as the Indian text alone.

Though phallic reproduction is not entirely necessary to India's genesis, the phallic pen is essential to its survival. The metonymic pen allows the author's imaginary India to endure while the central conceit of the Vedic body breaks down into dualisms. The pickle-phallus emphasizes Saleem's agency as a masculine writer and a "master" of the sheet linked to metonymic desire. This compensatory but ultimately triumphant formulation is evident when Saleem speculates that his auditor Padma has grown weary of his textual power and sexual impotence. He asks:

> Is it possible to be jealous of written words? To resent nocturnal scribblings as if they were the very flesh and blood of a sexual rival? I can think of no other reason for Padma's bizarre behaviour; . . . . Distressed, perhaps, by the futility of her midnight attempts to resuscitate my 'other pencil,' the useless cucumber hidden in my pants, she has been waxing grouchy. (121)

Saleem claims mastery over the sheet that dominated his grandfather, Aziz, by reversing the sexual roles: Padma is "spellbound" by his tale in progress just as his grandfather was mesmerized by the vision of a partitioned woman.

Shaul Bassi contends that while magic realism has served to "demystify hegemonic discourses, its metonymic relationship to the 'fantastic' involves a dangerous proximity to the code of romance, which . . . was a key genre in the construction of an imaginary India."[98] It is Rushdie's great skill to have generated metonymic production from his own belated romance with India; its operation allows him to claim the India from which he has long been separated by time, distance, and choice. In "Imaginary Homelands," he describes the novel's genesis in the idiom of reclamation and discovery, rather than as an expression of a suppressed identity. On a return trip to India after the failure of *Grimus*, the author conceived of the novel about his childhood home: "Bombay is a city built by foreigners upon reclaimed land; I, who had been away so long that I almost qualified for the title, was gripped by the conviction that I, too, had a city and a history to reclaim."[99] In the essay, as in the novel, metonymy acts as the primary mechanism of narrative, somatic, and political production, for India can be represented and embodied only through fragments. Just as the author, returning "almost" a foreigner to Bombay, "reclaim[s]" history without the continuing connection of residence, so does the nation-state emerge from fragmentary provinces and regions rather than from the "organic" evolution of the European political formation.

I contend that Rushdie's personal and professional relationship to India necessitates the novel's unilateral privileging of Saleem's openness. The image of the migrant as a "fragment" of India corresponds to the narrative metonymy of the novel's central conceit, produced by a fusion of multiple contexts. Migrancy appears in *Midnight's Children* not only through the figure of Aziz, the doctor-grandfather of the modern nation who also returns to India almost a foreigner, but most significantly through the absolute porousness of the Indian territorial "body." Though the metonymic dynamic, the author finds a narrative locus *within* the body he found almost foreign. In the same essay, Rushdie notes that his distance from India as he composed the novel also shaped his choice of mode: "Writing my book in North London, looking out through my window on to a city scene totally unlike the ones I was describing, I was constantly plagued by this problem, until I felt obliged to face it in the text, to make clear that ... what I was actually doing was a novel of memory and about memory."[100] Beginning with *Shame*, the migrant becomes a prominent figure in Rushdie's work, but *Midnight's Children* installs migrancy in the Indian body itself, generated from parts that excite imaginative and erotic desire. The dream of India, rendered concrete in Saleem's dissolution, dies as a result of this genesis. Though as always, the text offers other interpretations of its conclusion—the protagonist may be delusional, the nation may be reborn in the next mythical reincarnation—the conceit of the metonymically created, Vedic-inflected body as the vehicle of the nation-state bears too much weight to be resolved into mere individual fantasy or an abstracted mythic temporality.

Saleem's phallic, "pickled" pen acts as the nexus of exchange between the Vedic national and the textual migrant. *Midnight's Children* attempts to compensate for the premature foreclosure of the "actual" imaginary nation by preserving the text of memory as the "real" imaginary home. While Saleem's inability to reproduce biologically fits with the metaphor of national genesis from organically unrelated parts, the survival of his phallic pen, in the preservation of the text, at the expense of the incoporative, grotesque body, points to the particular gendering of the somatopsychic body as male and the value of porousness as circumscribed not just by univocality but also by the writer's need to assert the primacy of his textual India over the embodiment of the subcontinent and its writers. The position of migrancy that Rushdie explicitly acknowledges in subsequent novels, beginning with the justification of the distant writer's authority over the subcontinent in *Shame*, fundamentally shapes the conceit and dynamics of *Midnight's Children*. "Outsider! Trespasser! You have no right to this subject! ... Poacher! Pirate! We reject your authority!" hostile Pakistani versions of Padma say, deriding the narrator of *Shame*. To which he replies: "[I]s history to be considered the property of the participants solely?"[101] In *Midnight's Children*, the religious inflection of the subcontinental body allows for authorial inclusion in the Hinduized, absorptive Muslim corpus; this figure must be sacrificed not only to the Emergency enforced by Indira Gandhi, but also to the necessity of claiming authority for the writer who is "almost" a foreigner to the body that he imaginatively occupies.

•

"[I]t has become virtually impossible to look back at *Midnight's Children* from the late nineties without seeing the novel through the filter of events of the last fifteen years," writes Josna Rege. "It is hard to remember, or even acknowledge, the enthusiasm with which its publication was greeted in India."[102] Similarly, Meenakshi Mukherjee recounts, "It seemed to me then, as it must have seemed to many, that it was a landmark novel, attempting in a dangerously adventurous manner to stretch the possibilities of narrative fiction in general and of what could be done with Indian material in the English language in particular."[103] Rege and Mukherjee epitomize the initial reaction of many who experienced the novel not so much as a thoroughly "Indian" one as an assertion of Indian confidence, boldness, and originality in a literary language that seemed moribund. *The Satanic Verses* controversy, but also Rushdie's career and celebrity status, India's subsequent history, and the maturing of critical reception have all contributed to the change in this assessment, at the same time that critics such as Rege acknowledge the salutary effect that the novel had on Indo-Anglian literary production.

My aim in this return to Rushdie's "origins" in the metropolitan marketplace has been to show the ways in which his cosmopolitan location was altered through his embrace of the object "India" as a subject matter and the centrality of modern myth to his authenticity as a national insider. Harish Trivedi refers to a report that Martin Amis once asked Rushdie what he had that Amis did not; Rushdie replied, "India."[104] Whether one interprets such a reply cynically or not, Rushdie's turn from the allegorical myth of *Grimus*—a work that he also characterized as an attempt to take "a theme out of eastern philosophy or mythology and . . . transpos[e] it into a western convention"[105]—to an allegorical myth grounded in the subcontinental body, altered his profile and status utterly. Certainly Rushdie's success resulted to some degree from his occupation and display of a nativist body, even though no one, either reviewers or Rushdie himself, initially installed him as an unproblematically "Indian" writer. As I have shown, this transformation took place quickly as a result of popular and literary-critical success—particularly in the West, where he came to exemplify "Indian literature," and on the subcontinent, where he was seen as injecting the exuberance of contemporary Bombay cosmopolitanism into English language production. Uma Mahadevan-

Dasgupta recalls in a 2002 Indian *Statesman*: "[*Midnight's Children*] showed me that it was possible to speak in English, in our own slangy, colloquial, masala-filled Indian English, about the important themes—history, pain, struggle, love, and humour."[106] The sense of betrayal that accompanied Rushdie's academic revision into a "diasporan" or even an "exoticist" writer appears as a function of a mode of reception that, as I hope I have shown, has largely failed to imagine more capacious or nuanced categories of identity: Western readers continue to prefer metonymies of provincial literatures, as they did with Joyce. Though the tension between writing "about" and writing "for" India was enormously productive for Rushdie, the structure of betrayal seems written into the script of an imaginary claim on embodiment through a Western, English-speaking literary public enchanted by the display of minority spiritual practices. Exposing such bodies repeats a modernist trajectory for the minority author that, I argue, Joyce epitomizes and that the metropolitan literary milieu continues to reward. The controversy over *The Satanic Verses*, which I discuss at length in chapter five, revealed a claim on a religious body that the author has made since *Grimus*. Its possession has been crucial to his own aesthetic, and its "myth" has acted as a critically unmediated Herderian signifier of Indian authenticity.

The shock that accompanied Rushdie's comments in the June 23–30, 1997, issue of the *New Yorker*, in which he asserts the primacy of Indian literature in English over any production of the vernacular languages,[107] reflects the permutations of his profile: these observations are only slightly more pointed than the ones he made at the Commonwealth Club in 1982, in which Rushdie barely mentioned any Indian literary tradition or contemporary context at all. In 1997 he mentions a number of writers in the "'recognized'" languages of the subcontinent, but concludes the list with the observation that "there is only one Indian writer in translation whom [he] would place on par with the Indo-Anglian": the Urdu author Sadaat Hasan Manto, whom Rushdie compares with Joyce. But Rushdie precedes this somewhat measured statement—he is after all descrying the lack of English-language translations of these subcontinental authors—with the statement that the "new, and still burgeoning, 'Indo-Anglian' literature represents perhaps the most valuable contribution India has yet made to the world of books."[108] Positioned by 1997 as himself the father of two generations of "Indian" writers, Rushdie here again asserts a cosmopolitan provenance. It should come as small surprise that the celebrated "Indian" novel was not translated into Hindi until that year, the fiftieth anniversary of independence.[109]

I hope to have articulated the ways in which *Midnight's Children* enacts spiritually inflected embodiment and hence depicts a person that genuinely differs from that of the modern Western formulation of the "individual" as a subject-agent, even as this person catalyzes individualism. In the refashioning of Rushdie from a British to an Indian author, and even in the dismantling of this profile in wake of *The Satanic Verses* controversy and critical reassessments of his work, scholars have often assumed the cultural predicates of somatic representations. Early readings of the novel, dominantly Western and poststructuralist, neglected to examine the subject-agent that the narrative decenters. I have argued that the novel mobilizes at its base not just an assumed, default "individual," but also a "person" produced through portrayal of proto-religious bodily practices and understandings. *Midnight's Children* turns on the interplay between the conceit of a psychosomatically ill individual, fashioned as an autonomous agent funded by a deep psychic interior, and a person shaped by Vedic medicine and Hindu praxis, whose consciousness and sensations are more concrete and diffusely intermingled with internal and external contexts. The Vedic subject, with its implications for a particular somatic structure, agency, and relationship to the environment, registers presumptions about the person as material and actual and illuminates the metaphoric and relative nature of the "individual" as an historical embodiment. This argument shares the premise of cultural specificity with Alejo Carpentier's 1949 conceptualization of the fantastic as an outgrowth of particular histories in Latin American literature.[110] At the same time, the novel represents a specific mode of agency generated by spiritual practice and grounded in its epistemology. Finally, neither the magic realism that attached to the novel in its early academic reception nor the exoticism with which it was later charged adequately describes the text's allegiances or the author's professional profile. Rather than a "nativist" versus a "postmodernist," or an authentic versus an exoticist reading, I suggest that these paradigms produce a contemporary Indian subject-agent, one in whom the tension between the national and migrant, the provincial and the cosmopolitan, Indian is less explicitly at play than they are in Rushdie's later work. Such a procedure is not completely described as "othering," but rather as performative. It narratively resolves the dilemma that Rushdie faced as a metropolitan writer voicing India, and that his later career brought to the forefront of his image. To designate such transnational identities, we as readers must delve beyond binaries that continue to govern the mechanisms of reception and their institutions, which have produced Rushdie himself as an anxious, metonymic body.

3

Spirits Discipline *Ulysses*

Ulysses has been made to stand for many myths in its career of almost a century. Perhaps more forcibly than any other modernist work, it established the terms of opposition between art and religion, generated from the doctrine and practice of late nineteenth-century Catholicism. Not only the text, but also its own reception, secured this binary as a central axiom of literary modernism and its anthropological premises. I turn to the text of *Ulysses* to show the ways in which regulated belief produces as well as represses minority religious bodies. The narrative succeeds in imagining an integrated bodily habitus by abandoning a biological vocabulary as the primary paradigm for expressing interior psychic states. Rather than attempting to anatomize or transcend dependency and repression, as in *Dubliners* and *A Portrait,* Joyce allows discipline to make bodies through performative practices. Orthopraxy is central to the experiment of *Ulysses* in that bodies create their own epistemes, imitating techniques that ground collective, public knowledge through directed cognitive and physical acts. The new relation to Irish territory is intimately tied to Joyce's revision of alcohol as the sacred-material substance of masculine embodiment. The practice of excessive drinking gains the power to generate as well as to destroy the Irish-Catholic body and its art.

As I discussed in the first chapter, historicist Joyce criticism of the last decades largely ignored "religion" as a category of deep analysis. The rich vein of structuralist and poststructuralist interpretation of *Ulysses*, when it addresses the subject of spiritual belief, remains within a symbolic vocabulary, in which language acts the analogue of theology and ritual—even as the critic may challenge the auratic privilege of Joyce's language. Umberto Eco, for instance, in *The Aesthetics of Chaosmos*, states: "Like those who abandon a discipline but not its cultural baggage, with Joyce there remains the sense of a curse celebrated according to liturgical ritual."[1] While Eco seeks to reinterpret the evolution of Joyce's scholasticism and "medieval disposition," he treats "discipline" only as Catholic "instinct" or "sensibility" that models linguistic practice. Classic New Critical scholarship on Joyce's textual, intellectual, and personal relationship to religion includes William T. Noon's *Joyce and Aquinas*, Kevin Sullivan's *Joyce among the Jesuits*, and Robert Boyle's *James Joyce's Pauline Vision*.[2] According to the scholarly commonplace entrenched in the mid-century, Catholic theology serves a generative function for aesthetic metaphor and linguistic process in the novel. Somatic integration relates exclusively to the symbolic of Judaism, associated in the contemporaneous racial imaginary with "crass bodiliness," in Laura Doyle's phrase.[3] On the other hand, the "post-" and "semi-colonial" Joyce of the 1990s, for all its interest in retrieving a deeply Irish cultural and political context, addressed issues of race, class, nationalism, gender and sexuality—topics that bear upon Irish identity and embodiment—while treating religion institutionally and politically. Attention to the status, history, and symbolic of Jewish embodiment countered this general trend, notably in scholarship by Ira Nadel, Marilyn Reizbaum, Bryan Cheyette, and Neil Davison.[4] Recent studies oriented to historical and cultural particularism seek to locate Joyce in the specifically Anglo-Irish milieu from 1880 to 1920,[5] and attend to the Catholic educational system, as well as to Joyce's specific intellectual position within it,[6] but like other deeply historical and situated approaches to Joyce, they do not treat belief practices as a focus. Works such as Roy Gottfried's *Joyce's Misbelief* (2003), Geert Lernout's *Help My Unbelief* (2010), and Pericles Lewis's *Religious Experience and the Modernist Novel* (2010) have reengaged with this topic, with emphasis on more subtle readings of Joyce's belief in context and his representations of it. While scrutinizing the monolithic category of the secular, these studies continue to employ conceptions of belief based on orthodox, anthropological conceptions of "religion" as doctrine, assent, sentiment, and hermeneutic.[7]

In arguing that *Ulysses* uses religious belief to imagine an integrated and performative embodiment, I challenge the absolute equation of Irish Catholicism with doctrine and with sensual repression—terms rendered synonymous by Stephen, by Joyce, and by the critical response that the author inaugurated while he was composing *Ulysses*—and the assignation of corporeal movement to a Jewish symbolic alone. Instead, I contend, Judaism marks the disciplinary orientation of Irish Catholicism, signaling engagement with bodily practice as a crucible of belief and a fundament of corporeality. While in neither case does the analogue of religious practice signify assent to doctrine, faith in its fundamental precepts, or participation in a religious community, it does supply Joyce with procedures for intimately reformulating persons through regulated training. Irish Judaism and Irish Catholicism secure these transformations through the particular styles associated with each religion, Bloom with an erotic sensuality and Stephen-Simon with an inebriated one.

Crucial to this reinterpretation of the Irish-Catholic male body is a journey through the dead body of the Irish-Catholic mother. Stephen's melancholia traps him in the predatory maternal space of archaic religion. He occupies the position of the eighteenth-century gothic's persecuted daughter, enmired in a materialized tradition. Stephen's route to freedom from feminized abjection appears as a gothic descent into masculine dissolution, an inexorable fate determined by Irish history. A gothic social and biological trajectory, which the novel first links to the polluting effects of Judaism on the Christian body politic, degeneration casts the epic adventure as a reverse invasion of matriarchal Catholic Ireland, the Ireland that at once figures the foreign familiar within the English imaginary and the claustral engulfment of an outside inseparable from a psychic or physical interior. For nineteenth-century Protestants, "the supreme embodiment of the Catholic Other was not France but Ireland," Hugh McLeod asserts.[8] In this sense *Ulysses* opens with an inchoate nightmare of the inside-outside position that the author uses throughout the novel. The degeneration plot equally involves Simon Dedalus, who enacts a specifically Irish-Catholic mode of biological-social descent. As a corollary stock type, the drunken Celt stands with the sensual Semite as a racial-religious father who rescues Stephen by offering him a performative zone of somatic production. Just as Bloom's "degenerate" Judaism creates a highly visceral, inclusive sensorium, Simon's degenerate Irish Catholicism turns liquor into the blood of substantial transformation, equally mobile and material. In "Sirens," *Ulysses* privileges drinking as an Irish-Catholic bodily praxis, with the power to produce a fluid, celebratory "music of the body" as well as a momentary intersubjective community—on the basis of a compulsion that is destroying Dedalus and his family. As the parodic plot of degeneration subsequently moves Stephen into a night of prolonged drunkenness, he merges with the performative body of his father's art at the same time that he encounters the erotic conqueror, Bloom.

Unlike *The Satanic Verses,* in which the Joycean model is applied to Islamic scripture, *Ulysses* represents the body of belief by depicting epistemologies both produced from and governed by ordinary bodies. Yet the protocols of disciplined belief inform the sensory, psychic, and sensual representation of "realistic" characters who, in the early chapters, still possess a deep interiority. First, the perceptual apparatus appears relatively holistic as sight loses its modern primacy and segregation from the other senses, especially taste and smell. Joyce calls on the medieval sensorium as an emblem of sensory integration. Through this framework, he deprives vision of its contemporary powers of abstraction as well as its privileged status in racialist vocabularies. Secondly, the viscera and fluids of the body register as areas of awareness—not merely in grotesque effluvia, but also as elements integrally incorporated into cognition and perception. Finally, the exchanges between "interior" and "exterior," cerebration and sensation, thought and action, are rapid, frequent, and weakly differentiated from one another. These representational tendencies bear marked affinities to instrumental modes of belief, which do not strongly separate emotion from knowledge; which intimately investigate and direct psychic and physical states to re-form them; and which, according to Asad, comprehend physicality as an "ability," a "potentiality," or a "power" rather than a given material that expresses an individual or collective essence, as I discuss in chapter one.[9] The disciplinary practices of these religious modes ultimately produce corporeal dispositions as frameworks of knowledge and "persons" in relation to a distinct corporate embodiment. The agency that praxis makes does not coincide with the private subject, but rather with the community and the episteme that it has collectively made. The power of somatopsychic embodiment increasingly asserts independence not only from the subjectivity of particular characters, but also from the conception of characters as self-governing agents, housed in a bounded, autonomous, and expressive spatial structure. Each chapter's linguistic paradigm, acting much like a somatically generated spiritual episteme, determines the way in which subjects may register: as music, as zones of literature, as a theatrical roles, as elements, as machines, or as modes of discourse that arise from specific Irish histories and cultural forms. In this, Gibson contends, the novel moves simultaneously toward "liberation" and "revenge," constantly "driv[ing] Joyce back into the very structures from which he seeks to free himself."[10] Culminating in the mathematical catechism of "Ithaca," the narrative agency displays its fertile ability to make and reformulate subjects before returning to the fundamental lyricism of female "nature."

My reading of *Ulysses* restores religious practice to the center of Joyce's depiction of minoritarian Irish identity, a dimension often subsumed into racial or political categories. Even as the gothic religion of May Dedalus threatens throughout the day to overwhelm her son, *Ulysses* emulates the productivity of religious praxis to imagine masculine corporeality. Joyce uses a universalized conception of "religion," a rubric fundamentally shaped by the modality of modern Christianity, as an alibi for belief formations grounded in regulated physical practices and reads symbolically the bodily habitus that they make. Rejected as a vehicle of knowledge in the West by the turn of the century, religion as theology and affect becomes available for Joyce's elaboration of the modernist aesthetic, as has been well established. At the same time, I argue, the author exploits the instrumental inflection of Irish Catholicism to alter the dominant psychic and physical structure of the individual. If, as Donald Theall argues, "the new techno-culture ... permeated the content, construction, and spirit of Joyce's final works,"[11] bodily practices parallel as well as interact with inanimate mechanisms: that is to say, Joyce does not just imagine the corpus *as* and *through* machines, he also conceives of embodiment as a corporeal-epistemic technē. Sexual difference, rather than the inheritance of theology or natural "blood," forms the limit of the performative-technical corpus in *Ulysses*, as a number of feminist scholars have shown. Joyce's critique of Irish female embodiment enlarges the performative arena accorded to men while consigning women to an expressive corporeal mode. Like her husband, Molly achieves a somatopsychic inclusiveness of cognition, sensation, and sensuality; and unlike most of Joyce's Irish-Catholic women, she exercises considerable agency. Yet her representation remains grounded in a "core" biological identity and an expressive mode: her religious identity, her sensuality, and her alignment with earth are attributed to actual, "literal" circumstances.

Gothic Entrapment and Reverse Invasion

Both *Dubliners* and *A Portrait* use medical paradigms to depict a sectarian identity. In each, Joyce attempts to overcome the psychic immurement of Irish-Catholic life through his depiction of bodies, devising exemplary subjects to capture historical conditions. *Dubliners* diagnoses a chronic failure to achieve autonomy, *A Portrait* relates the psychobiological development of a hero imagined capable of surpassing this dependency. Both projects ultimately reproduce the segregation of sensuality and cognition that Joyce seeks to ameliorate: *Dubliners*, as I have shown, stylistically reinforces the drunkard's paralysis; *A Portrait* depicts Stephen's independent movement through physical removal, psychic rejection, and identification with an abstracted, mythic lineage. *Ulysses* returns to the project of representing the provincial body through another story of origins, now in the register of the family and the quest romance, according to Christine Froula.[12] Genealogy is at the forefront of the genre. "In the Romance," Robert Miles says, "the usurped and dispossessed find their rights restored; the lost are found, and a true genealogy reasserts itself." He continues by noting that "the issue of genealogy is of course inextricable from the question of political legitimacy."[13] *Ulysses* aims to restore masculine bodies, rather than rights, as the basis of both its aesthetic and its politics, but its little-explored gothic thematic does highlight the recovery of origins through a new configuration of the repressed and repressive past as a somatic legacy. The novel opens with a number of allusions to the gothic romance, which cast Ireland as an archaic religious territory. Its energies exercise considerable oppressive power. Uncanny and densely material in their figuration of the psychic, the gothic energies of "Telemachus" announce the project of working through Irish Catholicism as a somatic and geographic space, at once abjected and bereft. As Catholics, the novel's subjects are congruent with the villainous fathers and monks of the eighteenth-century gothic romance; as a colonized majority, they occupy the structural position of primitives in the imperial adventure. At the same time the long and complex history of English domination points to the imbrication of Irish genealogy in British narratives of national and imperial consolidation. In "Telemachus," Catholic Ireland appears as a half-assimilated and half-alienated "home," located on the very margin of romance binaries: the population is Christian but largely Catholic, white but still racialized as "not quite," located in a settler colony and a violently occupied territory encompassed by a kingdom. In this vertiginous sense, Joyce employs the gothic romance to depict the adventure as the reverse invasion of home and the return of the never separated. Gibson states, "Stephen's condition is actually one of painful belonging rather than of alienation."[14] Reference to gothic romance also echoes anti-Catholic literature and pamphlets produced in nineteenth-century Britain and America. "Roman Catholicism appears in England and America as foreign infiltration," Susan Griffin observes, but polemicists at the same time represent it as "a religion without a country . . . inimical to nationhood"[15] and assimilated to Judaism in its originary status.[16] In the Protestant imaginary, Catholicism—in Britain exemplified by the Irish rather than the formerly politically threatening French[17]—is "a religion of Holy Fathers who demanded unquestioning obedience, a cult fixated on the body, both as a site of penitential torture and as a target of sensuous appeal."[18]

Nash, after Derrida, describes the temporality of the opening of *Ulysses* as a "double time," one here related to the structure of Catholic confession. As autobiography, confession affords "a peculiarly specular form in which the younger subject is recreated, displayed, and viewed by a later self"—a relationship between the Stephens of *A Portrait* and *Ulysses* that Joyce renders as "opaque."[19] The pattern of rupture and resuscitation, of renunciation and retrieval of the never-lost, might also describe the gothic impulse. David Glover, in discussing Conrad's *Heart of Darkness* (1899), argues that "the Gothicisiation of the past stands as a sign of the radical unavailability of a definitive break with what has gone before."[20] Enmired in an emptied home and a failed plot, Stephen finds himself similarly stuck. Among the multiple ghosts entrapping him is that of the colonial *künstlerroman*. *A Portrait* depicts the family as a metonymy of the physical and psychic space of the colony: to achieve autonomous individuality, the colonial protagonist must separate physically from a formal political as well as an intimate familial state of dependency.[21] *A Portrait* fulfills the teleology of departure not by representing it directly, but rather by demonstrating its achievement through the existence of the novel itself, a narration shot through with retroactive awareness of a goal achieved. But "Telemachus" immediately cancels the proleptic logic of the previous *bildungsroman*, while its style enacts the already accomplished goal of a new representational flexibility, enacted though the dead (female) and resurrected (male) provincial Irish-Catholic body. Stephen has returned to the suspension of waiting to depart, now lacking both the destiny and the metaphysic that organized his initial, aborted launch.[22] Perched on the parapet of a tower, he is persecuted by the mock-priest Mulligan (later figured as a "monk")[23] and haunted by the dream-memory of his victimized mother: "Her glazing eyes, staring out of death, to shake and bend my soul. On me alone. The ghostcandle to light her agony. Ghostly light on the tortured face. Her hoarse loud breath rattling in horror, while all prayed on their knees. Her eyes on me to strike me down" (1.273–76). As Stephen is his mother's victim, she too is a prey of the colonizer, and the two meanings meet in his accusation, "Ghoul! Chewer of corpses!" (1.278). May received communion before her death and is now a ghost; she is also the food of a vampiric imperial mouth. "Proteus" explicitly links this specter to Dracula (3.397–400), aligning the Irish-Catholic mother with a foreign (male) monster who invades the domestic space to contaminate native (female) blood from within in an erotic reproductive siege. "No, mother!" Stephen thinks in reply. "Let me be and let me live" (1.278–79).

Froula argues that Stephen "wants to fashion a female textual body to animate a repressed female self,"[24] and Kristeva describes abjection as an insufficient or incomplete separation from the mother.[25] In his feminized immurement, Stephen appears to be stranded in the literary space of the British gothic, which conjures the setting of feudal, aristocratic Catholicism as a tyrannical male unreason in order to endorse rational institutions that are linked to female freedom, chief among them constitutional monarchy and Protestant reformation. Critics such as Miles, Donna Heiland, Margot Backus, and Helene Moglen[26] read the conventional entrapment of the gothic daughter as a dramatization of a conflict between individual choice and the requirements of kinship and inheritance, between female agency and patriarchal oppression. But "Telemachus" feminizes the demand for dynasty, for the absent mother continues to require assent to her religious belief. Joyce represents Stephen's internalized maternal demand not only through his vivid imagination of his mother's ghost, but also through his reading of the environment, as many critics have noted. The "dull green mass of liquid" that he views from the tower resembles the "green sluggish bile" (1.108–9) that she vomited in her illness and portends the close link between depictions of women and grotesque fluids in Stephen's mind and in later chapters.[27]

The novel's grotesque substitute for the sublime landscapes of the gothic—landscapes on which the interior of the gothic heroine is externalized and enlarged—parallels the representation of maternal death as unbound. In this, May's portrayal recalls Clare Kahane's psychoanalytic, feminist reading of the later gothic mother as a "spectral presence" for the heroine, an "archaic and all-encompassing . . . ghost signifying the problematics of femininity."[28] The maternal ghost materializes in the female body itself an "imprisoning biological destiny" that denies the subject the independence accorded men on the basis of sexual difference.[29] Stephen's struggle for differentiation, gendered female and domestic, foregrounds his need to achieve masculine independence through adventurous movement, the movement at which he has recently failed. Yet gothic binaries are staged only to be collapsed, for Stephen's assertion of individual choice against traditional authority also casts him as a male persecutor. Mulligan's accusation that Stephen "killed" his mother by refusing her dying request aligns the son with his victimizing father, an improvident drunkard, the "someone" who, Stephen believes, really "killed her" (1.90).[30]

But the major revision of the gothic family romance occurs when maternal Ireland assumes the guise of a nativist peasant and her oppressor that of a British patriarch, whose rationality rewrites gothic murder as the gathering of imperial knowledge. Mother Ireland now appears as a rural milkwoman, figured in Stephen's imagination as "silk of the kine and poor old woman," "a witch," and "a wandering crone" (1.401, 404–6, 435), a version of the sean bhean bhocht represented in Cathleen Ní Houlihan.[31] (A comic "gothic" servant as well, she initially believes that Haines is speaking French when he addresses her in Irish; like Mulligan's medicine, his tongue is a language for "them that knows," though he botches his translation [1.35].[32]) Joyce lampoons the organicism of the revival and self-consciously stages "types"[33] in this exchange, yet he also links antiquarianism to the gothic letter. The milkwoman replaces the British gothic's freedom-seeking, noble daughter with a figure of alienated servitude, divorced from the "culture" she is supposed to embody but attuned to the hierarchies of sex and class that subordinate her (the gender dynamics of which are lost on Stephen). Backus observes that Haines's antiquarianism is the "counterpart of British and continental Gothicism" through its "detached, quasi anthropological interest in extinct or dying cultural practices."[34] Exhumed to revive the present, antiquarianism appears as a discourse of power-knowledge, in which the imperial master catalogues and preserves the native past that he has helped to extinguish.

"However much Stephen might wish to be apart from the scene which he surveys, he is instead 'a part' in it," Nash observes,[35] and his inability to disengage, historically as well as personally, must eventually be articulated. The introduction of racial-national discourse revises the figure of the matriarchal Church during Stephen's subsequent conversation with Haines, whom Gibson links to the kindly face of the constructivist "Unionist project" of the Salisbury and Balfour cabinets of 1895 to 1905.[36] The landlord's characterization of religion in terms of the "personal God" and "miracles" encodes a familiar English reading of Catholicism as gothic superstition, a view that would seem to coincide with Stephen's memory of May Dedalus. Their common Christian background leads Haines to presume that Stephen shares his reflexive anti-Semitism. Both are the unexamined assumptions of the friendly, rational master whose presence makes Mulligan's "idle mockery" doubly problematic. The crass materialism of Mulligan, for whom a mother's corpse—whether May Dedalus, the Church, or Irish history—is merely "trip[e]," foregrounds the satiric detachment that threatens Stephen as much as incorporation into these gothic female bodies does (1.206). Mulligan's materialism ultimately parallels Haines's antiquarianism, in that each exerts power over the living through his knowledge of the dead (female) artifact. Their rational knowledge, directed at a dead object, recalls the narrative gaze of *Dubliners* on the Irish corpse, and constitutes a critique of it.

As Stephen leaves the tower and makes his way toward Dublin, the narrative has vividly portrayed the vital purchase of the gothic energies of feminized Ireland on male bodies. The empirical knowledge implicated in its deadening cannot help the Irish to separate from it.

"Telemachus" announces that the knowledge that *Ulysses* produces must be generated from, rather than imposed on, these bodies. The novel will do so by incorporating feminized theology and alienated tradition into a male somatic practice, one modelled on instrumental belief. The gothic assignations and tropes of "Telemachus," which represent agencies operating on the boundary of the internal and external, still act as the expressive traits of a psychologized subject-agent, shaped by a third-person narrator. But they anticipate the parodic "fate" that awaits Stephen as these agencies depart entirely from their lodging in the individual as a bounded, interiorized, and autonomous material entity. The journey into the "degenerate" masculine bodies of Dublin enacts their power.

Much as Stephen moves between the poles of victim and persecutor, Bloom moves between the roles of imperial conqueror and subjugated alien, through the conventions of a related romance plot. His role as a powerful yet degraded other is established in "Nestor," which introduces the discourse of degeneration as a physiological and political version of gothic threat. Speaking as a representative of institutional pedagogy, Deasy notoriously warns Stephen of the infestations of "jews" in England, "the signs of a nation's decay" who will "eat up the nation's vital strength," just as hoof and mouth contagion will destroy its vital cows (2.347–49). Deasy fits the model of the Ulster Unionist, though with "constructive Unionist" tendencies. He joins Haines in expressing British nationalist anxieties[37] and in anticipating the entrance of the ostensibly Jewish Bloom as a figure of contamination and mongrelization. Such depictions also recall the reverse invasion narratives of the 1890s, in which archaic-futuristic others penetrate and attempt to conquer England as a domestic space. Judith Wilt calls novels such as *War of the Worlds* (1898) and *Dracula* (1897) examples of an "imperial gothic," which gives voice to repressed fears of colonial revenge; a number of scholars have linked such works to theories of degeneration influential during the era.[38] Bloom thus follows a trail blazed by racial-national others such as Dracula and Laputa, the African nationalist who infiltrates Scotland at the beginning of John Buchan's adventure romance, *Prester John* (1910). Heirs to the eighteenth-century gothic in its spatial and temporal externalization of psychological idioms, both the imperial gothic and the imperial adventure romance inscribe time on space to represent encounters between the primitive past and the contemporary moment. Male bodies become metonymies of these temporally apposite territories: in the paradigmatic Victorian adventure out, H. Rider Haggard's *King Solomon's Mines* (1885), the modern, civilized man renews his masculinity by enacting an archaic warrior past, as McClintock and others have shown.[39] In the reverse invasion, the othered body brings the atavism of savage lands into the space of modernity. Just as British imperialists strip down to reveal the essential brute under the clothing of civilization, invaders such as Laputa and Dracula dress up in the knowledge of civilization in order to "pass" in Britain. Exemplary mimics, adept at disguising themselves and their plans through their knowledge of religion, technology, and even classical literature, both figures remain immune from the ameliorative influence of such knowledge.

If, as John Hoberman contends, "the exceptional status of the Jewish male has been his exclusion from a European ideology of adventure,"[40] Bloom represents the ultimate parody of such imperial heroes (and villains), an ambivalence long recognized in Joyce's choice of Odysseus as the antiheroic hero. Bloom's "perversity" may lie first in the explicit and central depiction of any sexuality, for the homosocial and adolescent emphasis of the adventure romance pushes even normative heterosexual relations to the margins or into the feminized "ground" of nature. Analogously, Bloom lacks the empirical and technical knowledge that allows the mimic-invader to manipulate his "host" culture and forward his own imperial aims. Not only his refusal of the role of warrior, but also his detachment from a strong political-religious identity, funds his ability to occupy the role of the fantasy imperialist, divorced from the power-knowledge nexus that figures such as Mulligan and Haines manipulate. In the ethnographic ruminations of the hero in "Calypso" and "Lotos Eaters," which parallel the unstable gothic binaries of "Telemachus," the novel underscores the mobility of Irish minorities within the imperial hierarchy. Bloom, as a consumer of imperial representations and commodities and as a white, Anglicized, Western subject, often dramatizes Irish affiliation with British racism. As Enda Duffy demonstrates, the Irish are the consumers, as well as the objects, of imperial fantasy, incorporating Orientalist and primitivist images into their knowledge and entertainment.[41] Bloom's reverie of an Eastern adventure, for instance, consists of stock features of the Orientalist narrative: "Somewhere in East: early morning: set off at dawn. Travel round in front of the sun, steal a day's march on him.... Walk along a strand, strange land, come to a city gate, sentry there, old ranker too, old Tweedy's big moustaches, leaning on a long kind of spear. Wander through awned streets. Turbaned faces going by. Dark caves of carpet shops, big man, Turko the terrible, seated crosslegged, smoking a coiled pipe.... Might meet a robber or two. Well, meet him." Bloom concludes that this scenario is "probably not a bit like it really," and his use of images such as the panto figure Turko the terrible is obviously comic.[42] Still, Bloom's adventure fantasy resembles his other readings of non-Western cultures and races, from which distinctions between the imaginary and the factual have entirely vanished (4.84–89, 91, 92). Bloom runs through a catalogue of exotic and primitive stereotypes,[43] when, for instance, entering All Hallows Church, he sees a poster announcing Father Conmee's sermon on St. Peter Claver and the African Mission. After considering that Catholics and Protestants are "the same" in their zeal for conversion, Bloom imagines that the "heathen Chinee" would "prefer an ounce of opium" to Christianity and wonders whether chopsticks might serve as a marketing device for Buddhism, as the shamrock does for Saint Patrick (5.325–27). Returning to thoughts of Conmee, he muses: "He's not going out in bluey specs with the sweat rolling off him to baptise blacks, is he? The glasses would take their fancy, flashing. Like to see them sitting round in a ring with blub lips, entranced" (5.333–36). Bloom's casual acceptance of racial stereotype also informs his recognition of Catholicism's imperial mission and fundamentally "primitive" practice. Observing mass inside the church, he ruminates on the Eucharist as an act of necrophiliac consumption and on Latin as a drug: "Corpus: body. Corpse. Good idea the Latin. Stupefies them first. Hospice for the dying. They don't seem to chew it: only swallow it down. Rum idea: eating bits of a corpse. Why the cannibals cotton to it" (5.350–52). He recalls Haines in forwarding an essentially gothic interpretation of Catholicism, combined with an image of savage Africa. But Bloom's disinterest and his lack of power infuse his speculations about Catholicism with an ecumenical comedy. Ethnographic distance and avowed innocence of precise knowledge accompany his repetition of imperial imagery.

Bloom's parodic embodiment of degeneration theory has been well established in the criticism, though the status of this discourse in Joyce's era has been the subject of some debate. In describing this relationship, I am concerned to point out Joyce's mobilization of literary tropes drawn from the imperial adventure in its gothic offshoots, as they retell journeys of degeneration in the idiom of the romance. Joyce destabilizes the binaries of these romance structures to characterize the Irish situation and depict the adventure as the reverse invasion of an uncanny "home." He uses gothic tropes to sketch a degenerate patriarchal genealogy for the Irish Catholic. I turn now to the performative dynamics that re-produce expressive gothic tropes as the creative and destructive energies of somatopsychic integration.

Orthopraxy's Production of the Minority Religious Body

Ulysses' first chapters use an idiom of interiority to cast Ireland as an anachronistic religious space, full of potent and unstable energies, as I have argued. Geographic and personal territories are haunted by omnivorous histories that refuse to release subjects from inexorable convention. Simultaneously, the spiritual forces depicted through psychological affect and textual allusion inform the integrated and mobile subject whose agency will move through various representational zones. Joyce portrays "religion" as theology and ritual while modelling its sectarian bodies on a different mode and formation of belief, centered on practice. As I discuss in the first chapter, Judaism, Islam, and some forms of Catholic monasticism, in contrast to the expressive emphasis of modern Christianity, orient belief toward disciplinary practice as integral to the disposition and episteme of moral formation.[44] Such instrumental modes of belief do not strongly separate emotion from knowledge, thought from act, or particular from communal flesh. Practice generates knowledge as a moral, somatic, and affective totality, training the adherent in concert with the community. The "orthodox," that is, doctrinally oriented, and affective formation of secularist Christianity assumes a corporeality a priori, through which sentiment and belief are expressed in relation to an accepted theology.

In contrast, praxis creates a totality of corporeality, knowledge, and belief through acts performed in the context of the community as a means of regulation.[45] Jean Leclerq provides an instructive example in the Benedictine contemplative's "active reading," which, compared to silent meditation on a text, illustrates the contrast between programmatic disciplinary praxis and "religious" practice in the more conventional current sense of observance and participation in rites and devotional activities. For the twelfth-century monastic, private recitation of scripture produced "a muscular memory of the words pronounced and an aural memory of the words heard." Rather than a primarily abstract or visual activity, recitation was often understood in terms of taste and nutrition, a "mastication" of scriptures that incorporated them somatically into the monk.[46] The meticulous and strict direction of physical acts—of gesture, movement, position, and interaction with the environment—distinguishes this mode from the symbolic one where the Christian-derived, secularist formation "religion" resides. In a similar vein, Sarah McNamer calls eleventh- and twelfth-century English devotional texts "intimate scripts"[47] for the production of feeling and sensory experience. Meditations on the Passion were designed to be "enacted" by readers and to "structur[e] a way of seeing" for women, who not only viewed the Passion as eyewitnesses, as did their male counterparts, but also experienced the events as lovers in the performative process of *spousa Christi*.[48]

As I discussed in the first chapter, post-famine Ireland witnessed an intensification of the Church's hold on the Irish Catholic body—not, in fact, a continuation of long-standing practices. Seamus Deane argues that the Irish "deployed Catholicism as a defensive strategy against state secularization and all its accompanying alienations" during the era, retarding in this way the movement toward independence that the famine propelled.[49] In this reading, Backus contends, the Irish "mortgaged bodily pleasure (the repression of which was the salient mark of Catholic difference) to retain cultural autonomy." In any event, nationalism, Catholic "piety," and "rigid moral rectitude" became more closely aligned during this period,[50] not least through the efforts of Paul Cullen (1803–1878) who, as bishop of Armagh, convened the 1850 Synod of Thurles to discipline and standardize Catholic practice in Ireland. Later archbishop of Dublin, he became Ireland's first cardinal in 1866. Though Backus and others have begun to interrogate the status of "libidinal repression" as the absolute signifier of Irish-Catholic embodiment, scholars have not similarly questioned its function in relation to bodily production. The Cullenite Church of the mid- to late nineteenth century also came to be regarded in some quarters as emulating a puritanical attitude and a worldly practicality associated with Protestantism at the same time that it was more militant and powerful.[51] Whatever the historical complexities of its sources and development, the residual orthopraxy of late nineteenth-century Irish Catholicism profoundly influenced the depiction of Irish-Catholic bodies in Joyce's work. Narrated in *A Portrait,* disciplined belief centrally informs the orthopraxy that *Ulysses* makes somatically generative through the symbolic of Judaism. Rather than portraying this yield in conjunction with actual religious practice, of course, Joyce employs it to redescribe the Irish male body as a particular mode of performativity grounded in perception and sensation. The author "reads" a performativity that, according to Asad, cannot be comprehended fully through the external viewing of ritual performance or its texts.[52] But Joyce's own development through such disciplines informs his portrayal of Irish masculinity through mutable performativity. *Ulysses* rejects the epistemology and sentiment of doctrinal Christianity but embraces orthopraxy as productive and repressive of Irish minoritarian bodies. The use of orthopractic Judaism and the material fluid of alcohol—that is, the bodily practices associated with Bloom and Simon Dedalus—underwrite the new formulation of somatopsychic investigation, knowledge, and performance. The rejection of these identities as in any way natural or uncomplicated—Bloom's adherence to Judaism, his strict definition as a Jew, or Stephen's belief in Catholic doctrine—affect not at all the power of the symbolic connected to the orthopractic modes of the narrative. Molly Bloom alone among the major characters bears straightforward, if multiple, identifications.

In first six chapters of the novel, as I have noted, this portrayal of embodiment registers through a relatively tightly integrated sensorium: vision in particular is depicted as countermodern, through its close relationship to the other senses. Martin Jay[53] and Jonathan Crary describe the historical genesis of modern sensory reorganization through accounts of the full embodying of vision. When the Cartesian model was displaced by new physiological knowledge and technologies, in concert with new disciplinary regimes and social conditions, vision became a fully contingent and subjective production, itself an object of knowledge and place of labor. This visual mastery was paralleled by "increasing standardization and regulation of the observer" and "forms of power that depended on the abstraction and formalization of vision," in Crary's description.[54] While *Ulysses* represents vision as fully embodied, the novel works to cancel its abstracted primacy. Stephen in particular acts as a vehicle for representing sound as equivalent to sight, for the narrative invests both with the proprioceptive sense of the body in movement, just as Bloom characteristically integrates vision with smell, taste, and touch. Though historically, and more recently, critics have argued for the visual modernity of *Ulysses*, I contend that the novel constantly and equally works to embed vision in the countermodern, integrated sensorium, in which smell, tactility, and taste are brought into closer alignment with an empowered vision. Sara Danius, for instance, states that *Ulysses* is "both an index and enactment of the increasing differentiation of the senses, particularly sight and hearing," derived in part from cinematography, phonography, and telephony.[55] I would argue that the bodily technologies of religious praxis equally inform the novel's innovations and increase the effect of their apparently "autonomous"[56] agency. Instead of separating and then reintegrating the senses in synesthesiac effects, *Ulysses* proceeds from an understanding of embodiment as a technology—that is, a set of practices and techniques for shaping the senses in themselves and in relation to one another. Danius glosses the depiction of sausage links as a concomitant operation of sight and smell, subject and object: "The shiny links, packed with forcemeat, fed [Bloom's] gaze and he breathed in tranquilly the lukewarm breath of cooked spicy pigs' blood" (4.142–45).[57] In my reading, however, the feeding of Bloom's sight and the parallel detection, by his nose, of the sausages' way of breathing both result from the prior embedding of his vision in smell, taste, tactility, and proprioception, in the imagined exchange of pork- and Bloom-breath. The feeding of Bloom's gaze is reminiscent of the Benedictine monk's mastication of scripture, just as the sausage encapsulates the meat's former life, production, and future consumption. To draw such a distinction is not to dismiss sensory agency or reproductive technologies, but rather to reorient them as grounded in bodily techniques derived from the model of disciplined practices: again, *Ulysses* understands embodiment itself as a technology, not just a historical and social situation shaped by technology.

Sight as a segregated and privileged form of knowing also pertains to the domination of the distanced gaze vividly dramatized in *Dubliners*. *Ulysses'* occupation of the insider-outsider relationship to its provincial Irish subjects demands a curb on the dominance of vision even as its agency is enhanced through mobility and exercised for its own sake. The primacy of a segregated vision is acutely perilous for a narrative that engages so heavily in racial and ethnic typologies, whose dominant historical idiom is an epidermal racialism, tied to the legibility of an essence. The novel avoids using physiognomy to characterize Judaism, for instance, preferring instead to cite the insignia or emblems of type in "Nestor," where Stephen recalls the "goldskinned" Jewish financiers on the steps of the Paris stock exchange through body language, sound, and dress rather than given physical features: their "maladroit silk hats," he concludes, are "[n]ot theirs: these clothes, this speech, these gestures" (2.66–67). Perhaps the most vivid example of racial typification through stereotyped physical features, the minstrel automata of the Bohee brothers, appears in "Circe" with "[f]lashing white kaffir eyes and tusks" and "smackfatclacking nigger lips" (15.419). After singing and playing the banjo, the brothers whisk black masks from their raw babby faces (15.422)—as if, Herr observes, "the skin itself were a kind of clothing."[58]

Instances of segregated ocular power crop up in the first six chapters of the novel and often accompany representation of the agency of hearing—especially in the chapters dominated by Stephen—and of smell, taste, or tactility—in chapters focused on Bloom. A locus classicus of the interrogation of sight, Stephen's walk on the beach in "Proteus" begins with an appeal to St. Ignatius Loyola, author of an orthopractic program of spiritual exercises (9.163), and continues by highlighting mystic and physiological perception: not only does Aristotle's empiricism trump Berkeley's idealism, for visible "signs" reside "in bodies" that register in Stephen's own, but the "ineluctable modalities of the audible" must accompany the "visible." He interrogates "seeing" as the absolute metaphor for "knowing," through tactility: "If you can put your five fingers through it is a gate, if not a door. Shut your eyes and see," he ruminates (3.8–9). The fundamental somatic sense of the body in movement connects to sound, for "rhythm begins" with walking, and feet ground poetic meter. Stephen moves through physical space "a stride at a time" (3.11). Throughout the chapter, his current experience and the memories that they spur prominently feature sound, voices, music, bells, wind, gunshots, barks, shouts, wind, crunching shells, and "wavespeech" (3.41, 457). Joyce represents the full range of bodily sensations through perception and movement, but it is ultimately the audible that registers in "Proteus" as the other primary sense through which Stephen conducts transactions with the world. Often, imagery that seems to be prompted by his sight actually gains propulsion through sonic and textual association rather than through highly visual "impression."

Prompted by a pun on a song, for instance, the conflation of the meanings of *mare* in French and English informs later metaphoric leaps: "Airs romped round him, nipping and eager airs. They are coming waves. The whitemaned seahorses, champing, brightwindbrindled, the steeds of Mananaan" (3.55–58). Though cast as a visual impression of the approaching water, the sonic and etymological connection spurs the imagination of "seahorses" as much as the visual link of the white waves to horses' manes does. The combination of "sea" and "horse" reappears in the series associating the "stagnant bays of Marsh's library" with the prophet Joachim Abbas, who "ran from [the rabble] to the wood of madness, his mane foaming in the moon, his eyeballs stars" as well as with the faces and nostrils of Swift's noble horse people, of Mulligan, and of other school fellows (3.107–12).

What registers in *A Portrait* as the sensory and sensual repression encouraged by Stephen's Catholic training reemerges in "Proteus" as a sensory and perceptual apparatus attuned to the solidity of sound, the tactility of sight, and the production of literature through the rhythmic music of the body in motion. Here the "gothic" qualities of the novel's opening become a generative practice of embodiment reminiscent of the medieval church. Embedded in Stephen's frequent allusions to scholastic philosophy, theology, and ecclesiastical history, the sensory experience of the walk along the beach recalls a medieval embodiment in which the senses have not yet been segregated. Caroline Walker Bynum notes that the materialism of medieval eschatology "expressed not body-soul dualism but rather a sense of self as psychosomatic unity." The medieval bequest of the "person," she continues, "was not a concept of soul escaping body or soul using body; it was a concept of self in which physicality was integrally bound to sensation, emotion, reasoning, identity—and therefore . . . to . . . salvation. Despite its suspicion of flesh and lust, Western Christianity did not hate or discount the body."[59] At the same time that Stephen, like Joyce, joins the legacy of this period with precisely this dualism, the representation of his sensory "making" in "Proteus" recalls a medieval "incarnated vision," which, according to Suren Lalvani[60] and Suzannah Biernoff,[61] was "tactile and kinesthetic" and more closely wedded to hearing, taste, and smell than was true for the reorganized vision that emerged in the early nineteenth century.

The chapter's project in fact seems to resemble that of Leclerq's "active reading," in which texts are incorporated into bodies. "Proteus" recasts the imaginative capacities of Stephen's sensorium in *A Portrait*. After the retreat, Stephen, believing himself in a state of mortal sin, meditates on sight, wondering how it damns so quickly through lust: "By seeing or thinking of seeing," he considers. "The eyes see the thing, without having wished first to see. Then in an instant it happens. But does that part of the body understand or what? The serpent, the most subtle beast of the field. It must understand when it desires in one instant, and then prolongs its own desire instant after instant, sinfully. It feels and it understands and it desires! What a horrible thing!" Stephen then poses another question, now conflating the snake with the eye: "Who made it to be like that, a bestial part of the body able to understand bestially and desire bestially?"[62] Earlier, in a less tortured vein, he recalls his former attraction to a priestly vocation as a sensual intensification of his experience of the mass: "In that dim life which he had lived through in his musing he had assumed the voice and gestures which he had noted with various priests. He had bent his knee sideways like such a one, he had shaken the thurible only slightly like such a one, his chasuble had swung open like that of such another as he had turned to the altar again having blessed the people."[63] Stephen's thoughts revolve around his occupation of the performative body as a form "aloof from the altar, forgotten by the people, his shoulders covered with a humeral veil, holding the paten within its folds . . . his hands joined and his face toward the people" as he chanted.[64] In "Proteus," the praxis of embodiment, while still speculative, is housed in the experiencing body. Rather than mimicking the bodies of priests to enhance his practice, or imagining himself inside them, Stephen is represented as corporally producing his senses while he meditates upon his immediate experience. As the "sands"[65] of eternal damnation become the possible "walking into eternity along Sandymount strand" (6.18–19), so does Joyce transpose the agency of each sense—to sin and to suffer—into the register of performativity.

To assert the relations of the senses as narrow in these instances is not to reassert the conventions of an "organic" body tied to realist codes. Instead I emphasize the production of embodiment through processes that allow for the display of each sense's agency and intentionality. The reception of Joyce's earlier fiction shows that the proximity of smell to sight particularly disturbs sensory segregation, and as I will discuss in chapter five, the early response to *Ulysses* points to a great unease between the narrative's power of somatic scrutiny and its equal insistence on holding subjects *in* an unabstracted, seemingly chaotic, perceptual and physical flux. Joyce's countermodern modernity, his depiction of a vivid contemporary moment made by technologies modelled on spiritual practice, accounts for the disruption of such oppositions, as I have been arguing. The dynamics of production recast the gothic binaries staged in "Telemachus" as an exchange between fluid and interpenetrating materials.

If Stephen's portrayal accents the new status of textual knowledge as embedded in and made from bodily experience, Bloom's highlights the production of worldly knowledge through imaginative empathy based on sensory experience and identification, as well as the investigation of a full sensory range. Activities and perceptions lack their conventional segregation. While "Proteus" features but does not highlight smell and taste, the Bloomiad constantly recurs to them by using descriptive synesthesia. "Calypso" famously opens with a description of Bloom's taste for the grotesque "inner organs of beasts and fowls," in particular "grilled mutton kidneys which gave to his palate a fine tang of faintly scented urine" (4.1–4). His visual perceptions frequently and quickly connect to taste and touch: the sight of the "dull, squat" (4.13) kettle quickly leads him to notice his mouth's dryness; his observation of the cat prompts him to consider her consumption of mice, the "gloss of her sleek hide," her "milkwhite teeth," the bristles of her whiskers, "shining wirily" (4.22, 33, 39), and the roughness of her tongue as well as the sounds of her licking, mewing, and purring. Bloom's brief attempt to inhabit the psychology and visual perspective of the cat infuse the narrative observation of her sentience.

Joyce depicts a corporeally expressive subject through Stephen's embodiment of text. Bloom's sensory observations counterpoint this production of knowledge. His respiratory exchange with the sausages is characteristic of his engagement with other animate creatures and with inanimate objects, as Danius asserts. His quick observations often lead him to speculate about the sensory position of other bodies, and in this act, he identifies with and briefly inhabits them: he thinks, for example, about the feel of the too-tight collar on a horse's neck, and the taste and texture of corpses to the vermin that eat them: "Saltlike crumbling mush of corpse: smell, taste like raw white turnips" (6.993–94). The investigatory inclination toward his own and other bodies has led critics to understand Bloom as an empiricist, yet his epistemology differs markedly from the medical materialism exemplified by Mulligan. "Hades," like "Telemachus," is set in the territory of death and is populated by ghosts, corpses, and memories of profound loss. But "Hades" expands on sensory identification and reformulation rather than exterior observation, on continuities and interrelationships rather than binaries, and on an incorporative and somatizing habit that draws on the organic proximity of life and death. Here embodiment is the gateway to imaginative identification. Bloom and his world result from an epistemology generated from his bodily experience as the basis of his compassion and comedy. Death, in the Bloomiad, is often figured as constitutive of the life cycle: the cat and Bloom, like May Dedalus and the vermin of the cemetery, are "chewers of corpses" who must eat to live and who will in turn become food. The depiction of these "expressive" and interiorized subjects as producers of somatic knowledge precedes their figuration as the mere subjects, rather than the subject-agents, of the bodily practices that they have illustrated. As these conventional characters become the mere subjects of various "instruments" of representation, they enter into epistemes made by their somatic practices. But individuals no longer govern these powers to any great degree. In staging the attenuation of and split between agency and "personal" subjectivity, the narrative grants the power accrued by the representation of somatic praxis to language as an episteme that controls material. That is, bodily agency creates its own fields of knowledge, extracted from collective praxis and enforced on the representational order of the material world.[66]

In the gothic-adventure plot of the journey, the imaginative "making" of bodies as intersubjective culminates in Stephen's religious-racial fathers while the son "degenerates" into drunkenness and sex. Parodying the "disciplines" of regulated religious practice, the somatic zones enjoin sensual indulgence. But they also imitate the psychic dissolution and somatopsychic totalization produced by regulated religious programs, even as they destroy the somatic and psychic dictates of the autonomous, bounded, and expressive individual. Because Bloom's "vulgar" embodiment and its status as Stephen's new paternal legacy have been amply explored in the criticism, I focus here on the largely unnoticed reformulation of his fellow father, Simon Dedalus, and the role of drink in *Ulysses*' revision of biological paternity and Irish-Catholic pathology.

Irish-Catholic Praxis and Alcohol

"[I]t is through immersion in Bloom as a sensual 'other' man that Joyce can reconstruct his bond to himself—that is, to himself in the person of Stephen, the fallen-away Catholic sensualist," Laura Doyle states.[67] But I contend that Stephen must reconstruct this bond through complementary immersion in the drunken Catholic father. The pathological "blood" of heredity and Eucharistic transubstantiation meet in the representation of alcohol. In its parodic plot of degeneration, *Ulysses* stages the descent into liquor as the biological destiny of the Irish-Catholic male. The alcohol as well as the body that the narrative depicts has, however, undergone transformation. Joyce's portrait of Stephen as a budding alcoholic is shocking in light of the assessment of chronic drinking in *Dubliners* and of the adolescent's contempt for his father's crass dissipation in *A Portrait*. In *Ulysses* the son gives himself over to the patriarchal Irish "disease" with a rapidity and intensity that implies a racial fate, transmitted through blood and enacted in the trajectory of Stephen's inebriated day. That Stephen is "the father of his own son" resonates with the seemingly inexorable decline of the mandarin "uncreated conscience of [his] race" into "another improvident Dublin character," in Kenner's phrase.[68]

Connected solely to paralysis and repression in Joyce's previous fiction, drink is speciously curative in both its sacred and profane forms. The author harnesses intoxication's *productive* and mobile energies in *Ulysses*. He extends his earlier depictions by dramatizing liquor's negative effects with great force, yet the poison of the Irish-Catholic male now functions as an elixir as well. "Poisons the only cures," Bloom notes in "Lotos Eaters." "Remedy where you least expect it" (5.483–84). The material aspect of a more fluid "blood," alcohol models the potency of bodies "disciplined" by its practice. The mobility of drinking as a linguistic signifier and a somatic state, rehearsed in its ultimately repressive and deadening effects in *Dubliners*, acquires a generative function in *Ulysses* by occupying drunkenness rather than largely observing its effects from an exterior, sober vantage. Alcohol's new powers direct much of the novel's late middle section, beginning with Simon's drunken song in "Sirens," proceeding through the Citizen's drunken aggression in "Cyclops," and cresting, at the peak of Stephen's drunk, in "Oxen in the Sun" and "Circe." Together the chapters illustrate the sweep of liquor's productions, as "spirit" meets "spirits"[69] in violence and communion, from the embrace of "Siopold" to the Citizen's rage. Notably, this equation first appears in *Dubliners* as a power of the female alcoholic. In "A Painful Case," the alcoholic Emily Sinico acquires these significations in death. In *Ulysses* the conjunction characterizes the live male body. The fluid properties of femininity, alcohol, and death are reimagined through the reigning paradigms of music and phallogocentric birth. Stephen enters into his father's bodily practice through drunkenness, registered in the epistemic and representational framework of "Sirens" as an acute auditory capacity and in "Oxen in the Sun" as a linguistic birth. In both chapters the physical basis of the tie between drunkenness and artistic production accompanies dissolution of the "individual" as a bounded psychic interior, for the agency of sound and speech made by bodies departs from the awareness and control of distinct characters. In "Sirens," the sober Bloom initially operates as a central subjectivity, but the language of the narrative overrides his viewpoint and his language to portray the intersubjective operation and constant movement of sound. Orthography, perspective, and "interior" reaction give way to the dictates of the chapter's revision of embodiment as the registration of ambient sound. At the same time, these enfleshments of song and language arise from particular circumstances that are coded with Irish communal resonances: the Feis Ceoil, or singing festivals, staged as musical revivals beginning in the 1890s, form a background to "Sirens" and the rise of an Irish-Catholic medical establishment, including the hospital for indigent women, act as the setting in "Oxen."[70]

Bloom depicts music and drunkenness as somatic analogues. Observing Cowley at the piano in the Ormond, the sober observer thinks that "he stuns himself with [music]: kind of drunkenness" (11.1191). Bloom similarly observes of Simon: "Glorious tone he has still. . . . Wore out his wife: now sings. . . . His hands and feet sing too. Drink. Nerves overstrung. Must be abstemious to sing" (11.695–99). Reminiscent of Stephen's attempt to deflect attention from the evidence of Simon's "shameful drinkingbout of the night before" in *A Portrait*,[71] tremors now also signify a music in Simon's body and music-making is a form of intoxication for Cowley. In spite of Bloom's prudent observation, Simon uses his voice to inhabit Lionel, and the quality of his performance pulls Bloom into the operatic role as well. At the climax of the aria, Dedalus and Bloom, auditor and singer, merge:

> —Co-ome, thou lost one!
> Co-ome, thou dear one!
> Alone. One love. One hope. One comfort me. Martha, chestnote, return!
> —Come . . . !
> It soared, a bird, it held its flight, a swift pure cry, soar silver orb it leaped serene, speeding, sustained, to come, don't spin it out too long long breath he breath long life, soaring high, high resplendent, aflame, crowned, high in the effulgence symbolistic, high, of the etherial bosom, high, of the high vast irradiation everywhere all soaring all around about the all, the endlessnessnessness. . . .
> —To me!
> Siopold!
> Consumed. (11.740–50)

The lyrical passage of the bird in flight, prompted by the emotional suspense between "come" and "to me," realizes the image of the lapwing, which represents Icarus' flight by the nets of country, church, and family at the end of *A Portrait*. It is the rejected biological father who now launches the lyrical, if highly overwrought, flight. The language describing it, incorporating fragments of the characters' thoughts, clearly emerges from a distant third "person" narrator, who represents a moment of "endlessnessnessness" that is pointedly temporary. Nonetheless, the conceit of the subject drunk on song refigures the city orchestrally, finding unexpected harmonies as well as critiques of the song's emotional fusions. The auditors' clapping comes to encompass the "clop" of the departed Blazes Boylan's horse as he heads toward Eccles Street in a cab, passing the statues of the imperialist-adulterer Nelson and the temperance advocate Father Mathew (11.757, 761–64).

The energetic literary pastiche of "Oxen in the Sun" applies alcohol's power to literary language, for Stephen creates his own art through "degenerate" paternal praxis. Rhythm, embodied in his earlier walk along the strand, underwrites both musical and literary production, propelled by the fluctuating registers of drink. The chapter builds on the sonic diffusions of "Sirens" by frequently rendering its subjects as a collectivity made by the body of British prose. Returning to the realm of mere materiality, Joyce here replaces the "foetus" carved into the desk in the Cork medical theater of *A Portrait* with a childbirth that dramatizes the reproduction of English in Stephen's newly embodied register.[72] The narrative styles, both ponderous and fluid, constantly convey sharp ironies through their distance from the subjects that they represent while the narrative uses them to demonstrate its facility. It is important to remember, as Duffy asserts, that the realistic donnée of the chapter is the childbearing of a poor Irish woman[73]—a woman in fact like May Dedalus, discounted by drunken Irish men just as she is exploited by phallogocentric English literary language. The dense, nearly impenetrable anthropological and bureaucratic language of the chapter's opening, which follows upon a Gaelic command, an epic invocation to the sun, and a slang exclamation announcing an Irish boy's birth, celebrates the continuation of the race through nation, custom, and tradition: "[I]t behoves every most just citizen to become the exhortator and admonisher of his semblables and to tremble lest what had in the past been by the nation excellently commenced might be in the future not with similar excellence accomplished if an inverecund habit shall have gradually traduced the honourable by ancestors transmitted customs" (14.21–26). This turgid tribute to the racial nation contrasts acerbically with the facts of colonization: the boy being born is no "citizen" but the member of a "race" whose increase may be undesirable to the country's rulers, whose family in all likelihood cannot support him emotionally or economically, and whose drunken "semblables" dramatize his "hereditary" fate. "Oxen" at the same time counters irony with the self-assertion of Irish English and Catholic upward mobility, as the National Maternity Hospital, established in 1894, is a Catholic one, given over to the aid of poor women. The "new, trained, and educated generation of young [male] Catholics" who treat them signify "an emerging managerial and professional class," Gibson observes: their insolence and poor manners are an expression of a democratic irreverence evidenced during this era.[74] Though the historical literary styles of "Oxen" have conventionally been described as a progressive evolution that declines into the drunken babble of modernity, the chapter from its opening dramatizes its episteme as a brash mimicry of an already debased production: Joyce engages with the politics of the literary anthology as a popular imperial instrument during the period.[75] The performative drunken male body meets with the naturally generative female one to enact any Irish production as a re-production. Male power is implicated in both biological and literary knowledge, for both the imperial and the colonial share patriarchy, if at different levels. In spite of their opposition to the sexual politics of the Church, which would always sacrifice the life of the mother for that of the child, the medical students describe women as sexual objects or maternal cows, even as the group enters into a complex dialogue with questions of population loss.[76] Bloom alone attends to the "woman's word" spoken by Nurse Callahan, who repeatedly asks the men to contain their roistering, and even he places this attention in the context of empathy for female pain rather respect for female authority: "The man hearkened to her words for he felt with wonder women's woe in the travail that they have of motherhood" (14.118–20). The chapter's final loss of structure reveals its "origins" in an outpouring of racial slur and aggression. After drinking the "mother's milk" of the cow and the "bull," the men traipse off to drink the mother's milk of alcohol at Burke's pub. The conclusion resonates with the assimilation of Irish soldiers into the British machinery of empire and the link between the emancipation of Catholics in 1829 and of black slaves in 1833.[77] The men's walk is presented in the language of the British army and its showhall representation: "March! Tramp, tramp, tramp, the boys are (attitudes!) parching. Beer, beef, business, bibles, bulldogs, battleships, buggery, and bishops" (14.1458–60). A variety of languages, dialects, and pidgins convey the action and voices: "Allee samee dis bunch," says one speaker, mocking a Chinese accent, and "Lou heap good man," imitating an American Indian (14.1448). Bloom, whose defense of women earlier earned him anti-Semitic insults, is now derided in minstrel accents that highlight theatrical sentiment and merge Irish colonials with American plantation slaves. "Ludamassy! Pore piccaninnies!" the narrator exclaims. "Thou'll no be telling me thot, Pold veg. Did ums blubble bigsplash crytears cos fren Padney was took off in black bag? Of all de darkies, Massa Pat was verra best" (14.1555–57). Derogatory references to various peoples are sprinkled throughout the pub crawl: "Jappies," "coon[s]," "injun[s]," "squaws," "chink[s]," and "sheen[ies]" are mentioned; Latin, French, German, Yiddish, and Spanish also appear, amid references to "Lapland," "Frenchy," a "Dutch oven," and a "Rooshian" (14.1560, 1504, 1483, 1501, 1528; 14.482, 1503, 1515, 1561). Using mimicry as a weapon against the master tongue, Joyce portrays it as an impure Hobson-Jobson, a mummery.[78]

Finally mimicry becomes the *ground* of the British canon, a demotic heteroglossia, born of the mongrel bodies that it erases and incorporates.

Discipline and Sober

The degenerative trajectories of the Semite and the Celt culminate in "Circe," where drunkenness turns gothic specter into delirious spectacle, and find their true "disciplinary" cancellation in the sober catechistical rigors of "Ithaca." Together these chapters suggest the scope of *Ulysses'* somatically produced epistemes and their extravagant alienation from any particular subject. "Circe" illustrates bodily practice at its most unrestrained, completing the arc of sensual indulgence created by the extremes of the novel's masculine Irish typology; "Ithaca" investigates and reduces human scale, representing the pathos of homecoming through withdrawal into an unrelenting inquiry. Sensuality and severity dispel the gothic powers of the novel's earliest chapters. Perhaps the most disembodied formulation of "knowing" in the novel, "Ithaca" sets the doctrinal model against the disciplinary one. Finally the protagonists become elements in a vast cosmic scheme that allows for their mingling in dispersion.

Like "Ithaca," "Circe" employs a graphically scripted genre. Cheryl Herr has shown that the chapter draws heavily on the resources of the panto, a popular theatrical form that highlights all manner of transformation—whether from text to text, poverty to wealth, lovelessness to romance, or forest to grotto.[79] Vision acts as the chapter's primary somatic mode. "Circe" stages biologically given identities as roles and costumes and ignores distinctions among persons and objects, death and life, desire and action. Yet this vision is strangely decontextualized and flattened,[80] not only through the theatrical conceit but also through its presentation as script. We are given a representation of a representation, more remote from actual theatrical event than a third-person, omniscient description of events would be. Here the archaic gothic powers depicted as psychic territories in "Telemachus" become liberated from any mooring in the human subject: drunken and erotic energy materializes any residue on which it alights, staging the raw drives of the Dublin males' unconscious. In spite of their completely independent agency, the gothic motifs that resurface here are curiously evacuated of their potency. The imaginary specter of May Dedalus reappears as a fully materialized imago, a horribly decayed corpse, and yet ultimately a ventriloquized puppet, repeating the melancholic thoughts that Stephen had in "Telemachus" as a melodramatic script. "Circe" depicts the "mother" as a Radcliffean ghost, an explained supernatural, to whom "Stephen" now voices his protest—"Cancer did it, not I" (15.4188)—before he finally smashes the chandelier with a Wagnerian "Nothung!" to dispel her, *"in the agony of her deathrattle"* (15.4238–45). Like the automata minstrels who show race is a costume when they finally *"whisk black masks from raw babby faces"* (15.422), the vampiric religious "mother" becomes fully visible in *Ulysses* as an evacuation of gothic essence. Though Stephen is still muttering about the "black panther" and "vampire," "Bloom" recognizes the features of May Dedalus in her son's face, as the "working through" of the gothic script has resulted in incorporation, though one that appears when Stephen is unconscious (15.4930, 4949).

Given Stephen's Luciferean declaration of "non serviam" against the archaic demands of matriarchal theology in "Circe," the catechistical structure of "Ithaca" seems drily sardonic: May's demand that her son serve her through assent to her faith is replaced by a narrative demand that the representational world submit to interrogation. The chapter's starkly impersonal agency appropriates omniscience as an end in itself, parodying divine power as authorial privilege in order to discipline the dissolute animation of "Circe" and correct the error-prone laxity of "Eumaeus." The questioner's indifference to human individuality—to human agency housed in a self-directing psychological interior—is expressed through a zeal for knowing every aspect of the characters' history, desires, plans, actions, and material circumstances. Focusing on the episteme of religious knowledge itself, "Ithaca" purports to abstract and repress human centrality and agency along with the individual subject: a doctrinal script demands rehearsal of codified knowledge, imitated through the marshalling of various disciplines, each of which renders information as determinate of representation. In essence, the narrative's minute scrutiny mimics the "production" of the somatopsychic subject as an effect of collective, public, and authoritative knowledge. While the expansive scope of the investigation has usually been read as a reduction of the male protagonists to elements in the city's water system, the globe's coordinates, mathematics, or the galaxy's constellations, it might also be seen to organize these mechanisms around them. In relating their educational histories, the narrative can generate "Blephen" and "Stoom" (15.49, 51) as interpenetrating technical-somatic "bodies" of knowledge.

The discounting of "religion" as a productive somatic paradigm for *Ulysses* has obscured the centrality of belief to Joyce's modernism. According to the conventional interpretation, Joyce adapts the orthodox mode of "religion" to serve as a figure for a sensuous art—an art that counters the physical and intellectual repressions exacted by belief. This reading, based on the dominant formation of modern Christianity, assumes a conception of "religion" as theology and ritual, in which belief is understood as the private affect of "individuals" whose somatopsychic structures are determined by other forces, as I have said. *Ulysses* draws on the religious mode of orthopraxy, and Joyce adopts its protocols to depict a performative embodiment for minority male subjects. In this belief formation, regulated practice fundamentally shapes adherents' bodies and minds as a whole in order to create from them an epistemic-emotional agency. Joyce imitates the productive capacities of religious discipline to portray somatic integration and dissolution, based on the mutable relations of agency and subjectivity.

The adaptation of disciplined practice affords the author a method of producing knowledge from bodies while overcoming the subject-object binary that constrains his earlier fiction. In the novel's early chapters, romance motifs illustrate the inability of knowledge imposed on subjects from an exterior vantage to release the Irish-Catholic man from pathological melancholy and stasis. Instead, he escapes entrapment by traveling through the racial-religious stereotypes that have defined provincial bodies. Formerly portrayed as pathologies, the degenerate practices of Irish men now also produce knowledge from somatopsychic experience and performance. As the conventions of realism subside, *Ulysses* depicts the gradual extraction of bodily power from the subject, assuming his agency to establish epistemes through which the narrative's subjects may register.

Ulysses owes a debt to the performative techniques of practical religion and so to the belief formations of contemporaneous Irish Catholicism and European-Irish Judaism. The "blood" of liquor as a material of transubstantiation, with both religious and chemical meanings, crucially accompanies the corporeal synthesis and mobility signified by Judaism: Joyce incorporates biological as well as spiritual-material corporeality into the reformulation. Performative embodiment gives the text a paradigm for "styling" minority Irish identity without essentializing it. The demotion of sight, determinative in the racialist discourses of the era, is particularly notable in Joyce's portrayal. Ultimately, the performative constitution of material meets its limit in binary sex. *Ulysses'* critique of the repressive mother administers the antidote of Molly Bloom as a sensual agent. Yet she adheres to a logic of expressive individuality, as the male protagonists do not. Joyce finally uses the critique of feminine repression in *Ulysses* to enlarge the performative capacities of men rather than to release women from their essential connection to nature.

Ulysses suggests the contingency of the essential somatic and psychic structure of the (male) "individual" signified by the conventions of realism. The novel proceeds from and returns to this model, which assumes a psychologized interior that governs a specific structure of embodied "selfhood."

But the journey of these male subjects suggests other, culturally inflected constructions of the person, and in particular illustrates the operation of spiritual belief formations in producing other kinds of relations among persons and of persons. In chapter five, I will take up the ways in which this recasting of the individual differs from its dominant Western construction. Before returning to the career of the novel, however, I turn to its successor, *The Satanic Verses*, in which Rushdie applies the orthopractic techniques of *Ulysses* directly to sacred bodies. In the text of *The Satanic Verses*, the mobility and plurality so prized by both Joyce and his acolyte meet their limit, as these values threaten to dissolve the power of minority religious bodies so crucial to their shared aesthetic.

4

Muslim Simulation and the Limits of the "Star Text"

"'To be born again ... first you have to die. Ho ji! Ho ji!'" sings Gibreel Farishta at the opening of Salman Rushdie's *The Satanic Verses*. Gibreel launches into his exuberant ghazal as he and Saladin Chamcha "tumbl[e] from the heavens" down to their reincarnation as the Muslim aliens of the British imaginary—the one a horned goat, the other a deranged zealot.[1] Like *Ulysses*, *The Satanic Verses* employs a gothic journey through degenerate male bodies. Here, however, Joyce's minority religious types are visually realized. When Rushdie's actors plunge from an exploding plane into the "sacred" territory of England, they undergo somatic and psychic mutations drawn from the vocabulary of Indian popular cinema,[2] and in particular from the genre of the Hindu mythological. Whether in history, transmigration, or dream, the Indian Muslims undergo reversions to become gothic and fantastic invaders of their own foundational narratives. In using Indian movies as the vehicle of these metamorphoses, *The Satanic Verses* merges the "instruments" of religious practice and visual reproduction to imagine the actors' bodies as sites of corporeal, geographic, and historical accretion. Muslim-Indian bodies become the platform for realizing visual practices that Rushdie draws from Hindu-saturated Indian popular film and its culture, chief among them impersonation, citation, and incorporation. The "parallel texts," or mythic and legendary narratives, that inform and compose their images produce each of the protagonists as somatic intertexts that not only allude to but also absorb other identities. It is Rushdie's masterstroke and master violation to use the Qu'ran as the dominant parallel text, and Muhammad as the central divine body, of the narrative: *The Satanic Verses* represents itself through the impossible genre of the Muslim mythological, an ideally syncretic medium that both exploits and surmounts the issue of impersonation borne by the Muslim symbolic in popular film. Yet in contrast to both *Ulysses* and *Midnight's Children*, *The Satanic Verses* qualifies the absolute privilege of mixture and movement tied to the technologies of minority religious practice. This value, so necessary to incorporation of the cosmopolitan migrant into the subcontinental body in *Midnight's Children*, diminishes here. *The Satanic Verses* illustrates the limits of the Joycean formulation of minority religion. Rushdie's novel exposes the indispensable role of a somatically grounded episteme of belief to the production of Anglo- and Indian-Muslim identities—and most particularly to his own authorial identity.

To claim any identity at all for his travelers, Rushdie relies on the praxis of Islam and the precepts of Hinduism. The actors' "technical" production by Indian film supplies the citational somatic image as corporate, fluid, and mobile, yet anchored in a characteristically Indian syntax. The loss of this context in a visual postmodernism, associated in the novel with Britain's reproductive media, reveals its areas of incompatibility with a "postcolonial" narrative of dislocation that still seeks to claim a "style" of identity in provincial religious-national embodiment. While Joyce's performative bodies resist a gothic nightmare of stasis and enclosure, Rushdie's must mitigate ceaseless movement. As many critics have noted, *The Satanic Verses* solves the dilemma through an aggressive conservatism, in which singular meaning is restored through what has been seen as an Oedipal conquest of the national by the migrant. I would add that the novel's conclusion resurrects the binaries of the Indian popular movie's melodramatic mode and the gothic novel's reinstatement of social order: Chamcha finally returns to his origins in India and in Islam, moves coincident with the deaths of the nationals, his father Changez and his rival Gibreel. But superseding simple envy of the national's claim to the literary territory of India is the narrative's fear of losing the religious modes of embodiment that distinguish its auratic aesthetic from the play of surfaces in (Western) postmodern simulacra. In working through this distinction, the novel ultimately transfers the discourse of degeneration onto referentiality itself and protects the narrative from absorption into it by staking its transcendence in the Prophet's body. The gothic reverse invasion of the body of prophecy enacts not only the cosmopolitan appropriation of the provincial religious body, but also the vampiric draining of its master signifier. The novel needs this prophylactic to protect itself from the appearance of exoticist or imperialist consumption, that is, to inoculate itself against the charge that Rushdie makes against cosmopolitan reproductive media. In my narrative of modernist literary history, the threat of the maternal vampire that opens *Ulysses* closes in the male cosmopolitan's claim on the blood of the provincial spiritual bodies of *The Satanic Verses*.

Gothic-Religious Embodiment and Indian Popular Film

Indian popular film operates as the preferred technology of somatopsychic embodiment in *The Satanic Verses*. Rushdie delivers his degeneration plots through emphatically concrete vehicles: histories that are typically evoked in *Ulysses* through nests of allusion take graphic shape, occupying a foreground itself allied with the Hindi cinema's delight in pulling diverse times and ontologies into a unified visual space.[3] The disciplined performativity of Muslim praxis is exuberantly parodied through the protagonists' reincarnations as monster and angel. Produced by the exemplary industry of the exemplary cosmopolis, the movies that Rushdie calls upon to fund these visible metamorphoses everywhere reflect and express the iconophilia of Hinduism pervasive in Indian visual culture and the context of sacralization carried by its mythic narratives.[4] At the same time they connote a political ideal in their creation of an Indian "public culture." Film critic Sumita Chakravarty "extrapolate[s]" from *The Satanic Verses* "the metaphor of *imperso-nation*," whose "ludic possibilities, as well as the anxiety generated by it, characterize the mode of Indian popular cinema's evocation and inscription of national identity."[5] In the larger context of Indian narrative traditions as well, "impersonation as a parable of social relationships has a long though uncharted history," she notes.[6] Like the pub in *Ulysses*, Indian cinema in *The Satanic Verses* constitutes an alternative arena of community.[7]

In combining the literary tradition of the English gothic, the idiom of the Hindu mythological film, and the origin story of Islam, *The Satanic Verses* takes on the specific problematic of Muslim representation in Bombay popular film. The symbolic of impersonation in this context suggests a threatening inauthenticity rather than a spectacular or communal playfulness. Quintessential "migrants" in Bombay as well as in London, the subcontinental Muslims register as abject zones of mobile signification because of their minority religious status, as well as their theatrical professions. The status of Muslim actors and subjects within the Hindu-dominated Bombay film industry further evacuates the identity that Rushdie depicts. Muslim stars have historically downplayed their religious identities, even when this affiliation is generally known, for the Muslim symbolic is "a problem but also a problem of (an always dubious) impersonation," one that "had to be exorcised again and again" in post-Independence Indian film, according to Parama Roy.[8] As emblems of representations of impersonation, Chamcha and Gibreel push Bloom's "degenerate" Judaism, linked with foreignness, rootless mobility, and disguise, to the extreme of counterfeit signification. Bloom's ultimate status, in "Ithaca," as an entirely disciplined signifier, a mutable mark, is the actors' point of departure in *The Satanic Verses*. Chamcha and Gibreel recall Jerrold Hogle's description of gothic signification as a progression of evacuated referentiality. Hogle contends that the ur-text of the English gothic, Walpole's *Castle of Otranto* (1764), "turns out to be referring back to a Renaissance symbolization of the self that was already 'counterfeit' in Shakespeare's day; hence the Gothic sign [is] the *ghost* of the counterfeit."[9] As the signified becomes more historically distant, the signifier seizes on ever more evacuated fragments of the past: Baudrillard's orders of representation are evident in the movement from the late eighteenth-century spectralization of the ghost to the Victorian simulation of the referent itself, epitomized in monsters such as Dracula and Jekyll-Hyde.[10] But while the British gothic that Hogle describes loses the authentic or "natural" referent through historical distance from it, *The Satanic Verses* treats this distance as physical as well as temporal. The visual and plastic modes of the novel's gothic-religious vocabularies reveal the fate of the "counterfeit" identity in simulation, a threat capable of absorbing the representational zone of transcendence that subcontinental Muslim bodies supply to Rushdie.

Most immediately, Rushdie merges gothic-religious and "filmi" idioms to depict particular psyches while they are interpellated into social and institutional narratives. As in *Ulysses*, in *The Satanic Verses* the protagonists' gothic roles represent the merging of exterior social and interior psychic projections and condition their eventual performative fates. The actors' transformations first register as arbitrary punishments, inflicted by political and religious authorities, at the same time that their mutations manifest psychic splits and repressions, "sins" against loyalty to their origins. Chamcha's flaw pertains less his long residence in England than it does to his rejection of any "Indian" identity whatsoever, an illusion of transcendence sustained through class privilege. Gibreel, whose migrant status pertains more centrally to the situation of Islam in India, loses his identity by losing his faith. While the protagonists suffer for renouncing their minority origins, *The Satanic Verses*, after Joyce, also interrogates the very notion of a unitary, natural "origin" to be violated. India's imperial legacy as well as the position of the religious minority within a Hindu state acts as a minus in the origin. Like Stephen in "Telemachus," the actors occupy an abject position because they eschew but cannot psychically separate from beginnings that never provided a stable or unitary point of departure. The actors' new embodiment merges the British racist imaginary, imposed from without, and the interior, psychologized condition, effloresced from within.

The technology of monstrosity allows Rushdie to revise these social and psychological "selves" by transporting them into the realm of the "person" formed by different cultural and religious protocols. Disciplinary agency does not dissolve the actors into somatic epistemes such as those that govern the depictions of Stephen and Bloom. Rather Gibreel and Chamcha manifest their loss of agency through somatic and psychic reinsertion into roles that they have previously inhabited. Gothic energies determine their plastic forms, parodically realizing the disciplinary production of bodies. In this the migrants recall Certeau's description of individualism as a "strategy" of embedding the self in a physical body: the organization of a central, bounded somatic space empowers agents against a distinct outside.[11] In *The Satanic Verses*, the bounded material body associated with the self of contemporary individualism becomes permeable, for technologies of the body and of visual reproduction overtake them. Rushdie's rendering of the spiritually saturated parallel texts of the Hindu cinema enables the actors' bodies to accrue other subjectivities, to enter into disparate plots, to ventriloquize others' voices, and to occupy others' forms as comic manifestations of both their gothic monstrosity and their disciplinary performativity. Through such accretions, the novel joins what Judith Halberstam calls a gothic "technology of subjectivity"[12] with Islamic practice as a technology of agency. Halberstam portrays nineteenth-century gothic monsters as metaphors for modern subjectivity in which "the self [is] a body which envelop[s] a soul"; it is "a body enthralled to the soul" formed and sought by the institutional apparatuses and discourses described by Foucault.[13] The gothic narrative that she describes is preoccupied with boundaries that are violated in the meaning machines of the monstrous bodies of *Frankenstein, Dracula, Dr. Jekyll and Mr. Hyde,* and *The Picture of Dorian Gray.* Yet the normative "self" presumed by the opposition of the human being and the deviant is actually "under construction within the stor[ies]," Halberstam argues: subjectivity becomes a "surface effect" in Stevenson and Wilde, for instance, as the narratives depict a "multi-formed" ego, in which "disguise becomes equivalent to the self in a way that confuses the model of subjectivity that each author maps."[14] Finally, "the hidden self subverts the authentic self as a notion," as an expressive, interiorized character becomes a "friction of surfaces" that might erase the self altogether.[15] *The Satanic Verses* places Chamcha precisely in this literary genealogy. The "authentic self" that this subgenre of the gothic challenges appears as a cultural construction not only because it subverts the stable, psychologized self of realist representation, however: the very "self" assumed in the revision differs because of the Muslim provenance of the monsters. In particular Gibreel's plot depicts an altogether different conception of what I have called the "person," modeled on the corporate Muslim body produced by orthopraxy as well as Hindu conceptions of mind-body relations, as I discuss in chapter two. Both protagonists manifest "corporate" identities connected with their specific media of transformation. Indian popular film enriches the person as a transactional and collective depth, while Western television represses the "individual" as the vehicle of subjectivity and produces only racialized surface as compensation. This difference forms the crux of the text's dilemma over the problematic of "migrant" mobility and its representational technologies, a dilemma that finally bears upon Rushdie's relationship to Indian Islam as an authoritative embodied voice.

Indian Popular Film and the Corporate Person

To reimagine a corporate Indian subjectivity in *The Satanic Verses*, Rushdie revises the Hinduized medical-religious conceits of *Midnight's Children* through the Hindu devotional movie.[16] It epitomizes popular cinema in the novel—indeed, the Indian film industry began with the mythological films of D. G. Phalke in 1913.[17] The visual and narrative idioms of the devotional film profoundly influenced the vernacular genres that quickly emerged from it. In the melodramatic mode that infuses these "filmi" genres, the transformational body bears dramatic meaning as a discursive signifier. Vijay Mishra explains that in this mode "the body [is] a marker of character or discourse," and as such "need not speak," for "it speaks itself."[18] The operation of parallel texts[19] also embeds all genres of Indian movies in auratic meaning. The term refers to the fusion of the star's roles with her off-screen identity as well as with the legendary narratives evoked by diegetic events or attributes. Conventionally, foremost among films' parallel texts is that of the star as a divinity of traditional epic.[20] Gandhy and Thomas explain, "The parallels between Indian stars and the gods of the Hindu pantheon are frequently remarked upon: both are colorfully larger than life, their lives and loves, including moral lapses, are the subject of voyeuristic fascination and extraordinary tolerance, and stars accept . . . an adoration close to veneration."[21] The Gibreel plot explicitly portrays the operation of the star text in producing him as an incorporative Muslim body. His stardom in what Rushdie names the "theological" explicitly employs the parallel texts of the Hindu epics, the *Ramayana* and the

Mahabarata (61). In vernacular film, Mishra observers, these epics supply the foundational "discourse that constructs the actor[s] and finds in the precursor texts" of traditional narratives "idioms and values that could be carried by them."[22] Before he becomes ill—the crisis that precipitates his flight to London—Gibreel is the godlike star. His portrayal is based on Ambitabh Bachchan,[23] but also recalls stars from earlier eras, such as M. T. Rao and M. G. Ramachandran,[24] popular and colorful personalities. Gibreel leads a secret "life of scandal and debauch" (25), chiefly of sexual licentiousness. But when his image disappears from its marquees, magazine covers, and screens during his illness, Bombay becomes the mournful site of *deus absconditus:*

> It was the death of God. Or something very like it; for had not that outsize face, suspended over its devotees in the artificial cinematic night, shone like that of some supernal Entity that had its being at least halfway between the mortal and the divine? More than halfway, many would have argued, for Gibreel had spent the greater part of his unique career incarnating, with absolute conviction, the countless deities of the subcontinent. . . . It was part of the magic of his persona that he succeeded in crossing religious boundaries without giving offence. . . . For over a decade and a half he had represented, to hundreds and millions of believers . . . , the most acceptable, and instantly recognizable, face of the Supreme. (16–17)

As an image, Gibreel gathers diverse identities in a popular commercial form that magnifies his virtues and offers an ideal public culture, as he, in Sara Suleri's phrase, "unites India in fandom."[25] The technical characteristics of this image contribute to its political and cultural function, for Rushdie presents the cinematic reproduction of Gibreel as a dynamic of metonymic expansion and projective absorption. The virtues discernable in his countenance overtake his screen image, in which his "real life" face, "in spite of profanity and debilitation . . . [is] a face inextricably mixed up with holiness, perfection, grace: God stuff," the narrator relates (17). The parallel text of stardom conflates the actor with his divine roles and the audience with his image of divinity, equations that dominate Gibreel's portrayal on-screen and off.

But Gibreel's ultimate incorporative "magic" is a purely invented, and highly significant, act of transcendence. He surmounts communalism by "incarnating" Krishna as well as the Grand Mughal on the screen (16–17). Because the mythological obviously cannot and does not treat the sacred text of Islam, *Verses* displays the actor's syncretic powers through his roles in Muslim historicals, the only popular genre in which Muslim subject matter routinely appears. Rushdie's actor has played "both the Grand Mughal and his famously wily minister in the classic *Akbar and Birbal*" as well as the Buddha and Krishna (16). Gibreel *is* singular in that his "Muslimness" signifies as an explicit element in his dominantly Hindu star text. Even though Muslim influence and participation are pervasive in popular cinema, inflecting its language, its parallel texts, and cosmopolitan aspirations, its presence is constantly hidden or subordinated in the actual film industry, as I have mentioned.[26] Gibreel's "impersonation" contrasts with the Muslim identity of Nargis, for instance, who maintained the public image created by her eponymous role in the nationalist epic *Mother India* (1957) by downplaying her sectarian affiliation, even though it was generally known.[27] Rushdie's character, in contrast, surmounts the issue of authenticity so thoroughly that he figures the nation as unproblematically as he does an ecumenical divinity. Before the star recovers, the narrator inquires: "If Gibreel died, could India be far behind?" (29). Gibreel's star text overcomes the impossibility of the metonymic production of nationality as imagined in *Midnight's Children*.

After the explosion of his plane by Sikh terrorists, Gibreel enters into the ultimate production of a nonsectarian film industry: a "Muslim theological." Into Hindu narratives Rushdie inserts the Qu'ran as the overarching parallel text of *The Satanic Verses*, and Gibreel as the central "impersonation" of Muslim India, in Rushdie's vision an ecumenical image of the divine. The novel stages the revelation of the Qu'ran as a film into which Gibreel is unwillingly and unknowingly thrust, whether this conjunction takes place in his mind alone, in a film, in history, or in yet another parallel text. Gibreel enters into the separate plot of Islam's founding through his "role" as the angel of revelation, who delivers the verses of the sacred text to the prophet. To represent this entrance, Rushdie confuses the body of the prophet with that of Gibreel through momentary shifts in Gibreel's visual perspective and oral control.

The saturation of the Indian popular film with religious meanings and dynamics, even when their subjects are not explicitly religious, supplies the author with the techniques of disciplinary performativity by merging them with the techniques of Indian vernacular film. This congeries is delivered as a gothic nightmare of interpellation into the historical founding of Islam. The visual context of the cinematic gaze allows for parody of the disciplinary merging of person and divinity, viewer and viewed. Central to *Verses'* full and extended fusion of the angel of revelation Gibreel and the prophet Mahound is its deployment of the darsanic gaze. According to the framework of darśana that shapes Indian cinematic practice, vision may act as a physical bridge between audience and icon, much like the "extrusive" and concrete gaze on the deity. "In practice," Vasudevan notes, "the devotee is permitted to behold the image of the deity, and is privileged and benefited by this permission, in contrast to a concept of looking that assigns power to the beholder by reducing the image to an object of the look."[28] In returning the gaze, the god may permit worshippers "to 'drink' divine power with their eyes" and assume "an extraordinary and revelatory 'point of view,'" according to Babb.[29] "[W]ho asks the bloody audience of a 'theological' to solve the bloody plot?" Gibreel asks when he finds himself in psychic communication with Mahound, who expects the angel to reveal God's message. But Gibreel's initial ability to view Mahound as an exterior body, even as they communicate mentally, disappears "as the dream shifts" and Gibreel discovers that "he's not just playing the archangel but also him, the businessman, the Messenger, Mahound, coming up the mountain when he comes" (108). The rapid cuts between perspectives suggest not only the merging of parallel texts, but also the action of an embodied gaze as a physical bridge of reciprocal communication.

The loss of agency that Gibreel feels in his initial lack of a script and in his later inability to locate the source of his own voice refers to the Indian cinema's practice of dubbing the actor's image with another actor's singing voice. The novel's opening lines allude to this practice when Gibreel "tunelessly" sings a filmi song rather than "only mim[ing] with playback singers" (3),[30] as he did in movies. Through the conceit of entrance into the mythological film itself, Gibreel thus "channels" a voice whose source is invisible and indeterminate, whose words come through his mouth and yet seem divorced from his thoughts. Rushdie's metaphor also recalls the celebrity status of the singers themselves, whose film tunes dominate popular music. Singers are often paired with particular stars, so that the singing voice of the actor remains constant through different movies. The parallel text of the actor thus includes the double-voicedness of song and speech as well as the body as the image of one actor and the sound of another. The singing voice comes through and joins with the visible image at the same time that it attaches to a voice not only understood to be separate, but also attached to a body visible in other contexts and familiar as a distinct identity.

In these ways Rushdie uses the technology of Indian film to represent the technology of disciplinary practice. They eventually "produce" Gibreel and Mahound as two subjectivities occupying one corpus. The novel's climatic fusion concretely portrays the aim of disciplinary practice by incorporating the prophet's body into the adherent's. As I will discuss in more detail later, *Verses* portrays this merging as conflictual rather than submissive, but the desire for knowledge of the prophet and his prophecies lies at the heart of the battle over the somatic episteme. While Ashley Dawson reads Gibreel's body as a "locus upon which the violent, sectarian disharmony of national reality is written," a "phantom bug" in the body politic,³¹ Gibreel equally acts as a meeting place of contradictory meanings. His citational spiritual-technological body resists the cohesive organic metaphor but collects significations, a somatic *differend*. Presented as a degeneration into psychosis from the standpoint of an interiorized individuality, in which a discrete body both contains and expresses a singular "self," Gibreel's reincarnation also encodes a conception of subjectivity as a "technical" production of religious embodiment and its visual reproduction. "The" body, a porous receptacle for mobile "souls" or psyches, acts as a platform for staging different or combined subjectivities rather than as a vessel for expressing an intrinsic, unique, and invisible interior. Scholars of Indian visual culture have articulated these formulations in varying ways, as they describe the premises of film, photography, and painting. Such protocols illustrate conceptions of the person that differ from the strategically organized individual that Certeau describes. According to Roy, popular film understands the relationship between the image and the subjectivity of the character it bears as "iconic" in Piercian terms: that is, the body bears a relationship of resemblance, rather than of "indexical" causation, to the interior. In this respect, the relation between body and character parallels that of the image and the actor depicted in Indian popular film. But Vasudevan complicates this semiotic through reference to the techniques of Indian theater and painting, in which iconicity condenses and "bind[s] a multi-layered dynamic into a unitary image."³² Similarly, the iconic in art historian Geeta Kapur's description is "an image into which symbolic meanings converge and in which moreover they achieve stasis."³³ As I discuss in chapter two, Christopher Pinney finds similar relations in the practices of popular regional photography, as well as the cinema that influenced it. He gathers evidence of a cultural conception of "the transience of the body and its status as a contingent receptacle for the soul" rather than an expressive vehicle for a distinct, grounded character, as I have said.³⁴ Sitters in the photographs that Pinney examines routinely assume different identities through props, backdrops, repetitions of the figure in a single frame, and allusions to mythic and historical figures (as well as through other media applied to the photographic surface). The portrait thus bears "fluid signs capable of succoring imaginary interiorities" that can be materialized through external citation. "Because the visible is not deemed to be anchored—in most cases—by an invisible realm of character (for there is usually a distinction between the two), the external body is freed from the constraints with which it is shackled in the Western tradition of painted portraiture. What can be captured [according to the popular Indian aesthetic] is a person's general physiognomy rather than the face as a trace of the interior character."³⁵ In Western individualism, the discounted third term globally diffuses a specific, intimate ipseity that mediates between agent and vehicle and is elided from the topography of psychic-corporeal space that visibly manifests it.

London's Monstrous Simulacra

If the Muslim theological enlarges Gibreel into a syncretic divinity, the Western media that reproduce Chamcha swallow and then degrade his identity. Strongly contrasting with the resourcefulness and depth of Indian cinema suggested by Gibreel's career, the Western media allied with Chamcha subsist primarily in the impoverished context of commodity. The same technical resources that produce Gibreel in Indian vernacular film produce Chamcha in English media: Chamcha ventriloquizes images, animates the altered imagery of his body as well as of objects, and acts as a congeries of attributional identities. But while Bombay and London possess the same technical capacities to dislocate, evacuate, and multiply identities, London's media present a stark contrast to the auratic context of Indian cinema. If Chamcha is viewed in terms of parallel texts, they would simply amplify his status as a surface of difference that propels the circulation of commodity. His image signifies his diminished status as a "person" because he ventriloquizes alienation and fetishization. In the Chamcha plot the exemplary processes of capitalism mesh seamlessly with the processes of the British racial imaginary.

The operation of the gaze in London illustrates the moral and political effects of these contextual differences. Chamcha's production as a commercial simulation highlights only the "blank" of his deracination (61), through a career centered on advertising and television. Chamcha, literally "spoon" or toady, learns the art of impersonation when he migrates to Britain as an adolescent, in an effort to "fool" the British "into thinking he was *okay*, he was *people-like-us*" (43); yet his class status in maturity helps to sustain his perception that he "'never ... belonged to a race'" (267). In his early days in London, Chamcha acts as a counterpart to the "playback singer" of Indian film, as he uses his skill at mimicry to voice products:

> [H]e was the Man of a Thousand Voices and a Voice. If you wanted to know how your ketchup bottle should talk in its television commercial, if you were unsure as to the ideal voice of your packet of garlic-flavoured crisps, he was your very man. He made carpets speak in warehouse advertisements, he did celebrity impersonations, baked beans, frozen peas. (60)

In contrast to the sacral contexts that everywhere inform Indian vernacular film, the British commercial animates the world by fetishizing commodities and understanding difference as consumer choice. Furthermore, the erasure of Chamcha's body from these images anticipates his function in other roles as a platform for staging superficial difference. Rushdie parodies the citational capacities of the actor's image in Indian film through Chamcha's Western production as a screen onto which attributes of the alien and the commodity are inevitably projected. His part as the extraterrestrial Maxim of *The Aliens Show*, for instance, dramatizes his parallel text as that of species difference rather than divinity. Derived from "*The Munsters* out of *Star Wars* by way of *Sesame Street*," the children's comedy reproduces his image as a trace of the dominant culture's gaze:

> What made the show a hit was its use of the latest computer-generated imagery. The backgrounds were all simulated . . . and the actors, too, were processed through machines, obliged to spend four hours every day being buried under the latest in prosthetic make-up which—once the video-computers had gone to work—made them look just like simulations, too. (62–63)

In Chamcha, Rushdie parallels the metonymic dynamic that globalizes Gibreel's "godstuff" in his screen image. But Chamcha's figuration as "ghoststuff" realizes his impersonation as erasure—in stark contrast to the mutuality of exchange between audience and actor in the darsanic gaze of Indian film. Chamcha functions much like Benjamin's actor, who "giv[es] up" aura to the camera in order to become an intersomatic surface, but here the transaction is filtered through Fanon. According to Benjamin, the film actor is "exiled from himself," for he "must operate with his whole living person, yet for[go] its aura," a process that entails the loss of corporeality to the shadow of the image.[36] The movie audience experiences this image as a sensuous identification, for their eyes become the conduit of a tactile projection into the screen. In *The Satanic Verses*, these "unconscious optics" serve as a point of identification of the other to be consumed as a commodity that has "swallowed" the image of a different subject. The cinematic or cybernetic image, like the ethnographic costume, acts as a disguise as well as a revelation of typified otherness.[37]

Chamcha, playing an alien who longs to be a television personality, also inhabits a metafictional narrative of himself as a simulation. Not merely a subject to be obliterated, he is also a body that supplies the raw stuff of representation. In the Western metropolis, the minority, like Pygmalien, "an artistic space-rock that could quarry itself for raw material, and then regenerate itself in time for the next week's episode" (63), acts as an infinite source to be plundered. The program displaces its own procedure of omnivorous consumption and mutation onto the invading extraterrestrials. Among the riot of animal and vegetable images are "Ridley, the most terrifying of the regular cast, who look[s] like a Francis Bacon painting of a mouthful of teeth waving at the end of a sightless pod" and "a coarse, belching creature like a puking cactus," named "Matilda, the Australien." Chamcha and his friend Mimi Mamoulian (the show's "Miss Piggy") consume voices as well as bodies, through quick, constant variation:

> [T]hey changed their voices along with their clothes, to say nothing of their hair, which could go from purple to vermilion between shots, which could stand diagonally three feet up from their heads or vanish altogether; or their features and limbs, because they were capable of changing all of them, switching legs, arms, noses, ears, eyes, and every switch conjured up a different accent from their legendary, protean gullets. (62)

The grotesque mouths of Ridley and Matilda, like the "protean gullets" of Mamma and Maxim Alien, register an anxious displacement of the indiscriminate, grotesque appropriation that characterizes the first-world media and marketplace. *The Aliens Show* recalls the invaders of H. G. Wells's *War of the Worlds* (1897), "the imperial gothic" in which an "inexorable" future revenge "exists already as an unchangeable extrapolation of the past."[38] But Rushdie connects the simulated images of Western commercial media with a loop of racialized labor and consumption. At the same time, Chamcha is "constructed" by the image in a Lacanian fashion, for the playful image of the extraterrestrial actually mirrors his cultural and psychological meanings to conceal the "lack" that constitutes him. The "surface" produced out of Chamcha covers the split around which he has organized himself as a secular Anglo-Indian Muslim in London.

In essence, Rushdie reserves his critique of vision for the media of the Western metropole, which employs the abstracted gaze that Crary describes as one of the products of nineteenth-century sensory reorganization. The primacy of sight over the other senses accords here with the hierarchy of white, Anglo-Britons over the darker, embodied objects of their gaze. Underneath the mobile surfaces of Western television, exemplified in *The Aliens Show*, lies an indexical corpus. The evolutionary logic that informs postmodern spectacles of the racial alien is made explicit in Chamcha's mutation into the wild man as a goat. It serves as a citational body, that is, a productive platform, for late nineteenth-century degeneration discourses and their embodiment. Chamcha subsequently "evolves" into various historical and technical images of the monster: he is "a figure out of a nightmare or a late-night T V movie" (49), "some sort of science-fiction or horror video *mutey*" (267), Mr. Hyde, Dracula (188), and Frankenstein's monster (282).

Gibreel and Chamcha finally enact disparate elements of the disciplined subject-agent. As expressive individuals, both migrants encompass diabolical and divine traits. In their gothic reincarnations, however, they realize different valences of disciplinary production, connected to the auratic capacities of the technologies that reproduce them. Gibreel is possibly psychotically deranged, so his body is "imprisoned" by his soul, in Foucauldian fashion. But in his portrait of somatopsychic fusions, Rushdie also realizes Gibreel as a mobile "person" in relation to discrete embodiments and individual perspectives. In this sense the somatic disciplines of religious technology liberate his "soul" from submission to social and discursive production. The "interiors" formed by scrutiny and regulation become detachable and energetic, capable of expansion through their use of bodies as vehicles of multiple and selected attributes. Chamcha, in contrast, exemplifies the disciplinary production of fixity, as his "soul" imprisons him in the form of the racial-religious totem. His liberation from a human body resolves in endless reproduction as a "type" of surface, a surface difference that endlessly circulates as a free-floating signifier. In the end, the horns that he sprouts are appropriated as novelty items, the detachable "attributes" of a racial protest based on a complete misreading of both Chamcha and a murderer with whom he is confused: even singular monstrosity simply re-enters capital circulation.

Reverse Invasion of the Patriarchs

Reversion to origin narratives, dramatized in the plots of Gibreel's interpellation into the sixth-century founding of Islam and Chamcha's embodiment as the racial-Darwinian beast of the nineteenth century, disrupts the univocality of monotheistic religion and racialist nationalism, in accordance with the Joycean model of cosmopolitan nationality. Rushdie, however, pursues the trajectory of degeneration through visual idioms that Joyce rejected as the dominant vehicle for depicting his minority religious types. The Lamarckian idea of acquired characteristics and the respectful agnostic's doubt are proposed as alternatives to the demand for submission to the racial stereotype and the authoritative Word of monotheistic religion. In spite of the demand to "submit" that dominates the representation of Islam as dictatorial and repressive, the novel revels in its generation of religious embodiment through the techniques of belief praxis and cinema. Aligning the devotional movie with Muslim praxis, Rushdie Hinduizes Islamic signification and imagines an auratic yet syncretic public culture for India. Though they too produce meaning, the Darwinian narratives that bear the weight of European teleology find no redemptive political feature. Lamarckian adaptation, connected to the possibility of some self-determination, does not overcome the power of commodity spectacle anchored in epidermal racism. Midway through the novel, Mohammad Sufyan, one of the proprietors of the Shaandaar B and B, offers an account of Chamcha's mutation that reconciles Lamarck and Darwin in an attempt to ameliorate this outcome. Sufyan claims that in the last edition of *Origin of Species,* "'even great Charles accepted the notion of mutation in extremis, to ensure survival of species; so what if his followers . . . repudiated, posthumously, such Lamarckian heresy, insisting on natural selection and nothing but.'" The former schoolteacher continues, "'—[H]owever, I am bound to admit, such theory is not extended to survival of individual specimen but only to species as a whole;—in addition, regarding nature of mutation, problem is to comprehend actual utility of the change'" (251). Sufyan points to misreadings of Lamarck in which the issue of species transformation merges with the dynamics of adaptation. Lamarck believed that external factors could cause modifications in organisms through pressures that created a need or "utility" that set internal fluids and forces in motion.[39] Nonetheless, adaptation cannot be distinguished from submission in the London plot of *The Satanic Verses,* where disciplining occurs as racial and social production of the totemic alien as a fetish as well as a citation. There is no position for Chamcha to occupy either in Rushdie's representation of Britain or in the productive possibilities that it offers the performative body. England's penetration by the "mere" body of the Muslim Indian, lacking Chamcha's former class protection, stimulates religious, scientific, legendary, and fantastic accounts of species difference. As I have said, Chamcha remains locked in the natural order, "fixed" in his gothic animality, while his image reenters the circuitry of representation, finally divorced even from the referent of his skin. In London, Chamcha's and Gibreel's objectification works toward their production not as agents but rather as subjects powerfully constrained by the racial and cultural discourses that they embody in their gothic incarnations. James English observes that "Rushdie's characters may strive for an individuality, an authenticity, a unique and sympathetic identity that could be enfolded in an antistereotypic discourse. . . . But this quest is always obstructed by their prior (and often self-conscious) insertion into a system of social relations that has only the most unoriginal, compromised, and politically dubious subject positions to offer."[40] In terms of "producing" somatic performativity for the migrant minority, Western technologies offer only the evacuated referentiality of Baudrillard's "simulation simulacra," a subgenre of science fiction in which the distance between the real and the imaginary disappears, "to be absorbed by the model alone."[41] Baudrillard associates this "cybernetic" process with the attenuation of historical representation, suggesting that in such an order of representation "the models no longer constitute either transcendence or projection, they no longer constitute the imaginary in relation to the real, they are themselves an anticipation of the real and thus leave no room for any sort of fictional anticipation."[42] *Contra* Baudrillard, Rushdie employs reversion to show "reality" or "history" precisely *through* the simulation. Here the rehallucinated past demystifies the technically enchanted pluralism of the contemporary moment as the black other breaks through the blank screen. At the same time, this realization of the monstrous material base simply reenters reproductive circuitry, subverting the very efficacy of protest by othered groups and reasserting the spectacle of surface. Chamcha's British identity is simulated whether he lives among the marginalized migrants of Brickhall or among the privileged cosmopolitans who "transcend" race, as he formerly imagined himself to do. His return to human form leaves him in a state of rage and "melancholy," a condition that Anne Cheng describes in minority American literature as coincident with the project of identity formation itself. "In melancholia," she states, "assimilation ('acting like an internalized other') is a *fait accompli*, part and parcel of ego formation for the dominant and the minority, except with the latter, such doubling is seen as something false ('acting like someone you're *not*'). The notion of racial authenticity is thus finally a cultural judgment which itself disguises the *identificatory assimilation* that has already taken place in melancholy racialization."[43] In contrast, *The Satanic Verses* figures the "fantasy stereotypes" that constitute and disguise the melancholic subject as gothic embodiments to be overcome. Furthermore, Rushdie's embodiment of the stereotype signals both "identificatory assimilation" and its irrelevance, for free-floating signifiers omnivorously consume subjective depth. Chamcha's melancholy encapsulates the dilemma of the novel itself, confronted with simulation as its idiom for migrant subjectivity and the performative bodies that produce it.

As I have stated, Rushdie stages the ultimate "Muslim historical" through the technical and textual apparatus of Hindu myth, making the Qu'ran a film that Gibreel enters and hallucinates after his reincarnation in England. As the parallel text of a faux Hindu devotional movie, the Qu'ran, understood as a singular text that is uncreated and untranslatable, becomes a religious text that, like the *Ramayana* and the *Mahabarata*, has no originary primacy over its retellings.[44] The novel's "cross-over" movie carries the narrative premises and the visual vernacular of popular Indian cinema into Islamic scripture and into the physical Muhammad so closely intertwined with it. More significantly, the combination of the bodily syntax of the popular film with that of Muslim practice allows the narrative to investigate, inhabit and finally to incorporate Muhammad into the communal "body" of Islam. Rushdie produces this fusion visually as a struggle and a conquest as well as a spectacle, a representation rather than an enactment, and a performance rather than a performative fact anchored in the adherent's body. Gibreel's star text incorporates Muhammad's, but also Rushdie's, as Muslim impersonations. The novel applies cinematic techniques to the totality of the prophet's body by removing the Prophet's body from its totality in the umma created by Muslim practice.

Rushdie's physical description of Mahound is a pastiche that draws on the *sham'il*. The Islamic literary genre focuses on praise of his physical beauty, which expresses his noble character.[45] Suleri notes that *The Satanic Verses* displays "rhetorical tenderness" toward Mahound in depicting him as a noble masculine figure.[46] The narrator describes him as he climbs Mount Cone: "The businessman looks as he should, high forehead, eaglenose, broad in the shoulders, narrow in the hip. Average height, brooding, dressed in two pieces of plain cloth. . . . Large eyes; long lashes like a girl's. His strides can seem too long for his legs, but he's a light-footed man" (93). Gibreel's contact with Mahound becomes increasingly close as the boundaries between the agency of each character become confused. In this, the novel investigates the Prophet's body as an intimate possession, in parallel to Muslim practice, which is understood to "internalize" Muhammad as a physical as well as a spiritual presence in the believer. But the narrative also *reverses* this practice by incorporating Mahound into Gibreel. The confusion of the text's agency with God's, with voices and "the Voice," becomes a dizzying interplay of subjectivities and agencies, enacted on the platform of the celebrity body. For all the novel's recourse to an allegory of origins, the agon between Mahound and Gibreel—like the explicitly contemporary narrative strand of the prophet Ayesha—encodes a modern conception of the Islamic "body" with which the writer struggles throughout the novel. Often assumed to be an originary conjunction, the equation of praxis with Muslim identity emerged from the decline of Muslim temporal power and resistance to European imperialism. "We know that it was only in the nineteenth century that the word Islam, of rare occurrence in the Quran and premodern Muslim texts in general, came to be used as a category of identity embracing all Muslim practice," says Faisal Devji. "Before this it had been used mostly to relate theological categories, such as obedience (*islam*) and faith (*iman*) to categories of Muslim identity such as religion (*din*), sect (*firqa*), school (*mazhab*) and mystical order (*tariqa*).... There was no idea of Islam as a totality of belief and actions that not only transmitted the remit of specific authorities like those of clerics, mystics, and kings, but also could become its own authority as an independent historical actor designating a new kind of moral community."⁴⁷

When Mahound returns to Mount Coney to verify the truth of the "satanic verses" that he first accepted as authentic, the narration shifts between first and third person, uses double-voicing, and calls upon the darsanic gaze to move between Gibreel's interior experience and a third-person, exterior visualization of the struggle between the men, which is witnessed by an audience of "djinns and afreets and all sorts of spooks sitting on the boulders to watch the fight." The combat between the two is a spectacle to folkloric and legendary creatures who sit on the fringe of belief. Gibreel himself experiences his interpenetration through a tactile vocabulary of interiority, which partakes of the Islamic tradition of reverent intimacy with the body of the Prophet as well as the mystical topos of revelation as displacement. He recounts:

> [O]nce again his wanting, his need goes to work, not on my jaws and voice this time, but on my whole body; he diminishes me to his own size and pulls me in toward him... and then Gibreel and the Prophet are wrestling, both naked, rolling over and over.... *As if he's learning me, searching me, as if I'm the one undergoing the test*.... [L]et me tell you he's getting in *everywhere*, his tongue in my ear his fist around my balls, there was never a person with such a rage in him, he has to has to know he has to KNOW and I have nothing to tell him... so we roll kick scratch, he's getting cut up quite a bit. (122–23)

Through the citational bodily syntax of Indian film, *Verses* represents the communal incorporation of the prophet's body as a singular one, in which Mahound and Gibreel become parallel "star texts" as their attributes fuse into a single form. The goal of Islamic practice, knowledge of the Prophet and of the sacred text, is dramatized as a struggle and, twice over, as a spectacle—not only over the truth of Islam, but over the Prophet's body as a production of performative worship, a performativity that Rushdie claims as crucial to his aesthetic technique and migrant identity.

Like the physical merging of Flapping Eagle, with Grimus, and of Saleem, with Shiva, Gibreel experiences a colonization of his consciousness, here represented as invasion by a *doppelganger*, Mahound. Unlike Rushdie's previous depictions of the physical fusion of male adversaries, however, the union of Gibreel and Mahound involves entire bodies, with emphasis on tactile contact and interpenetration. This scene, portrayed as a separation preserved in union, concretely reasserts the mobile depth of Indian visual culture's iconic bodies, in which the attributes of other selves allow for the "succoring of imaginary interiorities" that Pinney describes. At the same time, the scene shows Rushdie's insistence on his narrative as a parallel text of the Qu'ran and on his authority to appropriate its master signifier, Muhammad, as a surface or citation. In this the author deploys the equivocation that Vasudevan associates with the darsanic gaze of Indian film spectatorship, whose hierarchical presumptions may be manipulated to identify "new sources of authority."[48] Mahound "needs to know" Gibreel as much as Gibreel needs to know him. In a reformulation of Allah's instruction to Muhammad to "read" and "recite," Rushdie, through Gibreel, demands that Mahound "listen" and "acknowledge." At the conclusion of their struggle, Mahound "throws the fight" only to perform "his old trick," represented as a grotesque oral ejaculation reminiscent of Matilda the Australien. Gibreel concludes "[Mahound is] forcing my mouth open and making the voice, the Voice, pour out of me once again, made it pour out all over him, like sick" (122–23). If Chamcha is swallowed by simulation, Gibreel is bathed in a grotesque fluid of prophetic excess, which evacuates Mahound's exclusive claim on truth. Gibreel, like Chamcha, is eventually sent back into the circuit of simulation through union with another body. He returns to the screen in British versions of Indian mythologicals that dramatize elements of his "degenerate" visions—*Gibreel in Jahilia, Gibreel Meets the Imam,* and *Gibreel Meets the Butterfly Girl*—before he fully enters into a "fixed" identity as the angel Azraeel (345). The production of textual "doubt" that is the stated aim of Gibreel's struggle is finally less critical than the novel's conquest of Mahound's body, produced through the resources of the vernacular film's citational body and Islam's somatic practice. The excess of meaning that might be read into Mahound's oral ejaculation becomes the fluid that the repatriated migrant drains from the national-religious body.

It is through Gibreel's invasion and conquest of the prophet's body, and Chamcha's subsequent conquest of Gibreel, that *The Satanic Verses* prevents the postmodern (commercial and secular Western) surface from swallowing (spiritual Indian) aura.[49] In this connection, Slavoj Žižek contends, against Baudrillard: "[W]hat virtual reality threatens is *not* 'reality,' which is dissolved in the multiplicity of its simulacra, but, on the contrary, *appearance* itself." The Kantian sublime depends on the brief glimpse of the suprasensible, the noumenal, through the phenomenal, that is, the register of Joycean performative embodiment modelled on religious practice. In the simulacrum, "which becomes indistinguishable from the real, everything is here, so that no other transcendent dimension effectively 'appears' in or through it," Žižek asserts.[50] The merging of the Lacanian imaginary and the Real "at the expense of the symbolic" is precisely the zone that *The Satanic Verses* must defend to preserve the performative and citational embodiments that it generates from religious practices. The problem of the migrant's evacuated referentiality, tied to the production of postmodern simulation, is transferred onto the issue of Muslim "impersonation" in *The Satanic Verses*, and it is a problem that pertains to the position of the author as a cosmopolitan writer whose claim on the minority religious body stands between him and the exoticised simulacra.

Return of the Vampire

Suleri observes of *The Satanic Verses*: "A text that begins as Joyce ends as Dickens: it augments linguistic and cultural mayhem with the excesses of a sentimental resolution."[51] At the level of conceit, the cinematic parallel of the melodrama, a central mode of the Indian mythological and the literary mode of the gothic narrative, accounts for this dramatic shift. But the multiple Oedipal conquests of the novel's conclusion suggest an extraordinary pressure to rejoin the migrant signifier to a stable and uncomplicated signified of the origin. Chamcha's repatriation to India takes place in conjunction with the deaths of his father, Changez, and of Gibreel. Critics have noted that the "rage" of the minority toward Anglocentric Britain shifts when Chamcha and Gibreel direct their enmity toward one another. If the national often wounds the migrant in diasporan narratives, Chamcha's aggression against his twin enacts a fantasy revenge that restages the postcolonial as imperial *bildungsroman*. Spivak[52] and Suleri[53] have pointed out the novel's affinities with the homosocial agon and perpetual adolescence enacted in such romances, as well as their bearing on Gibreel's gothic intimacy with Mahound. But my point pertains not merely to the migrant's tenuous claim on India as a primary identity but also, more specifically, to the cosmopolitan narrative's need to claim the "body" of Indian Islam as the territory of performative religious embodiment, here tied to Indian popular film and its transactions with Muslim praxis. *The Satanic Verses* makes room for the migrant's return to his origins by draining the bodies of national and religious patriarchs, replacing the evacuated referentiality of the Muslim migrant's "gothic" simulation with the transfer of authoritative origins. As Simon Gikandi notes, at the novel's conclusion, "the name of the father is still in place" in a plot "that seeks to do away with *patria*."[54] Yet *The Satanic Verses* refrains from such struggle with the representative of contemporary belief in Ayesha, whom Gibreel also inhabits. In contrast to his congress with Mahound, Gibreel is "out cold" (226) during

Ayesha's trances, and she reports his messages through speech and popular filmi song, not scripture.⁵⁵

Ian Almond describes these and other instabilities in Rushdie's *oeuvre*, as the author seems to contest the "idea of a 'central' signifier for Islam, something which Islam must *necessarily* mean"⁵⁶ and to favor the mystical or demotic and skeptical strains of Islamic philosophy and practice, which allow for "freedom"—a freedom relentlessly associated with the artistic imagination in the Joycean paradigm. But Ayesha is also connected to the spectacular folk miracle—she is followed by butterflies that represent the fairies of the dastan narratives⁵⁷—rather than with the sacred word, with female multiplicity rather than male authority, and with a subcontinental rather than an Arabia-centered Islam. In this she offers a vehicle more hospitable to Rushdie's values and aesthetic. If, as Feroza Jussawalla argues on the basis of such moments, *The Satanic Verses* should be located in a high Indianized Islam though its attitudes and its narrative prose forms,⁵⁸ the Ayesha plot acts as more "dil-ruba"—or love—than "dastan"—or complaint—in its general tenor. It is here that the novel transforms the certainty of "disbelief" into the reverent opening of "doubt" (92), though a Muslim patriarch must die to accommodate this movement.

If Gibreel overcomes Mahound as the master signifier of Islam, Chamcha replaces Gibreel as the Muslim national. When Chamcha is a child his father represents cold authority, Muslim practice, and national residency. He lives in a gothic bedroom filled with "grotesque heads," "a horned demon," and "a leering Arab," all of which his young son hates as "portraits of Changez" (523). The darsanic gaze of Mahound onto Gibreel is paralleled in the interaction between the adult Chamcha and his dying father when Changez gives his son "a little nod of recognition." Chamcha exults, "*He heard me.*" The moment concludes their reconciliation: "To fall in love with one's father after the long angry decades was a serene and beautiful feeling; a renewing, life-giving thing, Saladin [Chamcha] wanted to say, but did not, because it sounded vampirish; as if by sucking this new life out of his father he was making room, in Changez's body, for death" (530).

The narrative makes room for Chamcha's return through such literalized removals, recasting his refusal to "submit" to Islam or to Indian identity as a reverse invasion of home. By draining the patriarchal bodies of life, the narrative allows for the incorporation of migrant simulation, not as an abjected margin but as a reverse invasion of origins that continue to fund the "transcend[ence]" of cosmopolitan art. Through the literal draining of Indian-Muslim fathers, *Verses* wards off the "swallowing" of deracination and its visual technologies. The question of commodified simulation, a question that potentially implicates Rushdie's own location as a British-Indian writer ensconced in the metropolitan literary market, informs the univocal significations of the novel's conclusion. Rushdie's interest in transcultural allusion, transformative bodily syntax, and enchanted simulation may promote much the same cybernetic absorption of the religious minority into the stereotyped image that British mass media do. From this standpoint, the modernist subversion of the Prophet's authority merely annexes difference to the marketplace in the manner of *The Aliens Show*: Islam becomes one more raw material to be processed and circulated in the metropole. Pacifying the anxiety of impersonation, the novel returns to the conventions of realism to assert the darsanic gaze as a new source of authority, granted by the patriarchs, and to "voice" the citational body of Indian Islam as an act of intimate aggression. It is through the invasion and conquest of the prophet's body, and Chamcha's subsequent conquest of Gibreel, that *The Satanic Verses* prevents the postmodern (Western) surface from swallowing (Indian) transcendence as the novel simultaneously asserts the migrant author as a parallel text of the Muslim and Indian body. Like Molly Bloom, the repatriated Chamcha anchors vertiginous mobility in a natural referent, though *The Satanic Verses* concludes with the melodrama of an Indian popular film.

●

Jean-François Lyotard differentiates the modern from the postmodern through each one's use of the sublime. While he states that the postmodern is "undoubtedly a part of the modern," the modernist aesthetic is "nostalgic" for the loss of presence: "It allows the unpresentable to be put forward only as the missing contents; but the form, because of its recognizable consistency, continues to offer the reader matter for solace and pleasure."[59] In contrast, the postmodern "would be that which, in the modern, puts forward the unpresentable in presentation itself" and so "denies itself the solace of good forms"—therefore blocking the collective experience of nostalgia and the "stronger sense of the unpresentable" that it produces.[60] Even so, Lyotard asserts that this nostalgia is not "a real sublime sentiment" but rather, in Martin Jay's phrase, "a lament for lost totality."[61] *The Satanic Verses* stages the Indian Muslim as the locus of such a narrative, in which the racial alien of the British gothic gains access to contemporary representation only as the "unpresentable"—a surface trace or attribute divorced from its function as a metonymy of religious national body. Rushdie's emphatic reassertion of modernist religious embodiment, dramatized in the "sublime turn" of unitary signification, responds to the threat of "swallowing" as a political as well as an aesthetic danger for the cosmopolitan author: what Lyotard understands as "nostalgia" for lost presence *Verses* translates into an aggressive register. The novel recovers India as an organic totality, drained of a little blood. *Midnight's Children* preserves its mode of aesthetic production even at the expense of India's actual survival. In *The Satanic Verses*, the "citational" performative body that arises from religious contexts must be preserved as the referent for the "postmodern" production of the cosmopolitan minority text. The novel makes explicit Rushdie's investment in Joycean modernism, in which religious practice funds the "style" of performative embodiment endangered by the spectacle of simulation as deracination. Stephen Dedalus' entrapment in gothic maternity thus ends in Chamcha's vampiric draining of gothic paternity; the gothic journey through abjection reestablishes the link of territory, authenticity, and filiative blood. In an Oedipal reversal, "home" becomes the ultimate object of the imperial conquest, as it supplies the evacuated signifier with content and depth. It was unforeseen at the moment of publication that the author's body would also be absorbed into the gothic plot, as he too became a star, embodying citations beyond his control. But the text of *The Satanic Verses* already encoded the threat to the Joycean paradigm that Rushdie had grappled with since the writing of *Midnight's Children*. As I will show, not the controversy over *Verses*, but the celebrity that attended it, led Rushdie to destroy this formulation.

5

Embodied Panic

Modernist "Religion" in the Controversies over *Ulysses* and *The Satanic Verses*

The Satanic Verses controversy of 1989 provoked an unusual literary interest in contemporary religious belief. Scholars and writers, like the Western popular press, understood the conflict as an allegory of freedom and repression, waged by the figures of art and religion. In using these terms to characterize the dispute, critics resumed an argument little changed since the scandalous debut of *Ulysses* in 1922, when religious and aesthetic epistemologies were similarly cast as absolute adversaries. Both debates associated modernity with the individual, defined as a sovereign agent who absolutely resists traditional or institutional authority—constraints that religion, the premodern arbiter of universal dogma, neatly epitomized. In fact, like all binaries, this one remains lively to the extent that its terms remain monolithic. In both controversies "art" and "religion" acted as frozen signifiers, emblems that condense and arrest complex movements of meaning. Ultimately the binary hid the challenge that *Ulysses* and *The Satanic Verses* posed to dominant Western understandings of subject formation. At issue were modes of agency in relation to embodiment. In each of the controversies, bodies depicted as externally regulated productions were set against "the" body as an autonomous, self-governed space. Regulated agency, connected primarily to the somatic and psychic disciplines of "archaic" religion, threatened to dissolve the representational integrity of sovereign individualism. Archaic religion functioned as the frozen signifier of repressive authority, whose display elicited panic over the loss of personhood.

The controversies provoked by *Ulysses* and *The Satanic Verses* catapulted each author from literary fame to popular celebrity, based on the transgression of a minority religious body before a cosmopolitan audience. While they could not have foreseen the scope—or in Rushdie's case the severity—of the reaction to the provocation of their work, the authors anticipated this culmination in their earlier careers. As I have said, Joyce and Rushdie pushed toward fuller investigation and exposure of the spiritually disciplined bodies that they identified as fundamental to their aesthetic practice and provincial identity. At the same time the writers denied that the knowledge generated by these representations was grounded in the productive capacities of belief. Their insistence on theological-aesthetic readings of bodily epistemes forwarded an entirely external and repressive understanding of orthopraxy. This depiction reinforced an anthropological and metropolitan framework, which associated minority belief with intellectual deficit and physical confinement, and contrasted it with imaginative and physical freedom. Close examination of the novels' early reception, along with attention to modes and histories of belief, reveals quite different issues are at stake. The binary of art and religion has occluded them for over a century.

The debates over *Ulysses* and *The Satanic Verses* highlight the persistent defense of a somatopsychic model of the person that is entirely conflated with the possibility of agency, as I establish in the preceding chapters.[1] This paradigm, which refuses any significant distinction among the terms "person," "agent," and "individual," lies at the center of the modernist conflict between "religion" and "art." In fact, each of the literary disputes involves *two* conceptions of agency and two modes of spiritual belief, their alliances determined by differing formulations of corporeality *as* agency. "The" body as a particular organization of affective, cognitive, and physical "space"—related to the model that Geertz[2] describes—contrasts with bodies in regulated practice, understood to be constituted by programs extrinsic to the imagined territory of personal government.

Revisiting the early response to *Ulysses* allows us access to the panic over somatic agency that the novel evoked, and, I am contending, that operated less obviously in *The Satanic Verses* affair. *Ulysses'* early admirers as well as its detractors persistently complain about the book's "obscenity," conveying dismay at its vulgarity and sexual frankness, but also encoding its more threatening dissolution of the somatopsychic organization of the individual that Geertz outlines, and which I discuss in chapter two. Whether or not they defend "religious" values, Joyce's readers often register alarm at his intrusion into a somatic interior that is equated with a psychic one: their panic does not arise from *Ulysses'* violation of a conventionally codified moral position, but rather from its instrumental treatment of bodies as agents. Reviewers align Joyce's approach with archaic religious ideas about the body's degraded status as well as with the modern machinery of surveillance. In these reactions, the ability to exert disciplinary authority links the historically disparate techniques of medieval Catholicism and technological modernity. Ultimately both primitive religion and contemporary machines subject readers to their own bodies and environments, robbing them of the autonomy that their normal boundaries ensure. In dominating his readers, Joyce acts as a punitive deity who abases his subjects to demonstrate his own mastery. He is free to reduce them to excrement and protoplasm, grotesque and reactive organic stuff.

This physically disturbing *Ulysses*, like the physically disturbing elements of the earlier fiction, had disappeared from view by the 1950s, a testament to the eventual triumph of the public-relations campaign that I describe in chapter one. Joyce and his coterie eventually transformed *Ulysses'* obscenely disorganized bodies into the raw material of Kantian sublation. The novel no longer posed a disciplinary threat to the body; instead it signified an intellectual challenge and an artistic triumph, "embodied" in the formal refinement of the material book, much as the author himself—first received as a cosmopolitan writer—came to signify a refinement of coarse and backward provincial bodies. While his early detractors portrayed Joyce as a sovereign individual who used his aesthetic power to subordinate his readers, later critics emphasized the human universality of his accomplishment. *Ulysses* realized the free exercise of an individuality that Joyce *shared* with his readers. Discourses of the body largely dropped out of the commentary, except to register the narrative's mimetic fidelity to life. It is this Poundian-New Critical *Ulysses* that continues to reign in the popular imagination, and the critical moves made to recuperate Joyce were readily mobilized in defense of Rushdie. Bodily regulation and disciplinary control, dispelled from the realm of "art" in the later reception of *Ulysses*, now belonged entirely to "religion." Thus in the reaction engendered by *The Satanic Verses*, Islam alone represented a disciplinary force that might violently eradicate the embodied individual—linked successively to the burned book, the endangered author, and the bounded, autonomous entity of the secular nation-state. Reference to bodily representations, evident in British Muslims' objections to the novel, appeared nowhere in British Christian defense of it. Instead this concern surfaced in fears of Muslim violence against the Anglo-British body politic. In May 1989, three months after Khomeini's decree, the London *Sunday Times* declared, "[I]t is now impossible to wish away or assimilate or suppress the potent living organism in the body of Britain itself."[3] The panic that ensued over sovereign national boundaries reprised the panic over sovereign individual boundaries so prominent in the earlier controversy.

Frozen in the binary of religion and art, the Joyce and Rushdie debates actually disclose a defense of "the" body as a particular organization of affective, cognitive, and physical space. The centrality of this formulation is underscored by its actual migration between the poles of opposition in the two controversies. Moral concerns about bodily depictions drove the protest against *Ulysses,* we have been given to understand; yet both explicitly religious and decisively secular readers objected to the novel's disruption of the somatic structure of the "individual." In *The Satanic Verses*' debate, the claim on this structure—typically understood to be a "religious" one in the Joyce affair—now characterized the defense of secular and artistic freedom against repressive religion. Allied with both "religion" and "art," the somatic structure of the individual emerges as the contested territory of these disputes. Certeau's "strategic" body, a central, bounded somatic space that empowers agents against a distinct outside, informs this formulation.[4] The strategy of embodied agency, set in both literary controversies against the power of external discipline, easily accommodates the religious mode of "secular" societies by assigning belief to a subordinate realm of choice, sentiment, and "free expression." In contrast, both nineteenth-century Irish Catholicism and twentieth-century Indian Islam to varying degrees challenge or even disorganize strategic embodiment through performative worship, as I have shown. With a critical emphasis on regulated bodily practice, this mode of worship significantly shapes agency, producing embodied knowledge that is ultimately public and communal. Hence Anglo-Muslims detractors experienced Rushdie's expressive, privately imagined representation of Muhammad as a severing of the communal body of Islam, while Anglo-Christians reacted to this complaint as an absolutist intrusion into a given, private space of individual choice.

The dominant Western religious formation accords fairly readily with most contemporary modes of Western Christianity, capitalism, and nationalism, as I have established. Religions that achieve belief through regulation contest the public and private split crucial to the current "secular" formation of Western nation-states, a difference that has triggered panic over the dispersal of Certeau's strategic power. The endless exchange of the frozen signifiers "art" and "religion," made synonymous with (metropolitan) freedom and (minority) repression, evades the more profound questions that these debates pose to Western methods of organizing and producing knowledge. Here I attempt to describe the aporia disclosed by the literary controversies, to linger at the moment of thought that such panic has effectively avoided.

The Disciplinary *Ulysses*

Ulysses disturbed a space of sovereign individuality that fit with the dominant Christian mode and formation of its day. Popular and literary periodicals reviewed *Ulysses* at its February 1922 publication as a book[5]—even though it was legally banned in the United States[6] and Britain as obscene and effectively, though not legally, censored in Ireland[7]—and again after Judge John Woolsey's 1933 repeal of the ban in America. In their comments, the novel's detractors echo the legal response, calling the book obscene or pornographic; comparatively few label it blasphemous. Yet even reviews in Catholic publications, which do employ the term, slide easily from spiritual and moral to social evaluation of the novel. Blasphemy violates sensibility rather than doctrine, manners rather than specific points of conviction. The emphasis on personal and social affront suggests a particular, and somewhat peculiar, orientation of belief, in which the sensibilities of the "self" override traditional concerns with epistemological error or with offense against God. In contrast, Muslim detractors of *The Satanic Verses* highlight precisely the issues of correct knowledge and divine injury, as I will discuss later. Joyce's early critics speak instead from a personal sensibility presumed to be socially normative and invoke this general standard to castigate blasphemy, obscenity, poor hygiene, and bad taste as synonymous violations. Additionally, whether or not they defend religious values or Irish nationalism, negative reviewers consistently focus on Joyce's somatic representations as the primary source of his offense. By subjecting readers to their bodies as their inescapable episteme, *Ulysses* enjoins a repulsive and disturbingly disorganized physicality. Brooker describes this response as a reaction to "the sheer indigestible materiality" of the novel, often experienced as an "ill-formed excess of matter."[8] Such complaints against Joyce's prose merely magnified comments about *Dubliners* and *A Portrait*, which were also criticized for their excessive interest in the physical realm, their partial view of life, and their shapelessness. As in the reception of these works, even admiring reviews of *Ulysses* may regret Joyce's investigation of bodies, particularly their smells and exudations. For example, Sisley Huddleston, a friend of Joyce's who published an influential comment in the March 1922 *Observer*, "becomes tired of the beastliness always breaking in."[9]

Reviewers often register disapproval through their own graphic characterizations, figuring *Ulysses* as bodily waste, especially as fluids, as dirt, or as receptacles for them, such as sinks, latrines, and sewers—tropes that began with reviews of *A Portrait*. Catholic commentators share the general tendency to couch moral complaints in physical terms. Hygiene, for instance, gauges spiritual rectitude, national purity, and aesthetic merit. In the Irish context, as Mullin shows, these metaphors pertained to a particular strain of reaction to English filth, though "the need to protect 'home' from the corruptions of 'abroad' was far from an exclusively Irish strategy."[10] This strain is evident in the two, nearly simultaneous reviews that Shane Leslie published in 1922: most significantly for my argument, Nash observes that "in the *Dublin Review* the offensiveness of *Ulysses* is specifically against Catholicism, but in the [English] *Quarterly Review* it is generally against 'all ideas of good taste and morality.'"[11] Leslie grounds his complaint more decidedly in a grotesque and proximate body in the Irish publication, where he asserts that "the spiritually offensive and the physically unclean are united" in the novel. As concerned with the book's threat to literary nationalism as he is with its religious transgressions,[12] Leslie recommends that the novel be placed on the Index Expurgatorius, for left to their own devices, the curious might be tempted to sample *Ulysses* "like so much rotten caviare." Bad taste finally results in regurgitation: the essay concludes with an image of Joyce himself as "a frustrated Titan . . . revolv[ing] and splutter[ing] hopelessly under the flood of his own vomit."[13] Also in a sectarian vein, Camille McCole, writing in the American *Catholic World* in 1934, makes a perfunctory nod to spiritual scruple when she observes that "[b]lasphemy and the most outrageous ribaldry both run riot through *Ulysses*." She complains at much greater length about the dominance of naturalistic, grotesque bodies, citing as examples the bile that May Dedalus vomits, the blood of squashed lice that reddens her fingernails, and the "'relish'" that Bloom displays in "'eating the inner organs of beasts and fowls.'" McCole concludes that "[i]n every instance the preoccupations of the author are most decidedly physical."[14]

Notably, readers who show little concern for sectarian or even conventional morality share the Catholics' disgust at the narrative's physicality. According to these reviews, *Ulysses* disorganizes even the obscene body. Arnold Bennett, in an influential 1922 piece that appeared in both the London *Outlook* and the New York *Bookman*, states that the novel blocks sexual excitement through its attention to the full range of bodily privacies. *Ulysses* is not pornographic, he asserts, but is "more indecent, obscene, scatological, and licentious than the majority of professedly pornographical books."[15] In an April 1922 comment in the British *Sporting Times* or "Pink 'Un"—a disreputable racing sheet—Aramis notes that "Ulysses is not alone sordidly pornographic, but it is intensely dull" and hence paradoxically "dreary" even in its filthy passages.[16] Bennett and Aramis imply that the erotically pleasurable body and the respectably bourgeois one assumed in other reviews share a single structure, to be upheld in the first instance and selectively violated in the second. This organization reduces the role of smell and certain kinds of touch, favoring (dry) surfaces; it is a given, passive, and nonproductive space; and it depends on separation and exclusion over synthetic apprehension or expression. *Ulysses* destroys the economy of eros just as it does the hierarchies of everyday public embodiment, for the narrative embeds sex completely in the full range of senses and products, in both male and female bodies. In contrast, Bennett and Aramis imply, effective obscenity highlights female sexual characteristics as contained sites of scopic and tactile consumption. Not only should male and female bodies be segregated representationally, but the female body should be depicted according to certain sensory dictates if it is to be consumed pleasurably—indecency, too, has its protocols. Finally, Joyce compounds his offense by canceling the more abstract pleasure that the work of reading difficult literature ought to yield. Productive and unstable, his grotesque and intimately depicted bodies interfere with aesthetic as well as erotic enjoyment of *Ulysses*. The novel denies readers both textual and sexual *jouissance* in order to offer them pus and vomit, menstrual and louse blood, feces and tainted food, disgust and boredom.

Critics such as Rebecca Walkowitz and Joseph Valente have recently read such objections to Joyce's vulgarity and excessive recording of detail as politically nuanced. Joyce's "cancelled decorum" and "tactical discourtesy"[17] signify a cosmopolitan strategy of trivialization that critiques nationalism through insubordination, in Walkowitz's reading; Valente observes that *Ulysses*' "promiscuous styles of attention"[18] constitute a refusal to observe literary, social, and national hierarchies. I share their desire to imagine the categories of modernist analysis as more expansive and flexible and also want to emulate the scrupulous attention to Irish history displayed by Mullin and Nash. But Joyce's more concrete and widespread disturbances of readers' comfort do not fall neatly into the oppositions of Catholic and anti-Catholic, provincial and cosmopolitan, or progressive and bourgeois audiences. They do reveal a conception of embodiment connected to shared codes of decorum that Joyce's method challenges and overwhelms. Most consistently, these comments reveal readers' physical unease. The sovereign agency embodied in the individual gains power from its quasi detachment from a body to which it belongs and yet merely bears. Typically, the reviewers suggest, privileged government of "the" body appears to be diminished in certain specific circumstances in which subjects feel most closely intermingled with their physicality, such as during sex. The novel not only forces readers to remain in this state by emphasizing bodily materiality, but it also generalizes the specific instances and types of mingling with materiality. In its productive and performative practice, *Ulysses* dissolves the internal structure of agency by totalizing functions or areas that should be distinguished, opening boundaries that should be closed, and rendering solid spaces fluid. The organization of the individual that *Ulysses* contests draws embodiment, agency, and subjectivity into a spatial autonomy that is the source of its potency. As I have noted, Certeau aligns the Cartesian locus recalled by this normative body with a "strategy," a set of techniques practiced by those in control of the modes of production. He defines the term as "a calculus of force relationships that become possible when a subject of will and power can be isolated from the environment." The "prope" of power constitutes "a victory of space over time" by articulating an outside over which agents exert control.[19] The historically distinct moments of producing the modern subject as an embodiment, as a "self," and as an autonomous agent that anchors them seems to be structured and melded through such a dynamic. It sediments "the" body as an expressive substance, suffused with a particular identity, at the same time that it allows for the body's maintenance as a property owned and mastered by a governing agent.[20] The bodily disposition set in individualism denies not the flesh, but its fluid and plural relations; asserts not "selfhood," which remains intact in either case, but rather autonomy. The normative corpus that emerges from this dynamic is a strictly demarcated homogeneity whose space remains stable only because its boundaries shift internally. That is, the "inside" and the "outside" of an autonomous body appear constant because its internal border shifts temporally. A suture as well as a perforation, this margin moves in accordance with situations that entail "being" as opposed to "having" a body.[21] An inner agent uses the slight but crucial disjunction to choose a relationship to its own substance, to bracket or unite with the body as a space. Through this movement, then, "the" body becomes a given, natural structure, protected in some degree from the vagaries of time and place, from the flux and disparities of bodies.

The acts that *Ulysses* enjoins upon readers eradicate the topography of the individual, a disorganization that elicits panic over the loss of ipseity. Later scholars, like Joyce's early defenders, have interpreted such reactions as hostility to the novel's modern techniques, displayed through *Ulysses'* affinities with psychoanalysis, cinema, and urbanization. But in fact, early detractors express much more ambivalence about technical modernity and their position in relation to it than these interpretations would suggest. The role of individual agency, rather than of modernity per se, is often the crucial determinant of such responses. When they represent *Ulysses'* somatic intrusiveness as visual inspection, most readers do imply that the novel enforces modern sensory regimes. Martin Jay,[22] Jonathan Crary, and others describe the historical genesis of this sensory reorganization through accounts of the full embodying of vision, as I discuss in chapter one. Contemporary reviews characterize *Ulysses* in similar terms when they describe its narrative "gaze": sight possesses the subjective, concrete, and empowered qualities of the new vision. The novel captures or reveals the somatopsychic interior in formerly unavailable ways, for Joyce "can open up thought as a surgeon does a body,"[23] "x-ray . . . the ordinary human consciousness,"[24] record incident and speech with "photographic accuracy,"[25] jerk the reader around with a "kinematographic" style,[26] and examine "all the overworked scenes of realistic narrative like drops of water under a microscope."[27] Grounds for wonder and praise in positive reviews, this scrutiny may also induce panic. Detractors stress that the power of sight granted through the managed corpus, as well as the pleasure of sight yielded by male scopic mastery, belongs to the author alone. Thus positive and negative reactions do not especially differ in their descriptions of Joyce's technical gaze; rather detractors assess it as an uninvited one, trained on a disoriented and immobilized victim. In this, *Ulysses'* dissolution of somatic boundaries and perceptual hierarchies resembles the effect of the stereoscope, an optical device of the 1830s that, Crary explains, "derang[ed] . . . the conventional functioning of visual cues" by providing "a hallucinatory clarity of particulars that never coalesce[d]."[28] Like the stereoscope—which quickly became allied with pornographic content—*Ulysses* seemed to "pin" the audience through a promiscuous barrage of sensation that would not itself be mapped by familiar signs. In a March 1922 review in the English *Daily Express*, for instance, S. P. B. Mais portrays *Ulysses* as a penetrating device. Mais first notes another reviewer's opinion that "the modern novelist's function [is] to 'follow life to places and recesses in the human soul and heart inaccessible to the camera.'" Joyce similarly "follow[s] it in *Ulysses* . . . to recesses which few of us altogether care to probe." Yet readers cannot avoid such mirrors, for "from his pages there leap out at us all our most secret and most unsavoury private thoughts."[29]

At the same time that *Ulysses* represents new visual powers, then, it denies readers a locus of identification with its movement or mastery, instead subordinating them through a welter of confounding information. Yet detractors also complain about the novel's insufficient segregation of sight. In *Ulysses* the proximity of other senses, particularly of smell, constantly narrows the separation of the senses from which the new power of vision had emerged historically and thus signifies readers' desire *for* the abstracted powers of reorganized sight, which Joyce withholds from them.[30] Wyndham Lewis's famous association of *Ulysses* with time bears upon the novel's ostensibly anti-visual impulse: he contends that Joyce "*thought in words,* not images," and hence neglected the "*entire* organism" for "the multitude of little details."[31] Joyce grounds the historically recent primacy of images by recurring to the alibi of the medieval sensorium, in which sight, smell, touch, and taste are more closely integrated, as I discuss in chapters one and three. *Ulysses* cancels out erotic titillation for readers such as Aramis and Bennett because the novel does not sufficiently privilege visual appropriation. Instead the narrative embeds sight in the realm of smell, the tactility of fluids, and the confusions of taste—in the "details" of materially productive bodies unmoored from their contemporary spatial hierarchies and domains.

As the site and producer of sensation, the form and object of knowledge, the normatively embodied individual feels endangered at the level of species and life form without control over visual fields, as over other sensory information. Whether this lack results from Joyce's technological gaze into psychic interiors or his refusal to allow readers the full power of visual abstraction, their comments register a loss of spatial privilege over phenomena. Camille McCole's alarm over the flow of bodily excrement in the novel, for example, migrates into equal dismay over the flux of dominating sensation, which eradicates human will. "No character in *Ulysses* ever *does* anything: every single one of them is merely the most passive of protoplasms actuated by no principle," she asserts, echoing early reactions to *Dubliners*.[32] Ultimately, *Ulysses* embodies consciousness too completely, rather than inaccurately, and does so by denying subjects any privileged platform of observation and direction, one linked to the capacities of reorganized, modern sight.

Joyce demonstrates absolute mastery of bodies through his revision of perception and subjectivity. In this, the author robs subjects of any transcendental power, epitomized in readers' ability to bracket the body, or at least to select the times and spaces in which they will acknowledge or engage with it. Worse, Joyce *chooses* to inflict this condition on his audience. Perhaps most galling to reviewers is his refusal to exercise his gifts to less punishing ends, for through his literary talent Joyce himself proves the existence of the sovereign observer as a transcendent margin over materiality. He appropriates agency solely to himself, extracting strategic organization from the individual to increase his own authority. The true "scandal" of *Ulysses* is its denial of a transcendental subjectivity that clearly exists, on the evidence of the author's genius. Joyce turns readers into the miserable subjects of an exacting God who annihilates the individual and hence human agency as such, leaving in its wake mere protoplasm.

Ulysses finally enjoins everyone to be a metaphorically united subject-body, removed from a sedimented autonomy and set loose among objects and forces without distinction from them. At the same time, this unity possesses none of the necessity that characterizes the metaphoric relation. Joyce's portrayals are experienced as radically contingent and yet endowed with the authority of metaphor, arbitrarily determined and yet absolutely enforced on readers. Some comments account for this disturbing combination through reference to Irish Catholicism, a lens that Joyce installed through his manipulation of commentary in the late teens, as I show in chapter one. Notably, Cecil Maitland and H. G. Wells understand Joyce's somatopsychic representations as the product of Catholic training. Maitland, writing in *New Witness* on "Mr. Joyce and the Catholic Tradition," attributes the author's perversity to Catholic praxis, which encourages a morbid preoccupation with the flesh. Joyce has merely lost the faith that allows adherents to transcend this baseness:

> This vision of human beings as walking drain pipes, this focussing of life exclusively round the excremental and sexual mechanism, appears on the surface inexplicable in so profoundly imaginative and observant a student of humanity as Mr. Joyce. . . . No one who is acquainted with Catholic education in Catholic countries could fail to recognize the source of Mr. Joyce's 'Weltanschauung.' He sees the world as theologians showed it to him. His humour is the cloacal humour of the refectory; his contempt the priest's denigration of the body, and his view of sex has the obscenity of a confessor's manual, reinforced by the profound perception and consequent disgust of a great imaginative writer.

Like Leslie and McCole, Maitland fears engulfment. Joyce "has reproduced the minds and imaginations of his characters so vividly that the reader finds difficulty in separating his consciousness from theirs; and thus his conception of humanity from the author's," he asserts. *Ulysses* challenges rational individualism by displaying its power to make fallen Catholics of all readers—that is, to enclose them in the degraded body "educated" by the morbidities of Catholicism.[33] In a similar reading of the relation between archaic religion and bodily debasement, H. G. Wells neatly sketches the distinction between worldly and private belief. Wells wrote to Joyce in 1928: "Your training has been Catholic, Irish, insurrectionary; mine, such as it was, was scientific, constructive, and, I suppose, English." In contrasting national minds, Wells portrays the Irish as equal parts Arnoldian Celt and Fenian ape, though the basis of their difference from the English is religious subjectivity:

> You began Catholic, that is to say you began with a system of values in stark opposition to reality. Your mental existence is obsessed by a monstrous system of contradictions. You may believe in chastity, purity, and the personal

God and that is why you are always breaking out into cries of [cunt], shit and hell. As I don't believe in these things except as quite personal values my mind has never been shocked to outcries by the existence of waterclosets and menstrual badges—and undeserved misfortunes.[34]

Irish Catholicism, as a false worldly knowledge, confuses "reality" with belief and facts with values; consequently those trained in this system must act out a discrepancy that is first epistemological. Catholics learn to totalize knowledge and religious beliefs, importing them wholesale into the worldly realm. The failure to demarcate the private from the public produces disorganized bodies—"cunt" and "shit" in the mouth—and perverse, obsessive minds. Proper understanding of these distinctions allows menstrual badges and toilets to exist outside or underneath the ideal, public, and masculine individual, such as Wells is.

Not modernity but agency, as well as the production of the body as a space of agency, functions as the criterion for these readers. As modes of somatic discipline, both instrumental science and archaic belief endanger the strategy of individualism by dissolving its spatial organization and hence its metaphysics of substance. Joyce, whether he wields a machine or the religious episteme represented in bodily praxis, subtracts agency from subjectivity when he deprives readers of the possibility of foreclosure on their physicality. Though when they invoke religion explicitly, these readers often speak in defense of belief, they reject representations that subject them to spiritual-technical discipline as a primary feature of embodiment. In this they accord with Maitland and Wells, who complain most pointedly not of Joyce's belief or lack of it, but rather of his fundamental formation by the wrong kind of religion, which leads to his need to display private matters. The wrong kind of Christianity *causes* Joyce's obscenity by warping his experience of his body and hence of the world. At issue in all these comments, as I have shown, is the ability to govern the oscillation of relations between self and material, to elect the times and occasions when "having" devolves into "being" a body. Implicitly, such autonomy is not fully available to male cultural-racial others or to women in general. In fact, *Ulysses* seems to force the privileged subject to occupy the fully material bodies of others.

Cosmopolitan Genius and Disembodiment

In his 1939 biography *James Joyce,* friend Herbert Gorman records and responds to many of *Ulysses*' early reviews, among them Cecil Maitland's. "If we consider Mr. Joyce's work from this point of view, it becomes clear that while [Joyce's] study of humanity remains incomplete, the defect is not due to any inherent lack of imagination on his part." Rather, Gorman reasons, Joyce's "failure" is "that of the Catholic system, which has not had the strength to hold him to its transcendentalism, and from whose errors he has not been able to set himself free."[35] Gorman's emphasis on Catholicism as an episteme turns Maitland's equal emphasis on bodily practice into an "error," continued by Joyce as a conception of the human being as "a specially cunning animal." Maitland, in spite of his highly sectarian condemnation of bodily investigation, points to the disciplinary mode of Irish-Catholic practice that Joyce made efforts to stress in the late teens. But in the subsequent reception of *Ulysses*, as Gorman's angle portends, religion detached from regulated training or physical production. Instead religion signified an abstracted theological knowledge or imaginative system. Accordingly, the novel came to stand for creative liberty rather than bodily license, and the material of the body shifted to that of book. Later commentary characterized *Ulysses* as a work of exalted consciousness rather than of physical subjection. The work became a source of knowledge about the universal human mind, a pure and human abstraction of the body. Ford Madox Ford anticipated this resolution in the December 1922 *English Review*, when he asserted that the "technical revolution" that Joyce initiated was a self-validating accomplishment. "In the matter of readers my indifference is the deepest," Ford asserts. "It is sufficient that *Ulysses*, a book of profound knowledge and profound renderings of humanity, should exist."[36] The book's inaccessibility, so resented in popular reviews, was supported through its transportation to a realm of texts that merit exegesis: the sacral-scholarly texts of Western culture.

Like Pound in his review of *Dubliners*, critics who applauded *Ulysses* frequently did so by contrasting it with the provincialism of the revival. The most influential early review of *Ulysses*—the review with which Ernest Boyd later took issue—took this tack. Valéry Larbaud, in the April 1922 *Nouvelle Revue Française*, called *Ulysses* the harbinger of an Irish cosmopolitanism and individualism: "[W]ith this *Ulysses* . . . Ireland is making a sensational re-entrance into high European literature." Joyce has done as much as "all the heroes of Irish nationalism to attract the respect of intellectuals of every other country toward Ireland,"[37] he famously contends. Joyce acts as a metonymy of the emerging nation, detached and reproduced through a modern and metropolitan aesthetic that transcends outmoded commitments such as nationalism and the Irish language. Accepting the view of *Ulysses* as an emblem of transcendence and freedom, but disagreeing with Larbaud's provenance, Irish critics such as Joseph Hone were quick to claim Joyce's origins as Irish and Catholic. Joyce "may be detached from our local passions; but it is not a detachment born of English influences or of cosmopolitanism," said Hone in a "Letter from Ireland" that appeared in the January 1923 *London Mercury*. "For us in Ireland," he asserted, "Mr. Joyce's significance lies in this, that he is the first man of literary genius, expressing himself in perfect freedom, that Catholic Ireland has produced in modern times. Mr. Joyce is as Irish as M. Anatole France . . . is French."[38] Walkowitz notes that both Larbaud and such critics write about Ireland as if it were a "valuable" and "coherent" object, aligned with nationalist politics against the artistic legacy of Europe; both parties contest the binary in that they want to broaden the nativist and "celebratory" character of Irish literary identity.[39] Nash, Booker,[40] and others highlight the particularly Catholic, and in this sense *in*coherent, element of *Ulysses*' identity: they point to John Eglinton's 1929 characterization of *Ulysses* as the first triumph of Catholic Ireland over "the Anglicism of the English language"[41] by a writer "Roman in mind and soul" throughout his work.[42]

"Genius"—in both the classical sense of spirit and the more modern one of a mastering intelligence, comprehensive as well as creative—acted as the pivotal concept in the transmutation of Joyce's dirty profanity into sacred artistry. This revision, enshrined in Eliot's "*Ulysses,* Order, and Myth," which appeared in the November 1923 *Dial*, is evidenced in much humbler and less laudatory quarters.[43] While reviewers frequently questioned the ends to which Joyce applied his talent, they never challenged the intrinsic value or essential construction of this ideology. The most virulent critics of the novel, such as Maitland and Leslie, acknowledge Joyce as a "Titan" and a "great imaginative writer." Rachel Bowlby observes that the successful 1960 trial of Lawrence's *Lady Chatterley's Lover* depended on a common acceptance of "clean and dirty, wholesome and unwholesome, moral and immoral" as the standards by which the novel should be judged. Defense of the book rested "on the grounds that [Lawrence's] writing is not dirty at all—neither in the words he uses nor in the forms of life that he advocates." Rather, she continues, Lawrence was presented as "more wholesome than his detractors, who ma[d]e of sex a 'dirty secret,'" while Lawrence restored the sacred importance of sexuality to marriage.[44] Joyce's redefinition similarly depended on shared assumptions between his opponents and his allies, but stressed "genius" and "lunacy" rather than sincerity as the crucial avenue of negotiation and erased altogether the perception of *Ulysses* as a representation of knowledge produced by bodies. Both genius and madness signified a freedom from normal constraint, a capaciousness of individual perspective—indeed a compulsion to follow the dictates of that perspective at the expense of all other considerations. As the secular analogue of godlike powers of creativity, located since the Romantics in the individual consciousness, artistic genius signified the unalienated labor of a sovereign individual able to fashion an objective correlative in language, animating mastery with spirit and shaping Irish material with European and classical form. In this sense *Ulysses'* reception follows the logic of assimilation, as the threat of the archaic, foreign, or gothic dissolves into the mixture of universal humanity and its knowledge while retaining its interesting flavor or charm. Joyce's purity resides in his devotion to depicting the truth of a degraded humanity and in his exercise of political and artistic freedom. For admirers, the novel is not chaotic, but encyclopedic; not obscene, but frank and detached, unsullied by its examination of the sordid aspects of existence; not coarsely mocking but scrupulously truthful. *Ulysses* was "comparable to the Bible," "ineluctably . . . true" to life, and "dazzlingly original" in its creative accomplishment. The novel possessed "absolute validity" in spite of its "local and private" focus.[45]

The Satanic Verses controversy mobilized a starker opposition between the sovereign individual body, now equated with the book, and the totalized subject of orthopractic belief, aligned with archaic (now non-Western and non-Christian) religion. The panic provoked by Joyce's performance of metaphoric relations among self, body, and context was in the later dispute elicited by the similar relations produced by the practice of Islam. In the Anglo-British imagination, a totalized Muslim agent sought to dissolve the boundaries between public and private knowledge that H. G. Wells had defended half a century before. Now, however, the archaic religious body attempted violently to dissolve the civil space of freedom, the Anglo-British individual as one sovereign national territory. The individual as a legal entity played a much more prominent role in *The Satanic Verses* controversy than it had in the *Ulysses* scandal, as both critics and defenders of the novel used freedom of speech and other civil rights to defend their positions. Anglo-British, and later American, reaction to the Anglo-Muslim protest demonstrated the confluence of Western national-civil subjectivity and artistic theology. The privileging of aesthetic form merged seamlessly with the right to freedom of expression, as both were synonymous with the institutional shape of individualism.

Whether depicted as a person, a book, or as the nation-state itself, the metonymic individual of these binaries is structured as a fetish. In this, the conception of agency recalls Žižek's equation of the transcendental subject with the commodity form. The subject, made of the same "sublime" material as money, possesses an "indestructible and immutable" body which outlasts physical embodiment.[46] But while Žižek describes the fetish structure of human relations as repressed in bourgeois society—it is displaced onto relations between things so that "free subjects" may emerge—I am placing the fetish structure in the civil and social production of embodiment itself as a historical mode of enfleshing the relations between his "sublime" and material bodies.[47] The metonymy that creates the individual from personal somatic matter also distinguishes the individual from the larger material world: that is, the positivist episteme that makes an exterior world of separate, inanimate objects also produces the subject as metaphysical substance rather than as mere stuff. In short, the individual is structured like a fetish not only "internally," but also "externally." Martin Krieger points toward this conclusion in his analysis of the experimental object of normal science: created through the pulling out of a part "still attached to the world," the power of the "dumb object" resides precisely in its production as a metonymy.[48] Similarly, when they imagine themselves as inextricably entangled with incoherent corporeality, Joyce's readers lose the power to separate from other people as well as to dominate inanimate matter. In *The Satanic Verses* controversy, the panic over this loss becomes geopolitical.

Ulysses Redux: Satanic Terror

Like *Ulysses, The Satanic Verses* impelled a confrontation between a totalized agent, who is connected to archaic religion, and the autonomous space of the individual. Externally directed disciplinary power once again endangered sovereign agency. But in the Rushdie affair the book's audience, rather than its representations or its author, posed the threat to individualism, and the civil space of privacy, rather than intimate bodily space, was felt to be vulnerable. If Anglo-Christian England understood the book's burning as a literal conflagration of the individual's authority, Anglo-Muslim protestors portrayed the novel's representations as an equally violent severing of Muhammad from the body-knowledge of Islam. In their view, the "pulling out" of properties to create the metonymic object—which I have characterized as producing the individual—rendered the metaphoric unity of Islam as a "thing" rather than an "act." Denny explains the distinction: "*Orthodoxy* is not the best term to use when characterizing Islam's sense of right religion. A better term is *orthopraxy*, which comes much closer to the reality of Muslim devotion and obedience to God." In comparison with Christianity, which "stresses doctrinal clarity and understanding by means of creeds, dogmas, and theologies," he continues, "Islam and Judaism . . . view religion as a way of life and a ritual patterning of that life under God's lordship."[49] The *salat* epitomizes the communal nature of the habitus that arises from Islamic orthopraxis. Observed five times daily, the *salat* unites the umma in "an intense, highly regulated, formal observance that features cycles of bodily postures climaxing in complete prostration in orientation toward the Ka'ba in Mecca," a center and focus of religious energy. (*Salat* is distinct from *du'a*, or private devotion, suggested by the translation "prayer.") One person may perform *salat*, but if he is joined by even one other worshipper, one of them must lead. This imam "acts as a pattern for the rest to follow, so as to preserve the required precision and order of the service."⁵⁰ The contrast between the metonymic and metaphoric modes of production also pertains to the distinction between performance and performativity that was central to the Muslim complaint against the novel. Detractors' comments suggest a critical difference between an act staged as a representation for an audience and an act undertaken as a productive end in itself.⁵¹ As Asad argues about the anthropological reading of monastic practice: "[A]lthough the formation of moral sentiments is dependent on a signifying medium, we cannot read off the formation from the system of significations that may be authoritatively identified and isolated as a distinctive semiotic phenomenon."⁵²

While not even Catholic commentators questioned the truth of Joyce's depictions, instead deploring their partiality, Anglo-Muslims stressed the factual inaccuracy of *The Satanic Verses*. The novel's imitation of scripture and tradition directly challenged the divine word as knowledge, untranslatable both linguistically and performatively. *The Satanic Verses* not only appropriated what Bobby Sayyid calls the "master signifiers" that unify the various expressions of Muslim worship—the Qu'ran, the hadith, and the sunna—but also traduced the communal body made in worship.⁵³ From this perspective Rushdie split Muslim subjectivity from agency, which is generated through collective praxis in relation to the sacred texts, and Islam from its multiple dispositional, textual, and moral frameworks. While Joyce's Catholic reviewers diffused religious offense into social and cultural categories—blasphemy, when specifically mentioned, encoded a generalized insult to group sensibility or social decorum rather than a violation of doctrine or practice—Muslims affronted by *The Satanic Verses* foregrounded the novel as a source of public knowledge. Its offense was first epistemological. In this, British Muslims spoke from the episteme proper whose mimetic effect had so unsettled *Ulysses'* readers.

In October 1988, according to Bhikhu Parekh, those who initiated the British protest asked that a notice be inserted in the book to inform readers that *The Satanic Verses* did not provide "an accurate history of Islam."⁵⁴ Rushdie "has intentionally and deliberately distorted the history of the Blessed

Prophet and his Companions," Syed Ali Ashraf states in an October 28 review published in the Muslim London weekly *Impact International*.[55] M. H. Faruqi, the paper's editor, comments in the same issue: "Fact of the matter is that not having the courage or ability of a scholar, Rushdie has simply tried to hide behind the realm of dream and fiction."[56] Others similarly call the novel a lie, a disfigurement, and a falsification of the Prophet, his companions, and his wives.[57] "Because of the importance Muslims themselves attach to the critical examination of the facts of the Prophet Muhammad's way of life [contained in the sunna], . . . The Prophet Muhammad can never be seen as a figure of fiction: he is a fact who lived in real time," contemporary scholars explain. This division pervades Islamic textual tradition, which "insistent[ly] emphasi[zes] . . . the separation of fact from fable so that the irreducible substance of faith can be known."[58] The Qu'ran manifests "the divine word inlibrate," and the hadith convey the sunna, or the Prophet's way of life, which have formed "the uniquely valid rule of conduct for Muslims" since classical times.[59]

Most obviously, Muslims contested the auratic and nonideological premises of literary fiction.[60] As in the *Ulysses* controversy, the audience often conflated blasphemy and obscenity. Unlike Joyce's detractors, however, Rushdie's stressed the profane content of the book even when they spoke of its physical and sexual representations. An ad that the Birmingham Central mosque placed in the *Times* compared Rushdie's depictions of Muhammad's companions to someone's portraying "Matthew and Mark indulging in indecencies and molesting children."[61] The novel's portrait of Islam's holy personages were comparable to characterizing Jesus as a homosexual engaged in orgies with the apostles, or Mary as a prostitute and Jesus as her client.[62] The sexuality of Muhammad per se was not at issue in such analogies; rather the obscene referred to the spiritual and cultural, as well as the epistemic, illegitimacy of their use.

Both the civil rhetoric and the Christian analogies that Anglo-Muslims deployed assume the separate, affective interior space of embodied individualism. Like the novel itself, these translations to some extent efface the public and performative dimensions of practical belief, even as they produced new forms of Anglo-Muslim identity in wake of the protest.[63] Religion, "either relegated to the private sphere, or read as a form of false consciousness," gained a new "national voice" for British Muslims.[64] Above all, *The Satanic Verses* initiated this development by splitting a communal body from the palpable Muhammad that it generated, severing from the community of believers the knowledge of Muhammad "internalised in every Muslim heart," in Ali Mazrui's phrase.[65] The physical and performative dimensions of Muslims' analogies, rather than their doctrinal content, more effectively convey this practical episteme. In Muslims' use of Christian scripture, transgressive sexual acts pervert affective and often physically intimate bonds, such as those between parents and children or prophet and disciple. Comic display compounds the betrayal as the novel destroys intimacy and trust to create a trivial amusement. From this perspective, Rushdie stages the somatically produced and incorporated Muhammad as an expressive performance or spectacle, a minstrelsy, just as he claims the Qu'ran as personal property. *The Satanic Verses* distorts belief as a performance "of" to render it as a particular performance "for," introducing the semiotic gap as an act of intimate physical aggression. Mazrui quotes Pakistani friends who compared the book to a "brilliant poem about the private parts of [one's] parents," read in the marketplace to the applause and laughter of strangers;[66] Mushahid Hussain likens Rushdie to "a Jew who tries to justify the Holocaust . . . and dismisses his crime in light-hearted humour at the expense of the victims of Auschwitz."[67] Rushdie, who had been raised as a Muslim, employed the knowledge and power of praxis against itself, detaching the "act" from its episteme to make a metonymic "thing" with its own potency. Speaking from a totalized bodily habitus[68] created through actions that sedimented believers' orientation to one another, to Muhammad, and to God, objecting Muslims felt that Rushdie split Muhammad, the model of active being in the world, from this unity. Ultimately, their comments imply that the novel disrupts the production of Muhammad as the primary power of the umma. Just as totalization dissolves the structure of the individual, here splitting depotentiates the body of Islam.

Much as the Muslim protest encoded resistance to the fragmentation of a totality, the majoritarian reaction described an autonomous space subjected and physically tortured by an Oriental despot.[69] The Bradford demonstration of January 14, 1989, brought the Muslim campaign domestic mass-media attention because participants burned a copy of *The Satanic Verses*. Rushdie, responding in an *Observer* article of January 22, made explicit the equation of book and body, art and theology. Here the author states that he possesses "the same God-shaped hole" that haunts Aadam Aziz in *Midnight's Children*:

> Unable to accept the inarguable absolutes of religion, I have tried to fill up the hole with literature. The art of the novel is something I cherish as dearly as the bookburners of Bradford value their brand of militant Islam. Literature is where I go to explore the highest and lowest places in human society and the human spirit, where I hope to find not absolute truths but the truth of the tale, of the imagination and the heart. So the battle over *The Satanic Verses* is a clash of faiths in a way. Or, more precisely, it's a clash of languages.[70]

Like *Ulysses'* advocates half a century before, *The Satanic Verses'* defenders presented artistic production as the supreme expression of individual freedom. "Dangers of a Muslim Campaign," an *Independent* editorial about the Bradford demonstration, states: "The Islamic campaign would be more understandable if Rushdie's novel were in any way trashy. But its literary merits are not in doubt." In the tradition of "the Inquisition and Hitler's National Socialists," the *auto-da-fé* was barbaric and uncivilized, the work of fanatics who refused to understand or respect British culture.[71] The editorial neatly conflates books and bodies in order to condemn the violent intolerance of heresy and fascism, using medieval Spain and genocidal Germany as the archaic and the modern emblems of foreign religiosity. Shailja Sharma observes that "the novel which told the stories of Britain's immigrants was proof that they could never become British."[72]

Thus Khomeini's death threat of February 14 merely completed the already established narrative of foreign violence penetrating sovereign national boundaries and the trope of the literary book as the substance of the persecuted individual. Though the symbolic of the book as the epitome of Enlightenment played a more prominent role in the Rushdie controversy, these nuances did little to disturb the basic formulation of strategic individual space revealed in the *Ulysses* affair. In defense of the exemplary individual, Rushdie and his supporters called upon the totemic book that eventually emerged from the *Ulysses* controversy. Anglo-Christian culture in Britain resurrected this book as the icon of the national-textual body. Similarly, Western authors found occasion to claim their profession as both spiritual and worldly. Speaking at a PEN American Center reading held as the novel was being released in the United States, Norman Mailer, for instance, echoed the charges of depletion and decadence levelled against the West by some Muslim critics. Calling writers an "endangered species" who usually injured only "each other," he asserted:

> But now the Ayatollah Khomeini has offered us an opportunity to regain our frail religion which happens to be faith in the power of words and our willingness to suffer for them. He awakens us to the great rage we feel when our liberty to say what we wish . . . is endangered. We discover that, yes, maybe we are willing to suffer for our idea. Maybe we are willing, ultimately, to die for the idea that serious literature, in a world of dwindling certainties and choked up ecologies, is the absolute we must defend.[73]

The Imam's threat had evangelically renewed writers' sense of artistic mission, offering the possibility of martyrdom *back* to them. Such responses suggest that metropolitan freedom had forgotten its vocation, only to be reminded by the textual fanaticism of Islam.

Conclusion

In the controversies over both *Ulysses* and *The Satanic Verses*, metropolitan modernist literature secured a phantasmal image of itself as worldly and public by violating the construction of "religion" as a crucible of, rather than an adjunct to, identity. The orthodox, secularist conception of religion, modelled on the liberal Christian formation, in fact modelled the theology of art as a semiautonomous symbolic. Western literature and religion did not compete as starkly opposite epistemologies, but rather as auratic sites of sensibility and expression, for both "art" and "religion" offered styles of elaborating the individual's foundation through access to tradition and to transcendent emotion. These acquisitions enriched rather than produced subjects, little affecting dominant epistemic regimes or the bodily dispositions that they generated.

Half a century after the *Ulysses* controversy, Rushdie and his defenders totalized genuinely epistemic differences in belief formations by casting Islam as archaic and absolutist, an omnivorous consumer of rights and boundaries. In attempting to elucidate the complexities of these disputes, I have aimed to stress the need for historicization and critical examination of the frozen signifiers that they mobilize. "What is missing from diasporic theory," writes Vijay Mishra in 2008, "is a theory of the sacred based not on the idea of the sacred as a pathological instance of the secular, in itself defined along purely modernist lines, but as a point from which interventions can take place."[74] Such interventions must begin with a reexamination of "religion" as a practice of reading cultural repression, productive only in the aesthetic recapture of theological figures.[75] This ideology continues to mask individualism, a deeply entrenched paradigm of Western spiritual, physical, and social identity formation, as a significant arena of both the earlier and more recent dispute. In both controversies, the challenge to this formulation of agency produced panic over the dissolution of "personhood." Minority literatures, as well as our public discourse, call for more considered responses to other realizations of the "person" and other productions of knowledge, for a genuine encounter with the difficult and compelling issues of difference that they pose.

6

The Religion of Celebrity

*P*opular celebrity relieved James Joyce and Salman Rushdie of the burden of representing the minority religious body as a provincial one, coincident with a particular geographic location. With the onset of international fame for Joyce and truly global notoriety for Rushdie, the authors themselves became signifiers of the energies of disciplinary religious praxis and their operation in the public realm. These belong to what Jaffe calls the celebrity "imprimatur," the author's trademark style of self.[1] Celebrity—auratic movement and diffusion through mass-media representation—funds the performative bodies that the writers generate in their subsequent work, which perpetually re-cites the surpassing of provincial origins. In *Finnegans Wake* (1939) and *The Ground beneath Her Feet* (1999), the techniques of producing the spiritual provincial body merge with those of producing the celebrity body. The *Wake* links the machinery of mass media representation and communication to the anatomy of sleep and its mental processes as well as to the analogue of drink. But the narrative also illustrates modernity as a product of the writer's body and the writer's body as a product of contemporary media: just as HCE is a radio transmitter and receiver,[2] Joyce is made as a technological emanation. In Rushdie's formulation of this nexus, celebrity becomes the epitome of movement and the basis of its embodiment. The torrent of representation acts a particular characteristic of modern celebrity. While Joyce remained—and to this day, as I have argued, to large extent still remains—in control of his public representation, *The Ground beneath Her Feet* suggests

Rushdie's loss of such power. Looking at the arc of the writers' careers shows the development of what James English analyses as "the economy of prestige," through which local and global networks reinforce one another.[3] Rushdie's case nonetheless also reveals a profound loss of local context, in the Hindu-Muslim Indian body. *Ground* illustrates Rushdie's loss of claim on the subcontinent, coincident with his loss of control of his physical safety. In *Joseph Anton*, Rushdie describes himself as a third-person character, born on the day that Khomeini called for the author's death. Like Chamcha, he is reborn as a devil as a result of violent trauma: "He was a new self now. He was the person in the eye of the storm, no longer the *Salman* his friends knew, but the *Rushdie* who was the author of *Satanic Verses*." He continues: "*The Satanic Verses* was a novel. *Satanic Verses* were verses that were satanic, and he was their satanic author, 'Satan Rushdy,' the horned creature on the placards carried by demonstrators down the street of a faraway city, the hanged man with protruding red tongue in the crude cartoons they bore." It was "easy . . . to erase a man's past and to construct a new version of him, an overwhelming version, against which it seemed impossible to fight."[4] Though in 2014 it might be argued that Rushdie, like his forerunner, has attained a stable profile of literary respectability, he now travels the circuits of pop representation as an image of terror overcome. Isaac Choitner observed, "Rushdie did not become a stylistically different writer under the fatwa, but in his later work, the larger subjects of religion and intercommunal warfare become secondary to his ostentatious prose."[5] John Updike connected this artistic change to Rushdie's own transformation from "an author" to "a cause célèbre and a free speech martyr."[6]

Finnegans Wake and *The Ground beneath Her Feet* encode the performative bodies generated by religious practice as entirely productive, based on epistemologies of mobile flux. Both works employ conceits of the earth as "ground" that dissolves or erupts in constant meaning-making. Instability characterizes the earth-body, which constantly accrues polyglot language, story, myth, and history through omnivorous association. The novels incorporate primary settings in territories aligned with minority religious bodies—Catholic Ireland and Muslim India—only to absorb them, so that these bodily "styles" resignify other continents, as the authors have done through the dissemination of their works and their images. Religious discipline abandons the repressive function in these works, just as the writer's own fully creative celebrity body absorbs the provincial one. Joyce and Rushdie now fashion the signifier celebrity as the writer's own myth travels the routes of popular representation, joining the company of ancient and contemporary divinities, Hibernating Britain and Europe and Indianizing the Americas. In this sense, the narratives complete the projects begun in *Dubliners* and *Midnight's Children,* in which the provincial religious body engenders fatality, for now not even death stops bodily production and reproduction. Unlike the *Wake* in relation to Irish territory, *Ground* dramatizes the abandonment of India as a geographic locus altogether and attempts to carry its praxis entirely through the celebrity body of migrant symbolization.

The cosmopolitan formulation of provincial praxis is reflected nowhere more completely than in the text of *Finnegans Wake*. Scholars' recent emphasis on the "potential" of the sleeper precisely coincides with the assumptions of religious praxis. The *Wake* unleashes the capacity of all bodies to make identities and their epistemologies in relation to one another. The daytime individuals suggested by the names Humphrey Chimpden Earwicker, an Anglo-Irish Protestant publican, and Anna Livia Plurabella, his wife and the mother of their three children, never appear in the text, as many readers have observed; rather the sleeping "somebody," the "one continuous present tense integument slowly unfold[ing]"[7] like parchment supplies the merest substratum of a physical-psychic location, node, or mark for the sleeper. The *Wake* is at the same time, Finn Fordham argues, "a comedy about some *notorious* figure, the autonomous subject who has overreached himself."[8] The historical-disciplinary making of this notorious-anonymous person appears in the trial of the Festy King, which, like "Proteus," examines the senses. Here, Bishop observes, Joyce puts on trial "all the exacting the rules of evidence by which the innately formless senses of sight and hearing have been disciplined over years of both personal and cultural history to bear witness on an 'audible-visible-gnosible world' held intelligibly in place by correlated institutional forces of *leg*ality, *leg*ibility, and *log*ic which Vico conceptually equates with intel*lec*tion and recol*lec*tion . . . by derivation from the common root *leg (to collect, to gather)."[9] The power of bodies produced by orthopraxy culminates in the malleability of words themselves as atomic-"Atemic" elements of somatopsychic production: sigla and initials suggest characters' identity as they migrate through various forms. The corpselike and presumably drunken sleeper's dream frequently narrates conflict, aggression, and crime, but never represses. As in Freud's dream logic, the text of *Finnegans Wake* adheres to principles of affirmation and inclusion, always "yes" or "and," rather than negation and causality. In this "nat" language, sound and association accrue surprising meanings not initially evident in a "denotative" reading for sense. Performativity owes much to the analogue of liquor, evidenced by the splash of whiskey that resurrects the corpse Finn and preoccupies the pubkeeper HCE. "Alcohol operates in *Finnegans Wake* as a cipher of the opiating powers of sleep," Bishop remarks,[10] and Theall argues that intoxication is "crucial" to

Joyce's Deleuzian somatic bricolage.[11] Here, as in *Ulysses*, "spirits" and "spirit" exchange their capacities for conversion and dissolution. The *Wake* supplies a microcosm of these dynamics early in the first chapter, when, after "The Ballad of Persse O'Reilly" is reproduced, the fates of the Rann-makers are being narrated. The "old stage thunkhard," a "stage drunkard" whose head has been thumped, is reported to have said, before his death in jail:

> Me drames, O'Loughlins, has come through! Now let the centuple celves of my egourge as Micholas de Cusak calls them,—of all of whose I in my hereinafter of course by recourse demission me—by the coincidence of their contraries reamalgamerge in that indentity of undiscernables where the Baxters and the Fleshmans may they cease to bidivil uns and . . . this outandin brown candlestock melt Nolan's into peese! (49–50)

The speech collapses "dreams" and "drams" (which may be "me" or "mine") to suggest the multiplication and dispersal of selves in death, or perhaps in extreme drunkenness. Like Earwicker and Finn, the drinker will be reproduced in new bodies and marks, which may not be perceivable by ordinary means—this "indentity" promises to reside in new combinations of forms. Such passages recall the "indentity" of Mrs. Sinico of "A Painful Case." Like the emanations of the *Wake*, Mrs. Sinico "transaccidenates" in death, though she does so only in Duffy's imagination. The fluid representational energies of femininity and alcohol lead to this potential in Joyce's early work; in his final one, the capacity of the female drunkard to transform the male body resides in Earwicker as the alive and dead (but still drunken) bodily "cask" of transformative liquid that produces endless representations. As I have argued about *Ulysses*, the text constantly displays the malleability of the "person," who becomes different manifestations through enactment. For instance, the narrator describes Shem as "his own individual person life unlivable, transaccidentated through the slow fires of consciousness into a dividual chaos, perilous, potent, common to allflesh, human only, mortal. . ." (186). Fordham is puzzled by the apparent redundancy of "individual person" in this passage, and reads "individual chaos" as a potentially tragic dissolution of agency.[12] From the perspective of orthopraxy, however, the terms describe performativity, staging the bodily power to reformulate through epistemic becoming: "dividual chaos" suggests freedom from the strategy of individualism in order to potentiate other performances of personhood, chaotic as they may be from the perspective of a liberal Western "self." Fordham actually hints at such productions in his reading of "transaccidentated," but remains committed to the concept of the individual as the sole container of a coherent personhood. In this he suggests that representations that "threaten to undermine and reformulate personal identity" might be read as openings to new forms of agency.[13]

Like *Ulysses*, the *Wake* produces the spiritual-material body by assimilating contemporary technologies to archaic ones. In contrast to the earlier novel, however, it incorporates the author as a technical representation, generated from the drunken sleeper and disseminated through his somatic techniques. The orthopractic method of *Ulysses* reaches a new level of technical synthesis by harnessing analogues such as the ontophone, which turns sight into sound, and filmic images, which favor neither space nor time, to produce sensory representation.[14] As much as he is a mythic and biological body, the sleeping someone is inseparable from the modes of mechanical reproduction and communication tied to the sleeper's senses. The senses are equated with, paralleled by, revised through, and even made by equipment of mass media and communication, as Theall investigates at length. A text powered by electromagnetism abounds with radios, telephones, telegraphs, television, cables, recordings, and movies.[15] They fill the air with gossip, rumor, and confusion. A major strand of the narrative concerns questions of guilt and reputation, hovering over the mystery of HCE's "exposure." The status of vision is notable in this regard. Colorful imagery, associated heavily with the feminine, is conjured in the blindness of sleep, at the same time that the text resists visualization,[16] yet relies on natural and electric light.[17] Like "Joyce," the sleeper is everywhere and nowhere in his self-portrayals. HCE makes but does not control the myths of himself, which circulate through mass media communication as well as private letters and speech. Their reach may not be truly global—the *Wake* alludes to only one Irish language work[18]—but suggests that the "myth" of the author circulates the world from the "tropped" head (34.2-6)—that is, the drunken, "too-much," metaphor-making, dropped *Kopf* of Irish English, the source of its technical achievement.

Jonathan Goldman argues that *Ulysses* initiates the process of Joyce's celebrity through a linguistic and visual branding reliant on extradiegetic codes. *Finnegans Wake* actually incorporates the mechanisms of publicity and celebrity into the diegesis of the text through such somatic and machinic technologies.[19] The *Wake* specifically depicts the embodiment that mass media circulate when Shem writes in ink made of his own shit (185.5-8). The passage, written in Latin, the language of the Church, mocks the orthopractic production of the text from bodily practice as well as the equation of *Ulysses* with excrement in the popular and literary press.[20] Indeed these passages show the indivisibility of bodily production and bodily representation for Joyce. His waste, like the rubbish heap of letters though which the hen picks, is as much a source of creation as his bodily parts. Feces, dung, and urine, the chief metaphors for *Ulysses* in its early reception, are incorporated into the body text, registering its "ewiges ja." The references to Joyce's earlier works similarly equate them with dirt and dung, policed by a "petty constable" linked to Shaun.

During the writing of *Finnegans Wake*, however, Joyce's image in the literary, and increasingly the popular, press had less and less to do with waste or with the bodily perversions connected to Irish Catholicism. The author's depiction as a contaminant whose "influence" threatened social and political and well as literary structures virtually disappeared during these years, as I have said. Increasingly, Joyce appeared as a monument or giant as well as a priest or prophet, a political or ecclesiastical entity of his own. When the issue of his Catholicism arose as a specific belief system, it was blamed for the author's defects. In the vein of H. G. Wells and Cecil Maitland, Herbert Gorman, in his 1939 biography of the author, insists that the "Catholic system" the rather than Joyce's imagination, should be held responsible for his "errors."[21] For the most part, however, the language of transcendence emerged through aesthetic analogies, as I discuss in the chapter five. Joyce's monumental genius or animating spirit expressed itself materially in the form of books. The writer was seen to constitute his own church, with a "cult" and "devotees," and his own sovereign nation. In the "Religion of Art," a January 1934 article that attempts to debunk elements of modernist hagiography, Malcolm Cowley states, "[Joyce's] birthplace was the lower middle class; his home, above which he seemed to have soared, was the twentieth century." Even war could not distract the Promethean author from his writing: "Europe was crumbling about his ears, thirteen million men died in the trenches, empires toppled over; he shut his windows and worked on, sixteen hours a day, seven days a week, writing, polishing, elaborating."[22] *Time* magazine, in a 1939 cover story that reviews *Finnegans Wake*, provides a later example of such sincere admiration: "In 1915 Joyce was so busy with *Ulysses* that he scarcely noticed that Italy and Austria were about to fight until frontiers began to close."[23] The cover depicts Joyce once again squinting at a page, through both spectacles and magnifying glass, as Europe once again heads toward war. Maurizia Boscagli and Enda Duffy observe that in this and other photographs taken by Gisèle Freund, "the aura of Joyce the famous modernist and internationally recognized artist is indistinguishable from the aura of the fetish presence of the star." The 1938 series, Boscagli and Duffy contend, negotiates the "ambiguous" relationship between Joyce the star commodity and the unique individual, the internationalist and the Irishman: "Making possible Joyce the cosmopolitan, haunting these photographs, is Joyce's Irish face."[24]

Like Earwicker, Joyce also becomes a figure of respectability far removed from embodiments in a text far more scatological and sexually transgressive than *Ulysses*. *Time*, which frequently pictures Joyce with his grandson Stephen in reviews and articles beginning in the 1940s, eulogizes him through the image of a grandfather who acts as a prophet, a natural force. His work serves as the aesthetic epitome of European culture in ruins. In a February 10, 1941, "Books" section, the magazine describes the emerging news of Joyce's death in terms of political ironies and religious analogies: "To many a baffled reader of *Finnegans Wake*, the death of Joyce meant merely that the 'cult of unintelligibility' had lost its chief prophet." To "friends" and "admirers," however, "Joyce's death seemed like some simple lapse in nature, grandly tragic and fitting" because it underscored the demise of a European cosmopolitan culture. The writer's work stood as "the most massive, inclusive, eloquent statement of Europe's intellectual and moral chaos, a chaos now audible and visible in the falling walls of Europe's cities." To die "in the midst of this downfall" was reminiscent of St. Augustine of Hippo's death "at the close of the Roman world[,] to the echo of Vandal swords against the city gates."[25] The article proceeds to recount the events of Joyce's flight from Paris to Zurich and his final Finnegan-like sleep: "*Nightnow! Tell me, tell me, tell me, elm! Night night!*"[26]

The autonomous artistic realm ultimately made Joyce safe for consumption, as his technical, literary virtues also displayed his political impotence. "In order to be a successful anarchist you must work within the order of society," John Murry wrote in 1922. "You have to use the time-tables and the language of ordinary men. By the excess of this anarchy, Mr. Joyce makes himself socially harmless. There is not the faintest need to be concerned about his influence."[27] This lack of political agency in fact later became a criticism of Joyce's work, particularly in the 1930s and 1940s in America, when Marxist critics attacked as bourgeois or elitist the very qualities that had been regarded as revolutionary or proletarian in the response of a decade before. Popular reviews, and reviews of the emerging scholarly criticism about his *oeuvre*, place Joyce in the company of Homer, Dante, and Dostoevsky as well as of the towering figures of European modernism, largely accepted as "giants." Even negative assessments continue to be couched in the familiar terms of monumentality and religion, with occasional nods to disease rather than vulgarity or filth: Van Wyck Brooks, for example, calls him "'a sick Irish Jesuit'"[28] and Cyril Connolly groups Joyce with Proust as "'very sick men, giant invalids who, in spite of enormous talent, were crippled by the same disease, elephantitis of the ego.'"[29] In contrast to works such as Gorman's, Harry Levin's *James Joyce* (1941), Richard M. Kain's *Fabulous Voyager* (1947), and William York Tindall's *James Joyce: His Way of Interpreting the Modern World* (1950), and collections of articles such as Seon Givens's *James Joyce: Two Decades of Criticism* (1948), installed the formalist cosmopolitan Joyce as exemplary. Many of these volumes themselves were reviewed or mentioned in mass-circulation newsweeklies. Popularizing of Joyce's work had begun much earlier, beginning with the Modern Library editions of *Dubliners* in 1926 and 1928, and continuing through Faber's 1942 *Introducing James Joyce: A Selection of Joyce's Prose* and Viking's 1947 *The Portable James Joyce*.[30]

The gestalt of the Joyce's celebrity cosmopolitanism has by this point been entirely freed from addressing the representation of minority embodiment *within* the works. Rather Joyce himself now "travels" as an imagination or intellect in spite of, or along with, the buried or surpassed fundament of his early formation. In its review of the monograph, *Time* quotes Harry Levin's *James Joyce,* stating that the author's "'imaginative constructions are . . . grounded on the rock of his buried religious experience.'" The review then paraphrases Levin by placing this experience even deeper underground: "Strictly speaking Joyce's religious experience was adolescent. He was barely out of his teens when he renounced Ireland and with it the Roman Catholic Church. Much has been made of his Jesuit education, of how his mind was formed by Catholicism and in particular by St. Thomas Aquinas. It is equally true to say that his mind was formed about as independently as any mind ever was."[31] As evidence of his autonomy, the article does not cite Joyce's departure from Ireland but rather his composition of "The Holy Office" (1904). The article succeeds in ignoring any reference to bodily functions in spite of the passage of the poem that it cites. Described as "crude" and a "boyish boast," the poem is said to illustrate the young man's devotion to Aquinas, rather than his interest in excrement: "*That they* [Joyce's 'Irish enemies'] *may dream their dreamy dreams / I carry off their filthy streams . . . / Thus I relieve their timid arses, / Perform my office of Katharsis . . . / Those souls that hate the strength that mine has / Steeled in the old school of Aquinas.*"

While Goldman argues that "the fantasy of self-production" evinced in his work "conveniently removes Joyce from the equally messy problem of cultural visibility,"[32] I hope I have shown the complex problematic of Joyce's personal "visibility." The display of the provincial spiritual body underlies the process, as Joyce's occluded biographical representation so clearly rests on exhibiting a provincial spiritual body *constantly in the act of being surpassed* by his public persona. Richard Ellmann's 1959 biography[33] solidified the triumph of the image of the transcendent, monumental genius first offered as a solution to the disturbing physicality of Joyce's work and attendant on his actual form during his lifetime. Ellmann's magisterial biography of Joyce still stands as a comprehensive reference work, in its revised, 1982 edition,[34] which avoids the word "alcoholism" in characterizing John Joyce's drinking, much less his son's.[35] Jane Lilienfeld speculates that Ellmann was "wary of the stereotypical view of alcohol addiction being endemic in the lives of the Irish family" and notes that Stanislaus saw his father's drinking as "culturally normative."[36] These investments and disavowals shape Ellmann's representation of Joyce, and even of his body, in ways consistent with the formulation of his transcendence of provincial Irish literature, Irish nationalism, and Irish Catholicism.[37] "Before Ibsen's letter [to him] Joyce was an Irishman; after it, he was a European," Ellmann writes, recalling the playwright's response to the essay "Ibsen's New Drama," which Joyce had published in the April 1900 *Fortnightly Review*.[38] The biographer asserts that Joyce's "'Celtic' melancholy" was "repugnant to his personality"[39] and that his character Leopold Bloom "achieves th[e] distinction [of being 'a cultured allround man'] in part by not belonging in a narrow sense, by ignoring the limits of national life; he is not so much an Irishman as a man."[40] When the Joyces were evacuated from Trieste in 1915, "Switzerland was more than a refuge [for them]; it was a symbol of artistic detachment."[41]

Joyce's own practices become problematic in this refinement of provincial character. As in the criticism, alcohol stands as a signifier not only of embodiment but of a particularly Irish form of it, stereotypical in the extreme. And yet, as I have argued, it is precisely this typification that Joyce claims and repeatedly uses in his fiction as a central element of the production of Irish Catholic corporeality. In the 1959 edition of his biography, Ellmann makes approximately fifty references to Joyce's drinking habits and preferences, noting in his introduction his subject's "regard for alcohol."[42] Excessive drinking caused Joyce much trouble with his wife and his brother, left him in the gutters of Rome, contributed to his financial troubles, exacerbated his eye problems, and did other damage to his health, according to Ellmann's own account. Yet when Jung, during his treatment of Lucia, discussed Joyce's consumption, Ellmann rationalizes: "It was not easy for Jung, who had been brought up in a 'fanatical anti-alcohol tradition,' to understand the attitude of Joyce, whose rearing was diametrically opposite. Joyce was abstemious during the day, and drank only at night. He drank with a nice combination of purpose and relaxation.... He engaged in excess with considerable prudence."[43] To admit Joyce's alcoholism might reduce him to the status of just another Irishman, one who escaped the fetters of religious repression only to fall prey to the other tyranny of his "race." Perhaps more important, attention to Joyce's consumption as well as to the pivotal role of liquor in his depiction of provincial embodiment suggests that overmastering genius had not allowed Joyce to transcend his origins as thoroughly as his cosmopolitan profile would demand. To contemplate such profaning of his metropolitan achievement is to realize the extent to which his minority identity has been occluded. In comparison with analysis of sex and sexuality—another dimension of embodiment—alcohol continues to be a relatively neglected topic in Joyce criticism, particularly in the many discussions of bodily and sensory representations,[44] and the suggestion of Joyce's use of the inebriate as an exemplary metrocolonial has in recent decades still caused concern over Joyce's nativist bona fides.[45] I have argued that this absence constitutes a significant aporia in Joyce's reception, one caused by the particular ways in which the author directed readings of provincial religious bodies *through* the stereotype.

Over twenty years after the call for his murder, Rushdie has achieved a celebrity profile that Joyce could not have imagined.[46] Knighted by Queen Elizabeth, married and divorced from a reality TV personality, Rushdie is a denizen of the Hamptons and the gossip pages as well as of the literary empyrean. He has increasingly meditated on fame, whether historical, as in *The Moor's Last Sigh* (1995) and *The Enchantress of Florence* (2008), or contemporary, as in *Fury*[47] (2002) and *Shalimar the Clown* (2005). Anshuman Mondal asserts, "Rushdie's . . . authority to speak *on* celebrity is bound up with his own status *as* a globalised celebrity."[48] *The Ground beneath Her Feet* constitutes the author's most sustained dramatization of celebrity. In this work—his third published after the fatwa and the first of these to be set in the contemporary world—Rushdie clearly represents the traumatic production of his own global fame and his transformation into an icon of persecution, as the novel recounts the proliferation of representations completely beyond the subject's control. If *The Moor's Last Sigh* rewrote the India of *Midnight's Children*, *Ground* merged *Verses'* metropolitan simulation and Indian filmi celebrity in the register of vertigo. Rushdie's fame after Khomeini's decree recalls Goldman's description of Oscar Wilde as the first modernist literary celebrity. In his early fame Wilde acted "like a commodity, a sign whose value accrues in relation to other signs" and whose "genius" entailed "no concept of interiority" but rather consisted of surface display, costumes, emblems, and even epigrams, a "shorthand" signifying wit. In this way Wilde became "a visible object of critique" who eventually disappeared by losing control of his meaning.[49] Rushdie's celebrity signification, both more violently imposed and more visually complicated, produced "invisibility" as itself a visible surface during his crisis. A Far Side greeting card published in 1991—*Ground* later alludes to it—neatly encapsulates Rushdie's change into an infamous signifier of invisibility and an absent presence, both associated with confinement and death. On the face of the card, Gary Larson portrays two men gazing out a window through the venetian blinds, in what appears to be a motel room, sparely outfitted with an armchair and an antennaed television. The bare light bulb hanging from the ceiling and the empty beer can and smoking ashtray, laid on the floor, emphasize the bleakness of the scene. The viewer looks in through the fourth wall, over the TV, onto the men's backs as they peep into the night. The one on the left is a plump white man in a white jumpsuit with a standing collar, ruffled cuffs, and bellbottoms. His hair rises in a pompadour over a face, shown in profile, that displays protruding lips. At the other end of the window stands a slightly tubbier but much shorter man, whose head is entirely turned to the window. More plainly but colorfully clothed, in a long sleeved, collarless orange sweater or shirt and green pants, he represents an "average" American man, his skin pinkish, his hair brown, in a short, standard male haircut. The drawing is slugged: "Roommates Elvis and Salman Rushdie sneak a quick look at the outside world," referring to Elvis's purported existence, long after his official death. Inside, the card says: "Haven't seen you in awhile. How's it going?"[50]

The Larson card serves as an almost dizzying signifier of Rushdie's celebrity status in wake of *The Satanic Verses* controversy. The card unwittingly anticipates the text of *Ground* in its specific content as well as its larger resonances. One of the novel's three principals, Ormus Cama, is, like Elvis, a huge rock star and a surviving twin, though the fictional Parsi Indian channels rock tunes sent to him from his dead brother. Ormus is mesmerized by his access to an invisible reality, an Orphic netherworld. Like Elvis after death, like Ormus, and finally like Ormus's wife and bandmate Vina Apsara, the Rushdie of the card exists in a celebrity half-life. But Larson's Rushdie is visually characterized solely through his proximity to the emblems of Elvis. The drawing divests the writer of even ordinary signifiers of his actual appearance, such as glasses, hairstyle, or physique. Rushdie operates as a visible absence, marked by the signifiers of *other* celebrities he has joined in the living death of "hiding" his body. Furthermore, as a prurient audience, we are complicit. Viewers of the card can see the celebrities' invisibility: we are peeping, even sneaking up on them, while they try to catch a glimpse of "real" life "outside" their enclosure in a signification that is as characterless as the room that they inhabit together.

In the transit zone of "transformation," Umeed "Rai" Merchant, the narrator of *Ground*, states, "we might have been trapped forever."[51] Rushdie's dilemma, as an author trying to peep out at the world from a separate enclosure, has remained, even though he long ago emerged from hiding to assume his role as a very visible celebrity, and later as a harbinger of the September 11th attacks.[52] The author has become the ultimate migrant territory, a meta-symbolic of the Indian sublime. As critics have noted, his latter representation of mobility and mixture entraps and strips as well as frees him. This shift in valorization results not only from a problematic evident in Rushdie's fiction since *Midnight's Children*, but also from the event of his own traumatic production as a globalized signifier severed from ordinary life. The perpetual mirroring of reference in the celebrity symbolic emerges as a crisis of representation in *Ground*.[53] "In stardom," the Muslim-born atheist Rai recounts, Ormus and Vina "entered into that zone of celebrity where everything except celebrity ceases to signify" (425). The celebrity-divinities transform constantly not only because of changes in their whims, images, and marketing, but also because of their rootlessness on earth and in the cosmos. In the narrative's delirious pastiche, Vina and her lover enact the myth of Orpheus and Eurydice as well as its puranic counterpart, the myth of Rati and Kama, so that the binaries multiply between locations and among the over-, under-, and extra "worlds" of death and life, human and alien. Celebrity extends the characters' migrancy through mass media that partake of science fictional and fairy tale as well as mythic and legendary motifs,[54] but *Ground* emphasizes the "global" idioms of 1960s and 24-hour news broadcasts of the 1980s. "Celebrity seems to render Vina post-racial, in parallel to her post-national position,"[55] Boyagoda observes of her mixed identity and pop image. After her death, however, this mutability becomes deeply disturbing to the narrative. Anyone can assign any meaning to Vina: her "cult," driven into hysterical replication of Vinas, exaggerates her own conjuring of new surfaces and identities during her life, yet compounds her death, as the "real" Vina known to intimates disappears doubly. Her lover and friend Rai relates, "[T]he astonishing afterlife of Vina Apsara is rapidly spiraling beyond the power of any authority, spiritual or temporal, to censure or control" (479). It signifies an earthquake more sublime than the one that killed her, as meanings become "aliens" and vampires, draining both the memories and the very bodies of her intimates of substance (488). Rushdie alludes to Larson's card when Rai bitterly recounts the public commentary eulogizing Vina, the fictional substitute for the living Rushdie: "Here is a Gary Larson cartoon of Vina and Jesse Garon Parker, the grotesquely Vegas-rhinestoned Fat Jesse of his latter, pill-popping, burgerizing days. They're alone in a motel room, looking out at the world through the slats of a venetian blind. What's this supposed to be, the dressing room of the undead? A zombie transit zone on the Far Side? Ha ha ha." Rai continues to lambaste the "lords of information" who have "been caught napping by the unexplained gigantism of the death and after-death of Vina Apsara." Vina's death engenders "a global struggle" whose "prize is meaning itself" (482). A comic and epic catalogue of commentators follows: "Madonna Sangria," speaking of "women's pain," a number of anonymous female fans, a (female)

American intellectual's essay on "Death as Metaphor," Christian and Muslim women, a male cultural-studies guru, British psychoanalysts, critics of every stripe, and residents of every place Vina ever lived interpret the meaning of her life and career. The novel even conjures a Baudrillard surrogate who discusses the "feedback loop" of television as a simulated simulacrum that evacuates every genuine emotion into "performing" rather than "acting": the bereaved are "[n]ot simply grieving but *performing grief*" (485).

Like *The Satanic Verses*, *The Ground beneath Her Feet* throws up a paradox in its treatment of representation. The unmoored mobility and self-referentiality of simulation and reproduction challenge the realm of the sublime, derived in Rushdie's most successful fiction from religious bodies and the epistemologies that their praxis generates. Rai finally pleads on behalf of the "living memory" of Vina that is consumed by these replications, "Don't make her a metaphor" (486). But this making of meaning is the province of Rushdie's fiction, the "creation" that the atheist Rai promotes to equal status with "Creation." In Rushdie's *oeuvre* to date, art and myth can manifest invisible truth, unite fractured communities, and act as the realm of the "soul." Here the journalist Rai's experiments with kirlian photography supply such a spiritualized metaphor. "To my surprise," the vehemently areligious Rai states, "I found that much of the imagery that came to me had religious overtones . . . I allowed myself the supernatural, the transcendent, because, I told myself, our love of metaphor is pre-religious." In contrast with double-exposure photography, which can reveal invisible bodily events as material—"a dying woman's out of body experience" or "a man suddenly explod[ing] into pure light," religion demands bodily submission, with angels "imprisoned . . . in aspic," freedom "nailed . . . to the ground," and knee "ben[t]" before god (447). Metaphor thus acts as the reservoir of the transcendent and as the agent of its demise, for the babble of news, gossip, and opinion replaces the revelatory voice or eye with emblems of celebrity and cancels any reverence for life or personal memory. In this formulation, only the claim to "ownership" of the actual separates the sublime from vampiric reproduction. Yet ownership of the actual, literal, or historical is the very ground of Rushdie's own contest with sacred texts such as the Qu'ran.

As metaphor replaces *Verses*' "doubt" as the productive source of transcendence, celebrity dispenses with the need for a territorial signified, that is, the India that allowed *Verses* to sustain sublime metaphor against the assault of soulless simulation. Vina and Ormus create their own myths even as they revise older tales of divinity. They absorb rather than embody or parallel prior narratives. Unlike the star texts of Indian popular cinema, however, these extradiegetic glosses diminish rather than enlarge the subject's meaning. In its travels among India, England, and the Americas, the novel emplots the chronological movement of Rushdie's image from a British to an "Indian" and to a metropolitan and "global" writer, decisively superseding provincial religious territory as the provincial body becomes paradigmatic, diffuse, and external. In contrast to Joyce, who absorbs and incorporates Irish geography, Rushdie, through Rai, stages a dramatic departure from India. It results from Rai's exposure of a criminal ring. Significantly, the exposé requires a journey into rural India, narrated, seemingly without irony, through the tropes of imperial adventure: "To journey down some of these tracks was to travel back in time for over a thousand years," Rai remembers (238). He discovers the absence of the requisite treasure in the cave: the goats for which a businessman receives large government subsidies do not exist. Rai escapes the death that met another journalist, whose corpse dangles over him as he awaits execution by the politicians' goons. He escapes, but the violent reprisals for his report drive him out of India. "Sure I'd go back. Things would cool down," Rai recalls thinking at the time. After all, "[r]eal life was not like an earthquake" (247). But politics determine a different outcome, and Rai ends this episode with a lengthy eulogy to India, his "*terra infirma*," "maelstrom," "cornucopia," "mother," "father," "fable," and "first great truth." Rai concludes: "India, fount of my imagination, source of my savagery, breaker of my heart. Good-bye" (249).

Rai follows the script of an imperial adventurer when he emerges to a "new life" after his near-death encounter with the "native" archaic. While Davy Crawfurd of *Prester John* and Allan Quatermain of *King Solomon's Mines* escape from African caves to see Eden or Scotland in the landscape, Rai experiences "disorientation" in his "loss of the East." It is the project of *Ground* to reorient the narrative by installing India as the origin of contemporary Western phenomena at the same time that India itself becomes a property of the cosmopolis, to be found everywhere.

In New York, Rai realizes, "A kind of India happens everywhere, and that's the truth too; everywhere is terrible and wonder-filled and overwhelming if you open your senses to the actual's pulsing beat" (417). Both prior and pervasive, India manifests itself through instances of wonder, contrast, metamorphosis, and sensory overload. Just as Ormus Cama's father Darius tries to syncretize the mythologies of East and West, *Ground* attempts to Bombay-ize London and more emphatically New York, through correspondences that are both comic and earnest. The twentieth-century American architectural style becomes art "dekho"; sixties counterculture mimics Indian mysticism; the music of rock in some sense has its origins in India, as the great hits of Elvis and the Beatles are first composed by Ormus's dead brother Gayomart and channeled to the living twin. When Ormus has an audience with a big-time producer, he develops a migraine and can't perform his own compositions. Instead "he s[i]ng[s] his Gayo ditties, those cover versions of the well-known hits of the day which he had so uselessly heard long before, in dreams; and so he was mistaken by the producer for a novelty act, a provincial echo of the big-city action, a hick" (190). While Randy Boyagoda argues that the novel installs America as both neoimperial and ideally heterogeneous,[56] these gestures seem desperate in their search for a replacement for the spiritual-technical fecundity of Hindu-Muslim national bodies. Provincial minority practice wants to act as exemplary in *The Ground beneath Her Feet*, but lacks the spiritual territory in which this practice has been anchored since *Midnight's Children*. In dispensing with this territory, the novel leaves unresolved the antithetical expressions of metaphoric representation, which both produces and destroys transcendence. Celebrity, endlessly capable of resignification, terminates the "half-evacuated referentiality" of the gothic in a seedy hotel room, a synecdoche of the writer's body. For all its inventiveness, *Ground* often lacks the sensuous quality of Rushdie's fiction since *Midnight's Children*. Though Rushdie continues to use familiar bodily tropes—Vina as the reproductive voice, Ormus as the Delphic ear and eye, Rai as the photographic one—the characters often seem to be conglomerations of references that insist on rather than perform sensual presence. In this aspect *Ground* resembles *Grimus*.

Rushdie disappeared for a time, like the "posthumous goddess" Vina, like Oscar Wilde, and like his own power over his representation. *Ground* seems to yearn for an "authority" to "control" the property of meaning (479). Finally Vina is colonized by her husband and lovers, who exploit other women in their desperation to simulate her. The novel ends with "ordinary human life" after the departure of "the mythic, the overweening, the divine," even though Ormus and Vina are still singing on TV (575). Rushdie, too, has reasserted stability in his life and career, but this narrative suggests an exhaustion of the sublime that Joyce devised and Rushdie adapted. The "ground" of disciplinary religious performativity ends, not in natural disaster, cosmic apocalypse, historical cycle, or ghosts, but in the more banal circularity of simulation and exploitation.

The role of belief, and more particularly orthopraxy, in minority religious literatures is by no means exhausted by the Joycean strategy that Rushdie adapted. Recognizing its dynamics may help metropolitan readers and critics to discern the multiplicity of belief formations and their nuances in emerging literatures. In this analysis, I have attempted to trace a major route through modernist literature that proceeds from anthropological premises. Joyce's use of religion as a formal analogue for art involved a particular relationship to the provincial minority body of his origins. While his elaboration came out of a broader, earlier aesthetic movement, I have attempted to show the critical role of minority belief praxis in his production of an experimental idiom of bodies as practices that generate epistemologies. Joyce exposed and denigrated Irish-Catholic male embodiment and agency in part to distinguish himself in the cosmopolitan milieu. As I have shown, when his readers initially failed to mark his work as sufficiently Catholic, he pushed this profile forward through commentary that he massaged. In what pop psychology calls an approach-avoidance relationship, Joyce always kept Catholicism as a visible aspect of his public identity, but kept it at a little distance from his body. In fact, as I have demonstrated, the premises of disciplinary belief centrally inform his experiment with bodily depiction throughout his career. Joyce's grasp of performative belief as a fount of epistemological change entirely based in physical production funded his revolutionary literary procedures. Rather than describing his discovery, as it emerged in *Ulysses*, he continued to "read" Catholic praxis as wholly repressive and this repression as aimed centrally at sexuality. Much like his treatment of alcohol as a poison and alcoholism as entirely deadening, his representation of orthopraxy changed in *Ulysses* with the realization of repression's productive capacities. But he never ceased to read performativity through the lens of doctrinal religion, whose premises dictated an understanding that accorded with the premises of individualism. The resolution of the scandal of *Ulysses* simply relocated this conception to a more abstracted register, one which allowed bodily excesses to be understood as privacies represented in the interest of truth and universality.

Salman Rushdie's execution of the Joycean project shows its continued vitality as well as its strains. Not only his works, in which the celebrity body of the author must carry the auratic power of praxis, but the writer's career itself dramatizes the widening political and aesthetic stresses on the Joycean formulation of belief. Given the many differences in their positions historically and culturally, a strong pressure on Rushdie's aesthetic comes from the unease with which its Joycean, modernist impulse sits with its more postmodern dynamics, a tension greatly exacerbated by the author's global notoriety. *The Satanic Verses* shut down the absolute value of hybridity when it confronted uncontrolled and commodified simulation. *The Ground beneath Her Feet* encountered the same dilemma with the difference that the author himself, as a hunted body, was the ultimate signifier of pop representation. Through the depiction of Vina, *Ground* suggests the need for some ownership of signification. Just as *The Satanic Verses* reunites migrant and country of origin to solve the dilemma of commodity reproduction, *Ground* subtextually concedes some validity to the Muslim complaint about *Verses*. When anyone can take ownership of a representation, some violence is done to the intimates of that person. In this sense *The Ground beneath Her Feet* returns us to the aporia of religion versus art but with a difference, with a suggestion of nuance. Finally, Rushdie's sacrifice of the Indian body as the source of his sublime has pushed his own work into the realm of the simulation simulacrum, as the hermetic signifier of celebrity finds no somatic "ground" in his subsequent fiction. This outcome does not mean that the Joycean formulation of provincial religion is spent, that it may not yet find future acolytes. But it does suggest that Western criticism and wider thought needs to crack open and scrutinize the imperial premises of "religion" as it has been understood in the twentieth century. As scores of writers from postcolonial and other marginalized cultures enter into the metropolitan marketplace of literature in English, the Western academy needs to attune itself to historical and cultural particularity in the portrayal of belief as practice and public identity, as well as aesthetic resource easily consumed as exotica. While the confluence of these global interactions produce new identities—just as *The Satanic Verses* controversy itself did—this need becomes even more urgent. Along with it comes a perhaps less obvious but equally pressing requirement that critics grapple with the masculinist focus of the Joycean project. In English, work such as Monica Ali's *Brick Lane* (2003) and Zadie Smith's *White Teeth* (2000), and in Persian Shahrnush Parsipur's *Zanan bedun mardan* (1989; translated into English as *Women without Men* [1998]) represent Muslim orthopraxy in quite different ways, with focus on women's praxis. Literary works that depict belief as a premise of agency and identity, one that rests upon conceptions of the person as not entirely or even primarily described by the strategy of individualism, coded male, must be met with a literary critical environment willing to give up its own prejudices and examine the contours of its repression of such productions.

Notes

Introduction

1. Alix Spiegel, "One Man Tackles Psychotherapy for the Amish," 18 March 2009, *All Things Considered*, National Public Radio, http:www.npr.org/templates/story/story.php?storyId=102053475.

2. Michel de Certeau, *The Practice of Everyday Life*, trans. Steven Rendell (Berkeley: University of California Press, 1984), xix.

3. See, in particular, David Spurr, *Joyce and the Scene of Modernity* (Gainesville: University Press of Florida, 2002), 55–76.

4. Andreas Huyssen, *After the Great Divide* (Bloomington: Indiana University Press, 1986).

5. Lawrence Rainey, *The Institutions of Modernism* (New Haven: Yale University Press, 1998).

6. Significant works in this vein include Joyce Piell Wexler, *Who Paid for Modernism* (Fayetteville: University of Arkansas Press, 1997); Jennifer Wicke, *Advertising Fictions* (New York: Columbia University Press, 1998); Mark S. Morrisson, *The Public Face of Modernism* (Madison: University of Wisconsin Press, 2001), and Kevin Dettmar and Steven J. Watt, eds., *Marketing Modernisms: Self-Promotion, Canonization, Re-reading* (Ann Arbor: University of Michigan Press, 1996).

7. James Buzard, *Disorienting Fiction: The Autoethnographic Work of Nineteenth-Century British Novels* (Princeton: Princeton University Press, 2005); John Marx, *The Modernist Novel and the Decline of Empire* (Cambridge: Cambridge University Press, 2005); Jed Esty, *A Shrinking Island: Modernism and National Culture in England* (Princeton: Princeton University Press, 2003); Ian Baucom, *Out of Place: Englishness, Empire, and the Locations of Identity* (Princeton: Princeton University Press, 1999).

8. See, for instance, Wicke, *Advertising Fictions*, 147, and Garry Leonard, *Advertising and Commodity Culture in Joyce* (Gainesville: University Press of Florida, 1998), 35–40.

9. Jenny Franchot, "Unseemly Commemoration: Religion, Fragments, and the Icon," in

Religion and Cultural Studies, ed. Susan Mizruchi (Princeton: Princeton University Press, 2001), 39.

10. Tal Asad, *Genealogies of Religion: Discipline and Reasons of Power in Christianity and Islam* (Baltimore: Johns Hopkins University Press, 1993), 125–67; Frederick Denny, *An Introduction to Islam,* 2nd ed. (New York: Macmillan, 1994), 67.

11. Claude Welch, *Protestant Thought in the Nineteenth Century,* vol. 2, 1870–1914 (New Haven: Yale University Press, 1985), 68.

12. Gauri Viswanathan, *Outside the Fold: Conversion, Modernity, and Belief* (Princeton: Princeton University Press, 1998), 12–13.

13. John Corrigan, *Business of the Heart: Religion and Emotion in the Nineteenth Century* (Berkeley: University of California Press, 2002), 3–4.

14. Welch, *Protestant Thought,* 2:104.

15. Denny, *An Introduction to Islam,* 67.

16. Asad, *Genealogies,* 125–67.

17. Judith Butler, "Performative Acts and Gender Constitution: An Essay on Embodiment and Feminist Theory," in *Writing on the Body: Female Embodiment and Feminist Theory,* ed. Katie Conboy, Nadia Medina, and Sarah Stanbury (New York: Columbia University Press, 1997), 401–17.

18. Asad, *Genealogies,* 125.

19. Asad's emphasis on the epistemic and somatic productivity of belief illustrates the persistence of this framework even in the theories that inform his argument: Asad clearly draws on Foucault's central insight about repression, yet Foucault himself never surmounted modern Christian premises to posit a "spiritual corporality" as well as a "political spirituality" in his thinking about religious practice. Jeremy Carrette states, "Foucault was unable to see how the religious body is shaped by, and shapes, belief in a nonbinary social operation." Hence he did not grasp that "belief 'is' the social positioning" rather than "a separate and distinct process of the social conditioning of bodies." *Foucault and Religion: Spiritual Corporality and Political Spirituality* (London: Routledge, 2000), 112–13; 6. See, for instance, Michel Foucault, *Technologies of the Self: A Seminar with Michel Foucault,* ed. Luther Martin, Huck Gutman, and Patrick Hutton (Amherst: University of Massachusetts Press, 1988), 18. For another approach to Foucault and spiritual practice, see James Bernauer, *Michel Foucault's Forces of Flight: Toward an Ethics for Thought* (Atlantic Highlands, NJ and London: Humanities Press, 1990), 158–84.

An illuminating discussion of Asad's Foucauldian-inflected argument is presented by Jon E. Wilson, "Subjects and Agents in the History of Imperialism and Resistance," in *Powers of the Secular Modern: Talal Asad and His Interlocutors,* ed. David Scott and Charles Hirschkind (Stanford: Stanford University Press, 2006), 180–205.

20. Robert Crawford, *Devolving English Literature,* 2nd ed. (Edinburgh: University of Edinburgh Press, 2000), 217.

21. Geert Lernout, *Help My Unbelief: James Joyce and Religion* (London: Continuum, 2010), 28–51.

22. Aaron Jaffe, *Modernism and the Culture of Celebrity* (Cambridge: Cambridge University Press, 2005), 20–31.

23. Jaffe, *Modernism,* 12–13.

24. Rebecca Walkowitz, *Cosmopolitan Style: Modernism beyond the Nation* (New York: Columbia University Press, 2006), 5.

25. Viswanathan, *Outside the Fold,* 60.

Chapter 1

1. Daniel Dubuisson, *The Western Construction of Religion: Myths, Knowledge, and Ideology*, trans. William Sayers (Baltimore: Johns Hopkins University Press, 2003), 14. For a counterargument based on a concern with praxis, see Russell McCutcheon, who contends that "religion" is as effective as any other arbitrary rubric, but he stresses that religious studies should focus on "a thoroughly reflexive historicization of the very existence of this sociocognitive category, regardless of its definition." *The Discipline of Religion: Structure, Meaning, Rhetoric* (London: Routledge, 2003), 235. Also see Tomo Masuzawa, "The Production of Religion and the Task of the Scholar," *Culture and Religion* 1 (2000): 123-30.

2. Asad, *Genealogies*, 29.

3. Notable exceptions are John Waldmeir, *Cathedrals of Bone: The Role of the Body in Contemporary Catholic Literature* (New York: Fordham University Press, 2009), and Amy Hungerford's *Postmodern Belief: American Literature since 1960* (Princeton: Princeton University Press, 2010). Hungerford, however, largely transfers the modernist ideology of the sacred text into the realm of writerly practice, and belief into the register of art. Also of interest is James Wood, *The Broken Estate: Essays on Literature and Belief* (New York: Picador-St. Martin's, 1999).

4. Crawford, *Devolving English Literature*, 217.

5. James Buzard, "'Culture' and the Critics of *Dubliners*," *James Joyce Quarterly* 37 (1999-2000): 55; Marvin Manganaro, *Culture 1922: The Emergence of a Concept* (Princeton: Princeton University Press, 2002), 105-50. In this the authors occupy a position related to that of Valente's Anglo-Irish "metrocolonial," who is subordinate to the imperial power and yet privileged against rural others. Joseph Valente, *The Myth of Manliness in Irish National Culture, 1880-1922* (Urbana: University of Illinois Press, 2011), 194.

6. Asad, *Genealogies*, 35. This terrain is staked out on political and aesthetic, rather than on religious grounds, by Richard Begam, "Joyce's Trojan Horse: *Ulysses* and the Aesthetics of Decolonization," in *Modernism and Colonialism: British and Irish Literature, 1899-1919*, ed. Michael Valdez Moses and Richard Begam (Durham: Duke University Press, 2007), 185-208.

7. Victoria Glendinning, "A Novelist in the Country of the Mind," in *Salman Rushdie Interviews: A Sourcebook of His Ideas*, ed. Pradyumna Chauhan (Westport, CT: Greenwood Press, 2001), 4.

8. Buzard, "'Culture,'" 55-56.

9. Susan Mizruchi, ed., introduction to *Religion and Cultural Studies* (Princeton: Princeton University Press, 2001), x.

10. Ibid.

11. Robert Cummings Neville, *Religion in Late Modernity* (Albany: State University of New York Press, 2002), 220-21; John Corrigan, ed., "Emotions Research and the Academic Study of Religion," in *Religion and Emotion: Approaches and Interpretations* (Oxford: Oxford University Press, 2004), 4.

12. See Wayne Proudfoot, *Religious Experience* (Berkeley: University of California Press, 1985), v, 2-3, for an influential formulation of the roots of protectionism. Corrigan, "Emotions Research," 5; Neville, *Religion*, 205-09.

13. Tomoko Masuzawa, *The Invention of World Religions, Or, How European Universalism Was Preserved in the Language of Pluralism* (Chicago: University of Chicago Press, 2005), 1.

14. Asad, *Genealogies*, 39.

15. Cf. Proudfoot, *Religious Experience*, xii.

16. Asad, *Genealogies*, 39.
17. Welch, *Protestant Thought*, 1: 60.
18. Ibid., 1: 63.
19. Friedrich Schleiermacher, *On Religion: Speeches to Its Cultured Despisers*, trans. Richard Crouter (Cambridge: Cambridge University Press, 1988), 22–23.
20. Andrew Dole, *Schleiermacher on Religion and the Natural Order* (Oxford: Oxford University Press, 2010), 23.
21. Corrigan, *Business of the Heart*, 4.
22. Viswanathan, *Outside the Fold*, 12–13.
23. Ibid., 153–63.
24. Denny, *An Introduction to Islam*, 67; Asad, *Genealogies*, 112. Cf. Jean Leclerq, *The Love of Learning and the Desire for God: A Study of Monastic Culture*, trans. Catharine Misrahi (New York: Fordham University Press, 1961), 90.
25. Asad, *Genealogies*, 112.
26. Butler, "Performative Acts," 401-17.
27. Asad, *Genealogies*, 125.
28. Talal Asad, "Religion, Nation-State, Secularism," in *Nation and Religion: Perspectives on Europe and Asia*, ed. Peter van der Veer and Hartmut Lehman (Princeton: Princeton University Press, 1999), 189.
29. Michael J. F. McCarthy, *Priests and People in Ireland* (London: Hodder and Stoughton, 1908), 625, qtd. in Lernout, *Help My Unbelief*, 50.
30. Lernout, *Help My Unbelief*, 30; Nicholas Atkins and Frank Tallett, *Priest, Prelates and People: A History of European Catholicism since 1750* (Oxford: Oxford University Press, 2003), 123–41, 182.
31. See, for instance, Luke Gibbons, "'Have You No Home to Go To?' James Joyce and the Politics of Paralysis," in *Semicolonial Joyce*, ed. Derek Attridge and Marjorie Howe (Cambridge: Cambridge University Press, 2000), 153–54.
32. S. J. Connolly, *Priests and People in Pre-Famine Ireland, 1780–1845* (Dublin: Gill and Macmillan; New York: St. Martin's, 1982), 275–76. For more information about the institutional church and the famine, see, for example, E. Larkin, "The Devotional Revolution in Ireland, 1850–75," *American Historical Review* 77 (1972): 625–52, and *The Roman Catholic Church in Ireland and the Fall of Parnell, 1888–1891* (Chapel Hill: University of North Carolina Press, 1979); D. W. Miller, "Irish Catholicism and the Great Famine," *Journal of Social History* 9 (1975): 81–98.
33. David Lloyd, "The Memory of Hunger," in *Loss: The Politics of Mourning*, ed. David L. Eng and David Kazanjian (Berkeley: University of California Press, 2003), 214–15.
34. Lawrence J. Taylor, *Occasions of Faith: An Anthropology of Irish Catholics* (Philadelphia: University of Pennsylvania Press, 1995), 195.
35. Marcel Mauss, *Sociology and Psychology: Essays*, trans. Ben Brewster (London: Routledge & Kegan Paul, 1979), 122, 101.
36. James Joyce, *A Portrait of the Artist as a Young Man*, ed. Hans Walter Gabler (New York: Vintage-Random House, 1993), 144.
37. Ibid., 141–42.
38. Katherine Mullin, *James Joyce, Sexuality, and Social Purity* (Cambridge: Cambridge University Press, 2003), 100, 106.
39. Christine van Boheemen, "Joyce's Sublime Body: Trauma, Textuality, and Subjectivity," in *Joycean Cultures/Culturing Joyces*, ed. Vincent Cheng, Kimberly Devlin, and Margot Norris (Newark: University of Delaware Press; London: Associated University Presses, 1998), 30.

40. Kevin Sullivan, *Joyce among the Jesuits* (New York: Columbia University Press, 1958), 10.

41. Garry Leonard, *Reading* Dubliners *Again: A Lacanian Perspective* (Syracuse: Syracuse University Press, 1993), 4.

42. R. B. Kershner, *Joyce, Bakhtin, and Popular Literature: Chronicles of Disorder* (Chapel Hill: University of North Carolina Press, 1989), 298.

43. John Nash, *James Joyce and the Act of Reception: Reading, Ireland, Modernism* (Cambridge: Cambridge University Press, 2006), 15.

44. Ibid., 21.

45. See Joseph Kelly, *Our Joyce: From Outcast to Icon* (Austin: University of Texas Press, 1999), 28–41. Kelly discusses the *Irish Homestead*, arguing that the *Dubliners'* stories that Joyce first published in the paper contained rural, folkloric elements as well as a new contemporary realism.

46. Ernest Boyd, "Concerning James Joyce," *New York World*, 25 January 1925, n.p., in *James Joyce: The Critical Heritage*, ed. Robert Deming (New York: Barnes and Noble, 1970), 320.

47. Ernest Boyd, *Ireland's Literary Renaissance*, rev. ed., 1923, 402–3, in Deming, *James Joyce*, 302. Nash points out that Boyd did not include Joyce in the 1916 edition of the work, which concentrated on poets and dramatists—the generic focus of the revival. Nash also contends that Boyd avoided a focus on Joyce's Catholic literary identity. "'In the Heart of the Hibernian Metropolis'? Joyce's Reception in Ireland, 1900–40," in *A Companion to James Joyce*, ed. Richard Brown (Oxford: Blackwell, 2011), 109–12.

48. Larbaud's influential review, which appeared in 1922, claimed that *Ulysses* showed "how little nationalistic a literary language can be." He generally praised the novel as superior to both Irish literature and politics in that it "restored . . . an artistic countenance, an intellectual identity" to the country. With *Ulysses*, Larbaud claims, "Ireland is making a sensational re-entrance into high European literature." "James Joyce," *Nouvelle revue française* 18 (April 1922): 387–88. The translation is taken from "The *Ulysses* of James Joyce," *Criterion* 1 (October 1922), 94–103, in Deming, *James Joyce*, 253.

49. Kelly, *Our Joyce*, 77, asserts that Pound is responsible for "the destruction of Joyce's profile as an Irish writer."

50. On 12 July 1905 Joyce wrote to his brother Stanislaus that he planned to follow *Dubliners* with a book entitled *Provincials*. *Selected Letters of James Joyce*, ed. Richard Ellmann (New York: Viking, 1975), 68.

51. Pheng Cheah and Bruce Robbins, ed. *Cosmopolitics: Thinking and Feeling beyond the Nation* (Minneapolis: University of Minnesota Press, 1998), 4. Cheah links this definition to Bhabha's notion of "hybrid cultural agency," which consists of "physical freedom from being tied to earth." "Given Culture: Rethinking Cosmopolitical Freedom in Transnationalism," *Cosmopolitics*, 301. For critique of this definition, see, for instance, Berthold Schoene, *The Cosmopolitan Novel* (Edinburgh: Edinburgh University Press, 2009), 2; Bishnupriya Ghosh, *When Borne Across: Literary Cosmopolitics in the Contemporary Indian Novel* (New Brunswick: Rutgers University Press, 2004); and Walkowitz, *Cosmopolitan Style*.

52. Valente, *The Myth of Manliness*, 194. See James Fairhall, *James Joyce and the Question of History* (Cambridge: Cambridge University Press, 1993), 64–77, for a precise class location of Joyce's subjects as well as a historical discussion of the rise of "paralysis" as a critical touchstone.

53. Arthur Kleinman, *Social Origins of Distress and Disease: Depression, Neurasthenia, and Pain in Modern China* (New Haven: Yale University Press, 1986), 56.

54. Qtd. in Valente, *The Myth of Manliness*, 233.

55. Valente, *The Myth of Manliness*, 195.

56. Joseph Valente, "Neither Fish Nor Flesh; or How 'Cyclops' Stages the Double-Bind of Irish Manhood," in Attridge and Howes, *Semicolonial Joyce*, 96–106.

57. Valente, *The Myth of Manliness*, 195.

58. Manganaro, *Culture 1922*, 105–6.

59. Cf. John Bishop, *Joyce's Book of the Dark:* Finnegans Wake (Madison: University of Wisconsin Press, 1986), 415–20.

60. For an extended analysis of popular and critical fashions in Joyce's reception, see Joseph Brooker, *Joyce's Critics: Transitions in Reading and Culture* (Madison: University of Wisconsin Press, 2004), and Kelly, *Our Joyce*.

61. Review of *Dubliners*, by James Joyce, *Academy*, 11 July 1914, 49, in Deming, *James Joyce*, 65.

62. Review of *Dubliners*, by James Joyce, *Everyman*, July 1914, 380, in Deming, *James Joyce*, 64.

63. Review of *Dubliners*, by James Joyce, *Athenaeum*, 20 June 1914, 875, in Deming, *James Joyce*, 61.

64. Gerald Gould, review of *Dubliners*, by James Joyce, *New Statesman*, 27 June 1914, 374–75; book review, *Times Literary Supplement*, 18 June 1914, 298, in Deming, *James Joyce*, 62, 63, 60.

65. Review of *Dubliners* by James Joyce, *Academy*, 11 July 1914, 49, in Deming, *James Joyce*, 65.

66. Review of *Dubliners*, by James Joyce, *Irish Book Lover* 4 (November 1914), 60–61, in Deming, *James Joyce*, 69.

67. Ezra Pound, "*Dubliners* and James Joyce," review of *Dubliners*, by James Joyce, *Egoist* 14 (July 1914), 267, in Deming, *James Joyce*, 66–67.

68. Kelly, *Our Joyce*, 79.

69. Scofield Thayer, "James Joyce," *Dial* 773 (September 1918), 202.

70. J. C. Squire, "Mr. James Joyce," review of *Dubliners*, by James Joyce, *New Statesman* 40 (April 1917), 40, in Deming, *James Joyce*, 99.

71. H. G. Wells, "James Joyce," *Nation*, 24 February 1917, 710, 712, in Deming, *James Joyce*, 86–87.

72. Manganaro, *Culture 1922*, 106–7.

73. A. Clutton-Brock, "Wild Youth," review of *A Portrait of the Artist as a Young Man*, by James Joyce, *Times Literary Supplement*, 1 March 1917, 103–4, in Deming, *James Joyce*, 89–90.

74. "A Dyspeptic Portrait," review of *A Portrait of the Artist as a Young Man*, by James Joyce, *Freeman's Journal*, 7 April 1917, n.p., in Deming, *James Joyce*, 98–99.

75. Review of *A Portrait of the Artist as a Young Man*, by James Joyce, *New Age*, July 1917, 254, in Deming, *James Joyce*, 111.

76. Thayer, "James Joyce," 202.

77. John Macy, "James Joyce," review of *Dubliners* and *A Portrait of the Artist as a Young Man*, *Dial* 42 (June 1917), 525–27, in Deming, *James Joyce*, 107.

78. John Quinn, "James Joyce, A New Irish Novelist," *Vanity Fair*, May 1917, 48, 128, in Deming, *James Joyce*, 104.

79. Van Wyck Brooks, review of *A Portrait of the Artist as a Young Man*, by James Joyce, *The Seven Arts* 2 (May 1917), 122, in Deming, *James Joyce*, 106.

80. Diego Angeli, "Un romanzo di gesuiti," *Il Marzocco* (Florence), 12 August 1917, 2–3, trans. James Joyce, *Egoist* 5 (February 1918), 30, in Deming, *James Joyce*, 115.

81. Deming, *James Joyce*, 16. In the headnote to Colum's article, Deming also—oddly—says that it is "the first to draw attention to the Catholic tradition and culture that shaped Joyce's early works," though the anthology contains Angeli's article, published in the previous year. Joyce's translation of Angeli's piece into English had even appeared several months before Colum's essay. Deming, *James Joyce*, 163.

82. Padraic Colum, "James Joyce," *Pearson's Magazine*, May 1918, 38–42.

83. Ezra Pound, "Joyce," *The Future* (May 1918), 161–63, in Deming, *James Joyce*, 168.

84. Julian Kaye, "The Wings of Daedalus: Two Stories in *Dubliners*," *Modern Fiction Studies* 4 (1958): 31.

85. Brewster Ghiselin, "The Unity of Joyce's *Dubliners*," *Accent* 16 (1956): 75.

86. Buzard, "'Culture,'" 46; Jaffe, *Modernism*, 34.

87. John Hagopian, "The Epiphany in Joyce's 'Counterparts,'" *Studies in Short Fiction* 1 (1964): 273.

88. Carl Niemeyer, "'Grace' and Joyce's Method of Parody," *College English* 27 (1965): 196.

89. One of the recent exceptions appears in Tracey Teets Schwarze's *Joyce and the Victorians* (Gainesville: University Press of Florida, 2002), 43–68. In exploring Stephen's "religion of unbelief" in relation to romanticism, however, Schwarze confines her discussion of belief to issues of theology.

90. Jane Heap, "James Joyce," *Little Review* 10 (April 1917), 8–9, in Deming, *James Joyce*, 117.

91. Manganaro, *Culture 1922*, 106–7.

92. Seamus Deane, *Strange Country: Modernity and Nationhood in Irish Writing since 1790* (Oxford: Clarendon, 1997), 168–69.

93. Nash, *James Joyce and the Act of Reception*, 41, 60.

94. Mullin, *James Joyce*, 19–20.

95. John-Charles Sournia, *A History of Alcoholism*, trans. Nick Hindley and Gareth Stanton (Oxford: Basil Blackwell, 1990), xii–xiv, 98–100.

96. This industry had greatly diminished in the south by the end of the century.

97. See Paul Townsend, *Father Mathew, Temperance, and Irish Identity* (Dublin: Irish Academic Press, 2002), 192–234.

98. Elizabeth Malcolm, *"Ireland Sober, Ireland Free": Drink and Temperance in Nineteenth-Century Ireland* (Dublin: Gill and Macmillan, 1986), passim. This turn-of-the-century agenda transformed an earlier nationalist binary, which generated the masculine discourse of autonomous citizenship against the image of the slave. The shift marked the emergence of a new historical stereotype, the feminized Celt incapable of self-government—a type immortalized in Matthew Arnold's "Celtic Literature." Malcolm, *"Ireland,"* 135.

99. Valente, *The Myth of Manliness*, 215–16.

100. David Lloyd, "'Counterparts': *Dubliners*, Masculinity, and Temperance Nationalism," in Attridge and Howes, *Semicolonial Joyce*, 137–38.

101. James Joyce, *Dubliners*, ed. Hans Walter Gabler (New York: Vintage-Random House, 1993) 77, 82. Subsequent citations from this source will appear parenthetically in the text. Frank Gifford, *Joyce Annotated: Notes for* Dubliners *and* A Portrait of the Artist as a Young Man, 2nd ed., rev (Berkeley: University of California Press, 1982), 74, C88, 93.

102. Arthur Kleinman, *The Illness Narratives: Suffering, Healing, and the Human Condition* (New York: Basic, 1988), 5–7.

103. Donald Torchiana, *Backgrounds for Joyce's* Dubliners (Boston: Allen and Unwin, 1986), 142; Lloyd, "'Counterparts,'" 145.

104. Margot Norris, *Suspicious Readings of Joyce's* Dubliners (Philadelphia: University of Pennsylvania Press, 2003), 123, 125–27.

105. Valente, *The Myth of Manliness*, 194–220.
106. Robert Scholes, "'Counterparts' and the Method of *Dubliners*," in James Joyce, *Dubliners: Text and Criticism*, ed. Robert Scholes and A. Walton Litz (New York: Viking-Penguin, 1996), 343.
107. Valente, *The Myth of Manliness*, 204.
108. Lloyd, "'Counterparts,'" 143. Lloyd sees the contemporary pub as a "heterotropic sit[e] within which drinking is articulated . . . as an Irish mode of countermodernity."
109. Norris, *Suspicious Readings*; Garry Leonard, *Reading Dubliners*; Tanja Vesala-Varttala, *Sympathy and Joyce's Dubliners: Ethical Probing of Reading, Narrative, and Textuality* (Tampere: Tampere University Press, 1999).
110. Valente, *The Myth of Manliness*, 215.
111. R. B. Kershner, *Joyce, Bakhtin*, 131.
112. Lloyd, "'Counterparts,'" 135.
113. Norris, *Suspicious Readings*, 197–99, suggests that Kernan may have been pushed down the stairs by a creditor, a possibility that leads to a somewhat different reading of the endless questions about who Kernan is and what happened to him.
114. Kershner, *Joyce, Bakhtin*, 131–32.
115. For a related reading of Kernan's mouth as a fetishized pictorial void, see Gerald Doheny, Dubliners' *Dozen: The Games Narrators Play* (Madison: Farleigh Dickinson University Press, 2004), 142–43.
116. Gifford, *Joyce Annotated*, 101, C154: 16–17.
117. See Torchiana, *Backgrounds*, 206, for theological definitions of "sanctifying" and "actual" forms of grace.
118. Jacques Derrida, "Plato's Pharmakon," in *Dissemination*, ed. and trans. Barbara Johnson (Chicago: University of Chicago Press, 1981), 97–99.
119. Kershner, *Joyce, Bakhtin*, 113.
120. Michel Foucault, *Madness and Civilization*, trans. Richard Howard (New York: Random House, 1965), 153–54.
121. Norris, *Suspicious Readings*, 169, glosses the story as a rewriting of the Charles Stewart Parnell affair with Kitty O'Shea as well as of the Oscar Wilde trial. Doheny, Dubliners' *Dozen*, 99, notes that "A Painful Case," like "Counterparts," turns on the notion of failed contracts.
122. Cheryl Herr, "The Erotics of Irishness," *Critical Inquiry* 27 (1990): 7–8.
123. Stuart Gilbert, ed., *The Letters of James Joyce*, rev. ed. (London: Faber and Faber, 1966), 62.
124. Nash, *James Joyce and the Act of Reception*, 31.

Chapter 2

1. Bruce Lincoln, *Theorizing Myth: Narrative, Ideology, and Scholarship* (Chicago: University of Chicago Press, 1999), xx.
2. Talal Asad, *Formations of the Secular: Christianity, Islam, Modernity* (Stanford: Stanford University Press, 2003), 37, 186.
3. Richard King, *Orientalism and Religion: Postcolonial Theory, India, and "the Mystic East"* (London: Routledge, 1999), 16–18. King draws on Michel de Certeau, "'Mystique' au XVIIe siecle: Le probleme du langue 'mystique,'" in *L'homme devant dieu* (Paris: Aubier, 1964), 2: 267–91.
4. Peter van der Veer, *Imperial Encounters: Religion and Modernity in India and Britain*

(Princeton: Princeton University Press, 2001), 132. For a discussion of the complicated relation between classical Sanskrit scholars and British orientalists, see Faisal Devji, "Apologetic Modernity," in *An Intellectual History for India*, ed. Shruti Kapila (Cambridge: Cambridge University Press, 2010), 52–67.

5. van der Veer, *Imperial Encounters*, 44–47.

6. Ibid., 126.

7. Emphasis later shifted to the Vendānta, the end of the Vedas, according to King, *Orientalism*, 119.

8. King, *Orientalism*, 69, 101, 107.

9. Eleanor Wachtel, "Salman Rushdie," in *Writers and Company* (New York: Harcourt Brace, 1993), 138–58, rpt. in *Salman Rushdie Interviews: A Sourcebook of His Ideas*, ed. Pradyumna Chauhan (Westport, CT: Greenwood Press, 2001), 128.

10. Salman Rushdie, *Joseph Anton: A Memoir* (New York: Random House, 2012), 50.

11. Salil Tripathi, "The Last—and the Best—Salman Rushdie Interview in India!" *Celebrity* (May 1983): n.p.; rpt. in Michael Reder, ed., *Conversations with Salman Rushdie* (Jackson: University Press of Mississippi, 2000), 25.

12. Shailja Sharma notes that Rushdie's "insider/outsider" position resembles Saleem's, and discusses the writer as a "native informant." "'Precious Gift/Piece of Shit': Salman Rushdie's *The Satanic Verses* and the Revenge of History," in *Scandalous Fictions: The Twentieth-Century Novel in the Public Sphere*, ed. Jago Morrison and Susan Watkins (Hampshire, Eng.: Palgrave-Macmillan, 2006), 140, 145.

13. Salman Rushdie, "Imaginary Homelands," in *Imaginary Homelands: Essays and Criticism, 1981–91* (London: Granta; New York: Viking-Penguin, 1991), 10–11.

14. Salman Rushdie, "The Empire Writes Back with a Vengeance," London *Times*, 3 July 1982, 8F. When pressed, often by interviewers, Rushdie has acknowledged the work of Indian nationals who write in English. See, for example, a 1983 interview conducted by T. Vijay Kumar, "Doing the Dangerous Thing: An Interview with Salman Rushdie," in Meenakshi Mukherjee, ed., *Rushdie's Midnight's Children: A Book of Readings* (Delhi: Pencraft International, 1999), 222–23. For a similar comment in a 2003 interview, see Gauri Viswanathan, "The Literary Rushdie," in *Midnight's Diaspora: Critical Encounters with Salman Rushdie*, ed. Daniel Herwitz and Ashutosh Varshney (Ann Arbor: University of Michigan Press, 2008), 25. Susheila Nasta, *Home Truths: Fictions of the South Asian Diaspora in Britain* (Basingstoke, Eng.: Palgrave-Macmillan, 2002), 137–47, discusses Rushdie's relationship to and significance among "Indian Writers in England" at the time.

15. Rushdie, "Empire," 8F.

16. For discussion of the local and global signifiers in marketing such profiles, see, for instance, Graham Huggan, *The Postcolonial Exotic: Marketing the Margins* (London: Routledge, 2001), and Sarah Brouillette, *Postcolonial Writers and the Global Literary Market* (Basingstoke, Eng.: Palgrave-Macmillan, 2007), 15–25, 44–76. Also see James English, *The Economy of Prestige: Prizes, Awards, and the Circulation of Cultural Capital* (Cambridge, MA: Harvard University Press, 2008), 312–20.

17. Jean-Pierre Durix, "Salman Rushdie," *Kunapipi* 4.2 (1982): 17–26, rpt. in Reder, *Conversations*, 9. Here Rushdie remarks, "This idea that there is a school of Indian-British fiction is a sort of mistake. Writers like Mulk Raj Anand and Narayan have many more affinities to Indian writers in the Indian languages than they do to a writer like me who just happens to be writing in English."

18. Michael Kaufman, "Author from Three Countries," *New York Times Book Review*, 13 November 1983, BR 22.

19. Bonny Mukherjee, "A Big City Novel," *India Today*, 16 May 1981, 126.
20. Rushdie, *Joseph Anton*, 54.
21. Meenakshi Mukherjee, introduction to *Rushdie's* Midnight's Children, 11–12.
22. Amitava Kumar, *Bombay London New York* (London: Routledge, 2002), 23–26, 65.
23. Kaufman, "Author," BR22.
24. Peter Tinniswood, review of *Grimus*, by Salman Rushdie, London *Times*, 21 February 1975, 8D.
25. David Wilson, "Fable-minded," review of *Grimus*, by Salman Rushdie, London *Times Literary Supplement*, 21 February 1975, 185.
26. Ibid.
27. Stuart Jeffries, "'I Am Funny—And So Are My Books,'" London *Guardian*, 11 July 2008, Features 4.
28. Kumkum Sangari, "Interview with Salman Rushdie," *The Book Review* 8.5 (1984): 247–53, rpt. in Pradyumna Chauhan, ed., *Salman Rushdie Interviews: A Sourcebook of His Ideas* (Westport, CT: Greenwood Press, 2001), 72.
29. Jean Ross, Interview with Salman Rushdie, *Contemporary Authors* 111 (1984): 414–17, rpt. Reder, *Conversations*, 4; Rushdie, *Joseph Anton*, 31
30. Sangari, "Interview," 72.
31. Brian Appleyard, "Why Don't We Love Science Fiction?" London *Times*, 2 December 2007, Features 8.
32. See Andrew Teverson, *Salman Rushdie* (Manchester: Manchester University Press, 2007), 112–15, for discussion of critics who have asserted the relationship of the "fantasy" element of *Grimus* and *Midnight's Children*. Judith Leggatt more aggressively questions the distinction between magic realism and science fiction fantasy in "Other Worlds, Other Selves: Science Fiction in Salman Rushdie's *The Ground beneath Her Feet*," *Ariel* 33.1 (2002): 105.
33. Charles Michener, "A Burst of New Fiction," review of *Midnight's Children*, by Salman Rushdie, *Newsweek*, 20 April 1981, 89.
34. V. S. Pritchett, "Two Novels," review of *Midnight's Children*, by Salman Rushdie, *New Yorker*, 27 July 1981, 84.
35. "Rushdie's Parallel View of India through a Brilliant Novel," review of *Midnight's Children*, by Salman Rushdie, *India West*, 12 June 1981, 7.
36. Bill Buford, "Swallowing the Whole World," review of *Midnight's Children*, by Salman Rushdie, *New Statesman*, 1 May 1981, 22.
37. John Leonard, "Books of the Times," review of *Midnight's Children*, by Salman Rushdie, *New York Times*, 23 April 1981, C21.
38. Elaine Feinstein, review of *Midnight's Children*, by Salman Rushdie, London *Times*, 23 April 1981, 10F.
39. Michener, "Burst," 89.
40. Leonard, "Books," C21.
41. Valentine Cummingham, "Nosing Out the Indian Reality," review of *Midnight's Children*, by Salman Rushdie, London *Times Literary Supplement*, 15 May 1981, 535.
42. Anita Desai, "Where Cultures Clash by Night," review of *Midnight's Children*, by Salman Rushdie, *Washington Post Book World*, 15 March 1981, 1.
43. Desai, "Where Cultures," 13.
44. Robert Towers, "On the Indian World Mountain," review of *Midnight's Children*, by Salman Rushdie, *New York Review of Books*, 24 September 1981, 28.
45. Maria Couto, "*Midnight's Children* and Parents: The Search for Indo-British Identity," *Encounter* 58.2 (1982): 61.
46. Ibid., 63.

47. B. K. Joshi and Victoria Glendinning, "It May Be Long But It's Not Overwritten," *Times of India*, 1 November 1982, 8.
48. N. J. Nanporia, "I Have Always Been a Public Property," *Times of India*, 3 July 1982, 8F.
49. Sunil Sethi, "An Indian Scheherazade," review of *Midnight's Children*, by Salman Rushdie, *India Today*, 16 May 1981, 126.
50. Ibid., 127.
51. Bonny Mukherjee, "Big City Novel," 126.
52. "Rushdie's Parallel View," 7.
53. Ibid., n.p. Gargi (1916–2003), actually wrote in Punjabi and earned renown as a playwright. His works were translated into English, as well as other languages.
54. Bonny Mukherjee, "Big City Novel," 127.
55. Ibid.
56. For a more recent treatment of Rushdie's representation of subcontinental history, with particular attention to feminist and grassroots movements, see Nicole Weickgennant Thiara, *Salman Rushdie and Indian Historiography: Writing the Nation into Being* (Basingstoke, Eng.: Palgrave-Macmillan, 2009).
57. Uma Parameswaran, "Handcuffed to History: Salman Rushdie's Art," *Ariel* 14.4 (1983): 34–45.
58. Wimal Dissanayake, "Towards a Decolonised English: South Asian Creativity in Fiction," *World Englishes* 4.2 (1985): 241.
59. John Stephens, "*Midnight's Children*: The Parody of an Indian Novel," *Journal of the South Pacific Association for Commonwealth Literature and Language Studies* 81 (1985): 184–208.
60. Parameswaran, "Handcuffed," 36.
61. Nancy E. Batty, "The Art of Suspense: Rushdie's 1,001 (Mid-)Nights," *Ariel* 18.3 (1987): 49–65.
62. C. Kanaganayakam, "Myth and Fabulousity in *Midnight's Children*," *Dalhousie Review* 67.1 (1987): 87, 92.
63. Jean-Pierre Durix, "Magic Realism in *Midnight's Children*," *Commonwealth Essays and Studies* 8 (1985): 57–63.
64. Francis Roh, "Magic Realism: Post-Expressionism," in Lois Parkinson Zamora and Wendy B. Faris, eds., *Magical Realism: Theory, History, Community* (Durham: Duke University Press, 1995), 15–31.
65. Stephen Slemon, "Magic Realism as Post-colonial Discourse," *Canadian Literature* 116 (1988): 9.
66. Ibid., 9, 12. For subsequent evaluations in relation to *Midnight's Children*, see for example, Wendy B. Faris, "Scheherazade's Children: Magical Realism and Postmodern Fiction," 163–190, and Theo L. Daaen, "Magical Realism and Postmodernism: Decentering Privileged Centers," 191–208, both in Zamora and Faris, *Magical Realism*; Neil ten Kortenaar, *Self, Nation, and Text in Salman Rushdie's* Midnight's Children (Montreal and Kingston: McGill-Queen's University Press, 2004), 48–60; Vijay Mishra, *The Literature of the Indian Diaspora: Theorizing the Diasporic Imaginary* (London: Routledge, 2008), 214–18; Ursula Kluwick, *Exploring Magic Realism in Salman Rushdie's Fiction* (Oxon, Eng.: Routledge, 2011).
67. Salman Rushdie, interview, "Charlie Rose Show," Public Broadcasting System, 30 June 2008.
68. Sangari, "Interview," 63–64.
69. Wachtel, "Salman Rushdie," 128.
70. Rushdie, "Imaginary Homelands," 16; Aijaz Ahmad, *In Theory: Classes, Nations, Literatures* (London: New Left-Verso, 1992), 11.

71. Timothy Brennan, *Salman Rushdie and the Third World: Myths of the Nation* (London: Macmillan, 1989). In the first monograph devoted to Rushdie, Brennan distinguishes him from earlier antinationalists to argue for his use of a critical postmodernism, aimed at the metropolis but aligned with a subaltern position.

72. Huggan, *Postcolonial Exotic*, 59–82.

73. Views of Rushdie as a pastiche appropriator or a critic of power structures—from variously designated locations—continue to dominate the critical landscape. For a more recent overviews, see Teverson, *Salman Rushdie*, 45–54. Vijay Mishra strikes a balance in his discussion of Rushdie's language, in "Rushdie-Wushdie: Salman Rushdie's Hobson-Jobson." *New Literary History* 40 (2009): 385–410.

74. Timothy Brennan, "The Cultural Politics of Rushdie Criticism: All or Nothing," in *Critical Essays on Salman Rushdie*, ed. M. Keith Booker (New York: G. K. Hall, 1999), 110, 122.

75. Kumkum Sangari, *Politics of the Possible: Essays on Gender, History, Narratives, Colonial English* (London: Anthem South Asian Studies-Wimbledon, 2002), 22. Sangari connects Rushdie's "doubleness" to his middle-class Indian parentage.

76. Bishnupriya Ghosh, "An Invitation to Indian Postmodernity: Rushdie's English Vernacular as a Situated Cultural Hybridity," in *Critical Essays on Salman Rushdie*, ed. M. Keith Booker, (New York: G. K. Hall, 1999), 129.

77. Clifford Geertz, "Deep Play: Notes on the Balinese Cockfight," in *Interpretive Social Science: A Reader*, ed. Paul Rabinow and William Sullivan (Berkeley: University of California Press, 1979), 181–223.

78. Salman Rushdie, *Midnight's Children*, 1981 (New York: Penguin, 1991), 11. Subsequent citations from this source will appear parenthetically in the text.

79. Owen Lynch, "Introduction: Emotions in Theoretical Context," in *Divine Passions: The Social Construction of Emotion in India* (Berkeley: University of California Press, 1990), 22. Owen contrasts the materialization or objectification of emotions with the tendency to "somatize" affect in China and to "internalize" it in the West. I argue that *Midnight's Children* uses both types of representation to embody the spiritual-medical hermeneutic.

80. Neil ten Kortenaar notes that Rushdie's metaphors often attribute physical qualities to abstracted or inner states. *Self, Nation, and Text*, 49.

81. Lynch, *Divine Passions*, 19.

82. Ibid., 10–11.

83. Kleinman, *Social Origins*, 56.

84. Lynch, *Divine Passions*, 22.

85. McKim Marriott, ed., "Constructing an Indian Ethnosociology," in *India through Hindu Categories* (New Delhi: Sage, 1990), 17.

86. Ibid., 18.

87. Kleinman, *Social Origins*, 55–56.

88. Unless otherwise attributed, the information about Vedic medicine in this and the previous paragraph is drawn from R. B. Amber and M. Babey Brooke, *The Pulse in Occident and Orient: Its Philosophy and Practice in India, China, Iran, and the West* (New York: Santa Barbara Press; London: Dawsons, 1966): 4–9, 52–54; P. N. V. Kurup and K. Raghunathan, "Human Physiology and Ayurveda," in *The Science of Medicine and Physiological Concepts in Ancient and Medieval India*, ed. N. H. Keswani (New Delhi: All-India Institute of Medical Sciences, 1974), 67–68; Richard Lannoy, *The Speaking Tree: A Study of Indian Culture and Society* (London: Oxford University Press, 1971), 95; and Judy F. Pugh, "Person and Situation in North Indian Counseling: The Case of Astrology, in *South Asian Systems of Healing*, ed. E. Valentine Daniel and Judy Pugh (Leiden, Neth.: E. J. Brill, 1984), 88–89.

89. Anki Mukherjee explores Saleem's sensorium as allied to technical media, and relates them to a Freudian understanding of psychic and somatic relations. "Fissured Skin, Inner Ear Radio, and a Telepathic Nose: The Senses of Media in Salman Rushdie's *Midnight's Children*," *Paragraph* 29.3 (2003): 55–76.

90. Christopher Pinney, *Camera Indica: The Social Life of Indian Photographs* (Chicago: University of Chicago Press, 1997), 199.

91. Ibid., 200.

92. Marriott, "Constructing," 18.

93. Rushdie, *Joseph Anton*, 54.

94. Meenakshi Mukherjee, "The Anxiety of Indianness: Our Novels in English," *Economic and Political Weekly*, 27 November 1993, 2608.

95. Rushdie, "Imaginary Homelands," 16.

96. Dieter Riemenschneider, "History and the Individual in Anita Desai's *Clear Light of Day* and Salman Rushdie's *Midnight's Children*," in *The New Indian Novel in English: A Study of the 1980s*, ed. Viney Kirpal (New Delhi: Allied, 1990), 188, 195–96.

97. David Kalupahana, *The Principles of Buddhist Psychology* (Albany: State University of New York Press, 1987), 198.

98. Shaul Bassi, "Salman Rushdie's Special Effects," in *Co-terminous Worlds: Magical Realism and Contemporary Post-Colonial Literature in English*, ed. Elsa Linguanti et al. (Amsterdam: Rodopi, 1999), 51. While I am proposing an interpretation at odds with her proposal of cinematic "special effects" to characterize these procedures, Bassi presents an astute anatomy of "magic realism," 59.

99. Rushdie, "Imaginary Homelands," 10.

100. Ibid., 11.

101. Salman Rushdie, *Shame* (New York: Knopf, 1983), 28.

102. Josna Rege, "Victim into Protagonist? *Midnight's Children* and the Post-Rushdie National Narratives of the Eighties," *Studies in the Novel* 29 (1997), rpt. in Meenakshi Mukherjee, *Rushdie's* Midnight's Children, 183.

103. Meenakshi Mukherjee, *Rushdie's* Midnight's Children, 10.

104. Harish Trivedi, "Salman the Funtoosh: Magic Bilingualism in *Midnight's Children*," in Meenakshi Mukherjee, *Rushdie's* Midnight's Children, 73.

105. John Haffenden, ed., "Salman Rushdie," *Novelists in Interview* (London: Metheun, 1985), 231–61, rpt. in Reder, *Conversations*, 43.

106. Uma Mahadevan-Dasgupta, "Milestone: Midnight Turns 21," *Statesman* (India), 21 October 2002, n.p.

107. Salman Rushdie, "Damme, This Is the Oriental Scene for You!" *New Yorker*, 23 & 27 July 1997, 52.

108. Ibid., 50.

109. Trivedi, "Salman the Funtoosh," 77. *Aadhi Raat Ki Sataneen* was published by Priyadarshan.

110. Alejo Carpentier, "On the Marvellous Real in America," in Zamora and Faris, *Magical Realism*, 75–88.

Chapter 3

1. Umberto Eco, *The Aesthetics of* Chaosmos: *The Middle Ages of James Joyce* [Le poetiche di Joyce. 1962], trans. Ellen Esrock, rpt. (Cambridge, MA: Harvard University Press, 1989), 4.

2. William T. Noon, *Joyce and Aquinas* (New Haven: Yale University Press, 1963); Sullivan, *Joyce among the Jesuits*; Robert Boyle, *James Joyce's Pauline Vision: A Catholic Exposition* (Carbondale: Southern Illinois University Press, 1978). Brooker, *Joyce's Critics*, 119–20, relates Hugh Kenner's early work to this tradition, through his view of *Ulysses* as "an anatomy of religious corruption."

3. Laura Doyle, *Bordering on the Body: The Racial Matrix of Modern Fiction and Culture* (Oxford: Oxford University Press, 1994), 175.

4. Ira Nadel, *Joyce and the Jews: Culture and Texts* (Iowa City: University of Iowa Press, 1989); Bryan Cheyette, *Constructions of 'the Jew' in English Literature and Society: Racial Representations, 1875–1945* (Cambridge: Cambridge University Press, 1993); Neil Davison, *James Joyce, Ulysses, and the Construction of Jewish Identity: Culture, Biography and 'the Jew' in Modernist Europe* (Cambridge: Cambridge University Press, 1998); Marilyn Reizbaum, *James Joyce's Judaic Other* (Stanford: Stanford University Press, 1999).

5. Andrew Gibson has been a leading practitioner of this approach, in *Joyce's Revenge: History, Politics, and Aesthetics in* Ulysses (Oxford: Oxford University Press, 2002), and in Gibson and Len Platt, eds., *Joyce, Ireland, Britain* (Gainesville: University Press of Florida, 2006). Also see Len Platt, *Joyce and the Anglo-Irish: A Study of Joyce and the Literary Revival* (Amsterdam: Rodopi, 1998).

6. Nash, *James Joyce and the Act of Reception*, 62–96; Platt, *Joyce and the Anglo-Irish*, 74.

7. Roy Gottfried, *Joyce's Misbelief* (Gainesville: University Press of Florida, 2008); Lernout, *Help My Unbelief*; Pericles Lewis, *Religious Experience and the Modernist Novel* (Cambridge: Cambridge University Press, 2010). Focused particularly on religious hermeneutics and genre are Gian Balsamo, *Joyce's Messianism: Dante, Negative Existence, and the Messianic Self* (Columbia: University of South Carolina Press, 2004) and Stephen Sicari, *Joyce's Modernist Allegory* (Columbia: University of South Carolina Press, 2001).

8. Hugh McLeod, "Protestantism and British National Identity 1815–1945," in *Nation and Religion: Perspectives on Europe and Asia*, ed. Peter van der Veer and Hartmut Lehman (Princeton: Princeton University Press, 1999), 47.

9. Asad, *Genealogies*, 125.

10. Gibson, *Joyce's Revenge*, 7.

11. Donald Theall, *James Joyce's Techno-Poetics* (Toronto: University of Toronto Press, 1997), 6.

12. Christine Froula, *Modernism's Body: Sex, Culture and Joyce* (New York: Columbia University Press, 1996), 90.

13. Robert Miles, *Gothic Writing, 1750–1820* (London: Routledge, 1993), 108.

14. Gibson, *Joyce's Revenge*, 39.

15. Susan Griffin, *Anti-Catholicism and Nineteenth-Century Fiction* (Cambridge: Cambridge University Press, 2004), 4.

16. Ibid., 5.

17. Linda Colley, *Britons: Forging the Nation, 1707–1837*, rev. ed. (New Haven: Yale University Press, 2009), 4, 8.

18. Griffin, *Anti-Catholicism*, 5.

19. Nash, *James Joyce and the Act of Reception*, 72.

20. David Glover, "The 'Spectrality Effect' in Early Modernism," in *Gothic Modernisms*, ed. Andrew Smith and Jeff Wallace (Basingstoke, Eng.: Palgrave-Macmillan, 2001), 32.

21. For a critique of the alignment of home with immaturity and hence premodernity, see Vincent Cheng, "'Terrible Queer Creatures': Joyce, Cosmopolitanism, and the Inauthentic Irishman" in *James Joyce and the Fabrication of an Irish Identity*, European Joyce Studies 11, ed. Michael Patrick Gillespie (Amsterdam: Rodopi, 2001), 27, n. 29.

22. Hugh Kenner, *Ulysses* (London: Allen & Unwin, 1980), 17; Doyle, *Bordering on the Body*, 172.

23. James Joyce, *Ulysses*, 1922, ed. Hans Walter Gabler, Wolfhard Steppe, and Claus Melchior (New York: Random House-Vintage, 1986). Subsequent citations from this source will appear parenthetically in the text.

24. Froula, *Modernism's Body*, 103.

25. Julia Kristeva, *Powers of Horror: An Essay on Abjection*, trans. Leon S. Radios (New York: Columbia University Press, 1982), 3–4.

26. Miles, *Gothic Writing*; Donna Heiland, *Gothic and Gender: An Introduction* (Oxford: Blackwell, 2004); Margot Backus, *The Gothic Family Romance: Heterosexuality, Child Sacrifice, and the Anglo-Irish Colonial Order* (Durham: Duke University Press, 1999); Helene Moglen, *The Trauma of Gender: A Feminist Theory of the English Novel* (Berkeley: University of California Press, 2001).

27. Joan Jastrebski, "Pig Dialectics: Women's Bodies as Performed Dialectical Images in the Circe Episode of *Ulysses*," in Gillespie, *James Joyce*, 167–68.

28. Claire Kahane, "The Gothic Mirror," in *The (M)other Tongue: Essays in Feminist Psychoanalytic Interpretation*, ed. Shirley Nelson Garner, Claire Kahane, and Madelon Sprengnether (Ithaca: Cornell University Press, 1985), 336.

29. Ibid., 347.

30. Nash, *James Joyce and the Act of Reception*, 73, 94, discusses the spectral presence of Joyce's mother, his first "audience," as an additional context. Balsamo, *Joyce's Messianism*, 83ff., examines the maternal vampiric in relation to negative theology.

31. John McCourt, "Queering the Revivalist's Pitch: Joycean Engagements with Primitivism," in *Irish Modernism and the Global Primitive*, ed. Maria McGarrity and Claire Culleton (Basingstoke, Eng.: Palgrave-Macmillan, 2009), 32. For recent discussions of Haines's ethnographic position, see Gregory Castle, *Modernism and the Celtic Revival* (Cambridge: Cambridge University Press, 2001), 213–17, and Vincent Cheng, *Joyce, Race, and Empire*, (Cambridge: Cambridge University Press, 1995), 151–62.

32. Nash, *James Joyce and the Act of Reception*, 44.

33. Ibid.

34. Backus, *The Gothic Family*, 97.

35. Nash, *James Joyce and the Act of Reception*, 45.

36. Gibson, *Joyce's Revenge*, 23, 35.

37. Ibid., 26.

38. Judith Wilt, "The Imperial Mouth: Imperialism, the Gothic, and Science Fiction," *Journal of Popular Culture* 14 (1981): 618–28.

39. Anne McClintock, *Imperial Leather: Race, Gender and Sex in the Colonial Contest* (London: Routledge, 1995), 240–45.

40. John Hoberman, "Otto Weininger and the Critique of Jewish Masculinity," in *Jews and Gender: Responses to Otto Weininger*, ed. Nancy Harrowitz and Barbara Hyams (Philadelphia: Temple University Press, 1995), 141.

41. Enda Duffy, *The Subaltern Ulysses* (Minneapolis: University of Minnesota Press, 1994), 154–55.

42. Cheryl Herr, *Joyce's Anatomy of Culture* (Urbana: University of Illinois Press, 1986), 9, 119–20.

43. See Vincent Cheng, *Joyce, Race, and Empire* (Cambridge: Cambridge University Press, 1995) for a discussion of primitivist and Orientalist imagery.

44. Asad, *Genealogies*, 130–31.

45. Ibid., 112.

46. Leclerq, *The Love of Learning*, 90.
47. Sarah McNamer, *Affective Meditation and the Invention of Medieval Compassion* (Philadelphia: University of Pennsylvania Press, 2010), 12.
48. Ibid., 12, 29.
49. Deane, *Strange Country*, 50.
50. Margot Backus, "Sexual Figures and Historical Repression in 'The Dead,'" in Gillespie, *James Joyce*, 114, n. 6.
51. K. Theodore Hoppen, *Ireland since 1800: Conflict and Conformity* (London: Longman, 1989), 144–52. Also see Gibson, *Joyce's Revenge*, 83, and Lernout, *Help My Unbelief*, 42, 48.
52. Asad, *Genealogies*, 130–31.
53. Martin Jay, *Downcast Eyes: The Denigration of Vision in Twentieth-Century French Thought* (Berkeley: University of California Press, 1993), 113, 151.
54. Jonathan Crary, *Techniques of the Observer: On Vision and Modernity in the Nineteenth Century* (Cambridge, MA: MIT Press, 1990), 150.
55. Sara Danius, *The Senses of Modernism: Technology, Perception, and Aesthetics* (Ithaca: Cornell University Press, 2002), 148, 152. Also see Theall, *James Joyce's Techno-Poetics*, for a discussion of machinic technologies, though he focuses primarily on *Finnegans Wake*.
56. Danius, *Senses*, 156–58.
57. Ibid., 152.
58. Herr, *Joyce's Anatomy*, 157–58. Also see Cheng, *Joyce, Race, and Empire*, 174, and Michael Pickering, on the status of blackface as a class and ethnic marker rather than an exclusively epidermal racial representation, "White Skin, Black Masks: 'Nigger' Minstrelsy," in *Music Hall: Performance and Style*, ed. J. S. Bratton (Philadelphia: Milton Keynes-Open University Press, 1986), 84.
59. Caroline Walker Bynum, *The Resurrection of the Body in Western Christianity, 200–1336* (New York: Columbia University Press, 1995), 11.
60. Suren Lalvani, *Photography, Vision and the Production of Modern Bodies* (Albany: State University of New York Press, 1996), 5.
61. Suzannah Biernoff, *Sight and Embodiment in the Middle Ages* (Basingstoke, Eng.: Palgrave-Macmillan, 2002), 97–98.
62. Joyce, *A Portrait*, 139–40.
63. Ibid., 158.
64. Ibid., 158–59.
65. Ibid., 131–32.
66. Cf. Asad, *Genealogies*, 16; also see Talal Asad, "Responses," in David Scott and Charles Hirschkind, eds., *Powers of the Secular Modern: Talal Asad and His Interlocutors* (Stanford: Stanford University Press, 2006), 239.
67. Doyle, *Bordering on the Body*, 188.
68. Joyce, *A Portrait*, 253; Kenner, *Ulysses*, 16.
69. Cf. Bishop, *Joyce's Book of the Dark*, 66.
70. Gibson, *Joyce's Revenge*, 104–6, 161–70.
71. Joyce, *A Portrait*, 93.
72. Feminist critics have long pointed to the chapter's phallogocentric topos as a portrayal of male anxiety and envy over female procreation: this literary language showcases its inability to depict an actual birth. See, for instance, Sandra Gilbert and Susan Gubar, "Sexual Linguistics: Gender, Language, Sexuality," *New Literary History* 16 (1985): 518–19, 534–35; Joseph Boone, "Staging Sexuality: Repression, Representation, and 'Interior' States in *Ulysses*," in

Joyce: The Return of the Repressed, ed. Susan Stanford Friedman (Ithaca: Cornell University Press, 1993), 202–3; Karen Lawrence, "Compromising Letters: Joyce and Women," *Western Humanities Review* 42 (1988), 4, 11; Froula, *Modernism's Body*, 172–96.

73. Duffy, *Subaltern Ulysses*, 185.
74. Gibson, *Joyce's Revenge*, 167–68.
75. Ibid., 177–82.
76. Ibid., 150–62.
77. Colley, *Britons*, 333, 330.
78. For related readings, see Marx, *The Modernist Novel*, 19–20.
79. Herr, *Joyce's Anatomy*, 104–20, 158.
80. Jastrebski, "Pig Dialectics," 153.

Chapter 4

1. Salman Rushdie, *The Satanic Verses*, 1988 (New York: Viking, 1989), 3. Subsequent citations from this source will appear parenthetically in the text.

2. Ghosh, *When Borne Across*, 15, notes the scene's resemblance to one from *Paris Ki Ek Shyam* [An evening in Paris (1967)]. Ashley Dawson, *Mongrel Nation: Diasporic Culture and the Making of Postcolonial Britain* (Ann Arbor: University of Michigan Press, 2007), 130–31, discusses Gibreel as a Bollywood hero.

3. Geeta Kapur, "Ravi Varma: Representational Dilemmas of a Nineteenth-Century Indian Painter," *Journal of Arts and Ideas* 17–18 (June 1989): 68; Ashish Rajadhyaksha, "The Phalke Era: Conflict of Traditional Form and Modern Technology," *Journal of Arts and Ideas* 17–18 (1989): 53–58, 67ff.; Rachel Dwyer and Divia Patel, *Cinema India: The Visual Culture of Hindi Film* (Newark: Rutgers University Press; London: Reaktion Books, 2002), 43–44.

4. Lawrence Babb, "Glancing: Visual Interaction in Hinduism," *Journal of Anthropological Research* 37 (1981): 387; Diana Eck, *Darśan: Seeing the Divine Image in India* (Chambersburg, PA: Anima Books, 1981), 7.

5. Sumita Chakravarty, *National Identity in Indian Popular Cinema, 1947–87* (New Delhi: Oxford University Press, 1998), 4–5.

6. Ibid., 7.

7. Christopher Pinney, "Public, Popular, and Other Cultures," in *Pleasure in the Nation: The History, Politics, and Consumption of Public Culture in India*, ed. Rachel Dwyer and Christopher Pinney (Oxford: Oxford University Press, 2001), 5–10; Sandria Freitag, "Visions of the Nation: Theorizing the Nexus between Creation, Consumption, and Participation in the Public Sphere," in *Pleasure in the Nation: The History, Politics, and Consumption of Public Culture in India*, 35ff.

8. Parama Roy, *Indian Traffic: Identities in Question in Colonial and Postcolonial India* (Berkeley: University of California Press, 1998), 155, 165; cf. Chakravarty, *National Identity*, 165.

9. Jerrold Hogle, "The Gothic Ghost of the Counterfeit and the Progress of Abjection," in *A Companion to the Gothic*, ed. David Punter (Oxford: Blackwell, 2000), 290.

10. Ibid., 299.
11. Certeau, *The Practice of Everyday Life*, xix.
12. Judith Halberstam, *Skin Shows: Gothic Horror and the Technology of Monsters* (Durham: Duke University Press, 1995), 2.
13. Ibid.

14. Ibid., 63–64.

15. Ibid.

16. Ana Cristina Mendes, ed., *Salman Rushdie and Visual Culture: Celebrating Impurity, Disrupting Borders* (Oxon, Eng.: Routledge, 2011) gives sustained attention to Rushdie's visual techniques and discourses. Of pertinence to my discussion here are Mendes's "Salman Rushdie's 'Epico-Mythico-Tragico-Comico-Super-Sexy-High-Masala Art' or Considerations on Undisciplining the Boundaries," 1–11; Florian Stadtler's "Nobody from Bombay Should Be without a Basic Film Vocabulary: *Midnight's Children* and the Visual Culture of Popular Cinema," 123–38; and Cristina Sandru's "Visual Technologies in Rushdie's Fiction: Envisioning the Present in the Imagological Age," 137–57, all in Mendes, *Salman Rushdie*.

17. Ravi Vasudevan, "Addressing the Spectator of a 'Third World' National Cinema: The Bombay 'Social Film' of the 1940s and 1950s," *Screen* 36 (1995): 311.

18. Vijay Mishra, *Bollywood Cinema: Temples of Desire* (London: Routledge, 2002), 38.

19. For an extended analysis of this term, see Vijay Mishra, Peter Jeffery, and Brian Shoesmith, "The Actor as Parallel Text in Bombay Cinema," *Quarterly Review of Film and Video* 11 (1989): 49–67.

20. Pinney, "Public, Popular, and Other Cultures," 12; Mishra, Jeffery, and Shoesmith, "The Actor as Parallel Text," 49–67.

21. Behroze Gandhy and Rosie Thomas, "Three Indian Film Stars," in *Stardom: Industry of Desire*, ed. Christine Gledhill (London: Routledge, 1991), 107.

22. Mishra, Jeffery, and Shoesmith, "The Actor as Parallel Text," 52.

23. Rushdie, *Joseph Anton*, 70.

24. Chakravarty, *National Identity*, 3; Mishra, *Bollywood*, 125–57; Roy, *Indian Traffic*, 152–53.

25. Sara Suleri, "Contraband Histories: Salman Rushdie and the Embodiment of Blasphemy," *Yale Review* 78 (1989): 618.

26. Mukul Kesevan, "Urdu, Awadh, and the Tawaif: The Islamicate Roots of Indian Cinema," in *Forging Identities: Gender, Community, and the State in India*, ed. Zoya Hasan (Boulder: Westview Press; New Delhi: Kali for Women, 1994), 246–53.

27. Roy, *Indian Traffic*, 165–68; Thomas 11ff. For more on the construction of Nargis' career and "star text," see Gandhy and Thomas, "Three Indian Film Stars," 116–23, and Rosie Thomas, "Sanctity and Scandal: The Mythologization of Mother India," *Quarterly Review of Film and Video* 11 (1989): 11–30.

28. Ravi Vasudevan, "The Politics of Cultural Address in a 'Transitional' Cinema: A Case Study of Indian Popular Cinema," in *Reinventing Film Studies*, ed. Christine Gledhill and Linda Williams (Oxford: Oxford University Press; London: Arnold, 2000), 139–40. See Hema Ramachandran, "Salman Rushdie's *The Satanic Verses*: Hearing the Postcolonial Cinematic Novel," *Journal of Commonwealth Literature* 40.3 (2005): 115, for a more conservative reading of the darsanic gaze.

29. Babb, "Glancing," 387–88.

30. See Ramachandran, "Salman Rushdie's *The Satanic Verses*," 105.

31. Dawson, *Mongrel Nation*, 131.

32. Vasudevan, "Addressing the Spectator," 307.

33. Geeta Kapur, "Mythic Material in Indian Cinema," *Journal of Arts and Ideas* 14–15 (1987): 82.

34. Pinney, *Camera Indica*, 199.

35. Ibid., 200.

36. Walter Benjamin, "The Work of Art in the Age of Mechanical Reproduction," in *Illuminations*, ed. Hannah Arendt, trans. Harry Zohn (New York: Schoken, Random House, 1969), 221.

37. Cf. Malek Alloula, *The Colonial Harem*, trans. Myrna Godzich and Wald Godzich (Minneapolis: University of Minnesota Press, 1986).

38. Wilt, "Imperial Mouth," 625.

39. Richard Burkhardt, *The Spirit of the System: Lamarck and Evolutionary Biology* (Cambridge, MA: Harvard University Press, 1977), 152–57.

40. James English, *Comic Transactions: Literature, Humor, and the Politics of Community in Twentieth-Century Britain* (Ithaca: Cornell University Press, 1994), 236.

41. Jean Baudrillard, *Simulation and Simulacra*, trans. Sheila Faria Glaser (Ann Arbor: University of Michigan Press, 1994), 121.

42. Ibid., 122.

43. Anne Anlin Cheng, "The Melancholy of Race," *Kenyon Review* 19 (1998): 55; also see Anne Anlin Cheng, *The Melancholy of Race* (Oxford: Oxford University Press, 2000), 125.

44. Mishra, *Bollywood*, 40.

45. Annamarie Schimmel, *And Muhammad Is His Messenger: The Veneration of the Prophet in Islamic Piety* (Chapel Hill: University of North Carolina Press, 1985), 32–34.

46. Suleri, "Contraband," 619.

47. Devji, "Apologetic Modernity," 55.

48. Vasudevan, "The Politics of Cultural Address," 140.

49. Stephen Morton, "Metaphors of the Secular in the Fiction of Salman Rushdie," reads this tension as a "significant . . . trope" of secularism's instability, in *Metaphor and Diaspora in Contemporary Writing*, ed. Jonathan P. A. Sell (Basingstoke, Eng.: Palgrave-Macmillan, 2012), 151.

50. Slavoj Žižek, "Cyberspace, or, How to Traverse the Fantasy in the Age of the Retreat of the Big Other," *Public Culture* 10 (1998): 485.

51. Suleri, "Contraband," 606.

52. Gayatri Chakravorty Spivak, "Reading *The Satanic Verses*," *Public Culture* 2 (1989): 79.

53. Suleri, "Contraband," 606ff; cf. Sara Suleri, *The Rhetoric of English India* (Chicago: University of Chicago Press, 1992), 112–113, 132–48.

54. Simon Gikandi, *Maps of Englishness: Writing Identity in the Culture of Colonialism* (New York: Columbia University Press, 1996), 200.

55. Spivak, "Reading," 83; Suleri, "Contraband," 620–21.

56. Ian Almond, *The New Orientalists: Postmodern Representations of Islam from Foucault to Baudrillard* (London: I. B. Tauris, 2007), 107.

57. Feroza Jussawalla, "Rushdie's *Dastan-e-Dilruba: The Satanic Verses* as Rushdie's Love Letter to Islam," in *Critical Essays on Salman Rushdie*, edited by M. Keith Booker (New York: G. K. Hall, 1999), 100.

58. Ibid., 81–84.

59. Jean-Françoise Lyotard, *The Postmodern Condition: A Report on Knowledge*, trans. Geoff Bennington and Brian Massumi (Minneapolis: University of Minnesota Press, 1984), 77. For a discussion of the novel's postmodernity in relation to the gothic sublime, see Maria Beville, "The Gothic Postmodernist 'Waste Land' of Ellowen Deeowen: Salman Rushdie's Nightmarish Visions of a Postmodern Metropolis," *Nebula* 4. 1 (2007): 1–18.

60. Lyotard, *The Postmodern Condition*, 79.

61. Jay, *Downcast Eyes*, 582.

Chapter 5

1. Cf. Asad, *Genealogies*, 16.
2. Geertz, "Deep Play," 229.
3. "Is Rushdie Just the Beginning?" London *Times*, 28 May 1989, 22; qtd. in Dawson, *Mongrel Nation*, 122–23.
4. Certeau, *Practice*, xix.
5. See Adam Parkes, *Modernism and the Theater of Censorship* (Oxford: Oxford University Press, 1996).
6. For treatments of *Ulysses*' career in America, see Paul Vanderham, *Joyce and Censorship* (New York: New York University Press, 1988); and Jeffrey Segall, *Joyce in America: Cultural Politics and the Trials of* Ulysses (Berkeley: University of California Press, 1993). Joseph Brooker describes the full arc of the novel's popular and critical career in *Joyce's Critics*.
7. Brooker, *Joyce's Critics*, 186–87, notes that *Ulysses* was not an officially proscribed book, according to the Irish censorship board, and therefore was initially excluded from circulation under British law. For discussions of *Ulysses*' reception as indecent and therefore anti-Irish Catholic, see Katherine Mullin, "English Vice and Irish Vigilance: The Nationality of Obscenity in *Ulysses*," in Gibson and Platt, *Joyce, Ireland, Britain*, 68–82. Also pertinent is Celia Marshik, *British Modernism and Censorship* (Cambridge: Cambridge University Press, 2006), 126–66. Significant work on these issues also includes Katherine Mullin's *James Joyce, Sexuality, and Social Purity*; John Nash's *James Joyce and the Act of Reception*; and John Nash, ed., *Joyce's Audiences* (Amsterdam: Rodopi, 2002).
8. Brooker, *Joyce's Critics*, 28, 32.
9. Sisley Huddleston, "*Ulysses*," review of *Ulysses*, by James Joyce, *Observer*, 5 March 1922, 4, in Deming, *James Joyce*, 216.
10. Mullin, "English Vice," 78.
11. John Nash, "Irish Audiences and English Readers: The Cultural Politics of Shane Leslie's *Ulysses*' Reviews," in Gibson and Platt, *Joyce, Ireland, Britain*, 146. Nash supplies a full description of Leslie's career and cultural location.
12. Notoriously, in the English periodical, Leslie compares *Ulysses* to a Fenian bomb on the prisonhouse of the British canon. He states, "English critics will be divided [about the novel]. . . . Ireland's writers, whose own language was legislatively and slowly destroyed by England, will cynically contemplate an attempted Clerkenwell explosion in the well-guarded, well-built classical prison of English literature." Review of *Ulysses*, by James Joyce, *Quarterly Review* 238 (October 1922): 234.
13. Shane Leslie [Domini Canis], review of *Ulysses*, by James Joyce, *Dublin Review* 171 (July–September 1922): 113, 119.
14. Camille McCole, "*Ulysses*," review of *Ulysses*, by James Joyce, *Catholic World*, March 1934, 725, 724.
15. Arnold Bennett, "Concerning James Joyce's *Ulysses*," review of *Ulysses*, by James Joyce, *Bookman* [New York], August 1922, 570.
16. Aramis, "The Scandal of *Ulysses*," *Sporting Times*, 1 April 1922, 4, in Deming, *James Joyce* 192, 194.
17. Walkowitz, *Cosmopolitan Style*, 58–59.
18. Joseph Valente, "James Joyce and the Cosmopolitan Sublime," in *Joyce and the Subject of History*, ed. Mark Wollaeger, Victor Luftig, and Robert Spoo (Ann Arbor: University of Michigan Press, 1996), 61–62.
19. Certeau, *Practice*, xix.

20. Cf. Nikolas Rose, *Inventing Ourselves: Psychology, Power, and Personhood* (Cambridge: Cambridge University Press, 1998), 38; Michel Foucault, *The History of Sexuality*, vol. 3, *The Care of the Self*, trans. Robert Hurley (New York: Pantheon-Random House, 1986), 66; and Michel Foucault, *Technologies of the Self: A Seminar with Michel Foucault*, ed. Luther Martin, Huck Gutman, and Patrick Hutton (Amherst: University of Massachusetts Press, 1988), 18.

21. Kleinman, *The Illness Narratives*, 26.

22. Jay, *Downcast Eyes*, 113, 151.

23. Laurence Emery, "The *Ulysses* of Mr. James Joyce," review of *Ulysses*, by James Joyce, *Claxon*, (winter 1923–24), 15, in Deming, *James Joyce*, 293.

24. Edmund Wilson, "*Ulysses*," review of *Ulysses*, by James Joyce, *New Republic*, 5 July 1922, 164.

25. Joseph Collins, "James Joyce's Amazing Chronicle," review of *Ulysses*, by James Joyce, *New York Times Book Review*, 28 May 1922, 6.

26. "A New Ulysses," review of *Ulysses*, by James Joyce, London *Evening News*, 8 April 1922, 4, in Deming, *James Joyce*, 194.

27. Robert Cantwell, "The Influence of James Joyce," *New Republic*, 27 December 1933, 200.

28. Crary, *Techniques*, 125–127.

29. S. P. B. Mais, "An Irish Revel: and Some Flappers," review of *Ulysses*, by James Joyce, London *Daily Express*, 25 March 1922, n.p., in Deming, *James Joyce*, 191.

30. Cf. Crary, *Techniques*, 67.

31. Wyndham Lewis, *Time and Western Man* (Boston: Beacon Press, 1957 [1927]), 122, 118.

32. McCole, "*Ulysses*," 723.

33. "Mr. Joyce and the Catholic Tradition," *New Witness*, 4 August 1922, 70–71, in Deming, *James Joyce*, 272–73.

34. H. G. Wells, *Letters of James Joyce*, letter, rev. ed., ed. Stuart Gilbert (London: Faber and Faber, 1966), 274, 275.

35. Herbert Gorman, *James Joyce: The First Forty Years* (New York: Farrar and Rinehart, 1939), 297.

36. Ford Madox Ford, "*Ulysses* and the Handling of Indecencies," *English Review* (December 1922), 539.

37. Valéry Larbaud, "James Joyce," *Nouvelle revue française* 18 (April 1922): 387–88. The translation is taken from "The *Ulysses* of James Joyce," *Criterion* 1 (October 1922): 94–103, in Deming, *James Joyce*, 253.

38. Joseph Hone, "Letter from Ireland," *London Mercury* 5 (1923): 306–8.

39. Walkowitz, *Cosmopolitan Style*, 60–61.

40. Nash, "In the Heart," 108–22; Brooker, *Joyce's Critics*, 191–92; Kelly, *Our Joyce*, 180–225.

41. John Eglinton, "Dublin Letter," *Dial* 86 (May 1929), 417–20; in Deming, *James Joyce*, 459.

42. John Eglinton, "The Beginnings of Joyce," in *James Joyce: Interviews and Recollections*, ed. E. H. Mikhail (Basingstoke, Eng.: Macmillan, 1990): 34; qtd. in Booker, *Joyce's Critics*, 192.

43. The essay was anthologized in Sean Givens, ed., *James Joyce: Two Decades of Criticism*, (New York: Vanguard, 1948), 198–203.

44. Rachel Bowlby, "'But She Would Learn Something from Lady Chatterley': The Obscene Side of the Canon," in *Decolonizing Tradition: New Views of Twentieth-Century 'British' Literary Canons*, ed. Karen Lawrence (Urbana: University of Illinois Press, 1992), 123–24.

45. Emery in Deming, *James Joyce*, 293; Huddleston in Deming, *James Joyce*, 216; Bennett, "Concerning James Joyce's *Ulysses*," 570; Gilbert Seldes, review of *Ulysses*, by James Joyce, *Nation*, 30 August 1922, 212.

46. Slavoj Žižek, *The Sublime Object of Ideology* (London: Verso, 1989), 16, 18.

47. Ibid., 26.

48. Martin Krieger, "Making Physical Objects: The Law of the Excluded Middle, Dumbing-up the World, & Handles, Tools, and Fetishes," *Configurations* 2.1 (1994): 111–12.

49. Denny, *Introduction*, 67, 113.

50. Ibid., 119–121.

51. Cf. Asad, *Genealogies*, 141; Butler, "Performative Acts," 278.

52. Asad, *Genealogies*, 131.

53. Bobby Sayyid, *A Fundamental Fear: Eurocentrism and the Emergence of Islam* (London: Zed; New York: St. Martin's, 1997), 54.

54. Qtd. in Malise Ruthven, *A Satanic Affair: Salman Rushdie and the Wrath of Islam*, rev. ed. (London: Hogarth-Chatto & Windus, 1991), 75. Sharma, "'Precious Gift,'" summarizes the British context, 138–43.

55. Syed Ali Ashraf, "Nihilistic, Negative, Satanic," review of *The Satanic Verses*, by Salman Rushdie, *Impact International*, 28 October 1988, in Lisa Appignanesi and Sara Maitland, eds., *The Rushdie File* (London: Fourth Estate, 1989), 25.

56. "Publishing Sacrilege Is Not Acceptable," *Impact International*, 28 October 1988, in M. M. Ahsan and A. R. Kidwai, eds., *Sacrilege versus Civility: Muslim Perspectives on* The Satanic Verses *Affair* (Leicester, Eng.: Islamic Foundation, 1991), 145.

57. See, for example, "Rushdie Has Fallen into Total Moral Degradation," *Independent*, 21 February 1989, in Appignanesi and Maitland, *The Rushdie File*, 23–24; Mughram Al-Ghamdi, Open letter from UK Action Committee on Islamic Affairs, 28 October 1988, in Appignanesi and Maitland, *The Rushdie File*, 58.

58. Ziauddin Sardar and Merryl Wyn Davies, *Distorted Imagination: Lessons from the Rushdie Affair* (London: Grey Seal; Kuala Lumpur: Berita, 1990), 155, 151.

59. Sardar and Davies, *Distorted Imagination*, 26; Schimmel, *And Muhammad Is His Messenger*, 24.

60. Asad, *Genealogies*, 301–2.

61. "The Rushdie Affair," advertisement, London *Times*, 3 March 1989, in Ahsan and Kidwai, *Sacrilege versus Civility*, 187.

62. Ali Mazrui, "Novelist's Freedom versus Worshipper's Dignity," *Impact International*, 28 April 1989, in Ahsan and Kidwai, *Sacrilege versus Civility*, 217.

63. Pnina Werbner, "Stamping the Earth with the Name of Allah: *Zikr* and the Sacralizing of Space among British Muslims," in *Making Muslim Space in North America and Europe*, ed. Barbara Daly Metcalf (Berkeley: University of California Press, 1996), 181.

64. Sharma, "'Precious Gift,'" 138.

65. Qtd. in Ruthven, *Satanic Affair*, 29.

66. Ali Mazrui, "The Moral Dilemma of Salman Rushdie's *The Satanic Verses*," lecture, Cornell University, 1 March 1989, in Appignanesi and Maitland, *The Rushdie File*, 220–28.

67. "The Rushdie Affair: A Muslim's Perspective," *Index on Censorship*, April 1990, 13.

68. Mauss, *Sociology*, 122, 101.

69. Dawson, *Mongrel Nation*, 123.

70. Salman Rushdie, "Choice between Light and Dark," *Observer*, 22 January 1989, in Appignanesi and Maitland, *The Rushdie File*, 75.

71. *Independent*, 16 January 1989, in Appignanesi and Maitland, *The Rushdie File*, 67–69.

72. Sharma, "'Precious Gift,'" 143.
73. Norman Mailer, lecture, PEN American Center, New York City, 22 February 1989, in Appignanesi and Maitland, *The Rushdie File*, 173–75.
74. Mishra, *The Literature of the Indian Diaspora*, 233.
75. Cf. Viswanathan, *Outside the Fold*, 60.

Chapter 6

1. Jaffe, *Modernism*, 34.
2. Theall, *James Joyce's Techno-Poetics*, 77–78.
3. English, *The Economy of Prestige*, 312.
4. Rushdie, *Joseph Anton*, 5.
5. Isaac Choitner, "How the Mullahs Won: Salman Rushdie's Artistic Decline," review of *Joseph Anton*, by Salman Rushdie, *Atlantic Monthly*, December 2012, 98–103.
6. John Updike, "Paradises Lost," review of *Shalimar the Clown*, by Salman Rushdie, *New Yorker*, 9 September 2005, http://www.newyorker.com/archive/2005/09/05/050905crbo
7. James Joyce, *Finnegans Wake* (New York: Viking, 1939), 185–86. Subsequent citations from this source will appear parenthetically in the text.
8. Finn Fordham, *Lots of Fun at* Finnegans Wake: *Unravelling Universals* (Oxford: Oxford University Press, 2007), 226.
9. Bishop, *Joyce's Book of the Dark*, 46.
10. Ibid., 139.
11. Theall, *James Joyce's Techno-Poetics*, 15, 26.
12. Fordham, *Lots of Fun*, 48.
13. Ibid., 225.
14. See Theall, *James Joyce's Techno-Poetics*, 81–82, 149.
15. See ibid., 31, for a complete list of the technologies represented in the work.
16. Bishop, *Joyce's Book of the Dark*, 219.
17. Theall, *James Joyce's Techno-Poetics*, 111.
18. James Atherton, *The Books at the Wake: A Study of Literary Allusions in James Joyce's* Finnegans Wake (New York: Viking, 1960), 89.
19. Jonathan Goldman, *Modernism Is the Literature of Celebrity* (Austin: University of Texas Press, 2011), 59–61.
20. Robert Boyle, "*Finnegans Wake*, Page 185: An Explication," in *Critical Essays on James Joyce's* Finnegans Wake," ed. Patrick McCarthy (New York: G. K. Hall-Macmillan, 1992), 262.
21. Gorman, *James Joyce*, 297.
22. Malcolm Cowley, "Religion of Art," *New Republic*, 10 January 1934, 218.
23. "Silence, Exile, and Death," *Time*, 10 February 1941, 72.
24. Maurizia Boscagli and Enda Duffy, "Joyce's Face," in Dettmar and Watt, *Marketing Modernisms*, 133–59.
25. "Silence," 72.
26. Ibid., 11.
27. John Murry, "Mr. Joyce's *Ulysses*," review of *Ulysses*, *Nation & Athenaeum*, 22 April 1922, 124.
28. "Portrait," *Newsweek*, 10 November 1941, 76.
29. "Traveling Joyce," *Time*, 17 February 1947, 109.
30. Kelly, *Our Joyce*, 80, 212.

31. "Traveling Joyce," 109.

32. Goldman, *Modernism*, 74.

33. Richard Ellmann, *James Joyce* (Oxford: Oxford University Press, 1959). The first references are to this edition.

34. Richard Ellmann, *James Joyce*, rev. ed. (Oxford: Oxford University Press, 1982).

35. Jane Lilienfeld, *Reading Alcoholisms: Theorizing Character and Narrative in Selected Novels of Thomas Hardy, James Joyce, and Virginia Woolf* (New York: St. Martin's, 1999), 93.

36. Ibid., 93; Stanislaus Joyce, *My Brother's Keeper*, ed. Richard Ellmann (London: Faber & Faber, 1958), 63, 74, 98.

37. See Brooker, *Joyce's Critics*, 100–12, and Kelly, *Our Joyce*, 141–75, for discussions of Ellmann's approach and sources. Lilienfeld, *Reading Alcoholisms*, 156, argues that while Ellmann heavily relied on Stanislaus Joyce's *Complete Dublin Diary* in many respects, the biographer mitigated Stanislaus's accounts of his father's drinking habits and their effects on the family. For other challenges to the representations of John and James Joyce's drinking practices, see, for instance, Hélène Cixous, *The Exile of James Joyce*, trans. Sally Purcell (New York: David Lewis, 1972), 136–42; Ira Nadel, "The Incomplete Joyce," *Joyce Studies Annual* 2.1 (1991): 89, 95–98; Richard Pearce, "Simon's Wild Irish Rose: Famine Songs, Blackfaced Minstrels, and Women's Repression in *A Portrait*," in *Joyce and the Return of the Repressed*, ed. Susan Stanford Friedman (Ithaca: Cornell University Press, 1993), 130–32; Brenda Maddox, *Nora: A Biography of Nora Joyce* (New York: Fawcett-Columbine, 1988), 68–69, 181, 185–86; and Carol Loeb Schloss, *Lucia Joyce: To Dance in the Wake* (New York: Farrar, Straus and Giroux, 2003).

38. Richard Ellmann, *James Joyce*, 78; rev. ed. 75.

39. Ibid., 227; rev. ed. 218.

40. Ibid., 372; rev. ed. 362.

41. Ibid., 397; rev. ed. 86.

42. Ibid., 5. Most of these remain in the revised edition, though not this one. In his new introduction, Ellmann cites Lucia Joyce's medical papers, which record Joyce's description of himself as "a man of small virtue, inclined to extravagance and alcoholism," 6 n.5.

43. Ibid., 693; rev. ed. 680. Ellmann quotes Ernest Jones's 1955 biography, *Sigmund Freud*.

44. This is not to say that scholars have entirely ignored the topic. See, for instance, Mark Osteen, *The Economy of* Ulysses: *Making Both Ends Meet* (Syracuse: Syracuse University Press, 1995), 262–71, and David Earle, "'Green Eyes I See You. Fang, I Feel': The Symbol of Absinthe in *Ulysses*," *James Joyce Quarterly* 40 (2003): 691–709.

45. See, for instance, Vincent Cheng, *Joyce, Race, and Empire*, 32–34, and Len Platt, "The Buckeen and the Dogsbody: Aspects of History and Culture in 'Telemachus,'" *James Joyce Quarterly* 27 (1988): 78–79.

46. For descriptions of Rushdie's popular and critical image during his years in hiding, see, for instance, Anouar Majid, *Unveiling Traditions: Postcolonial Islam in a Polycentric World* (Durham: Duke University Press, 2000), 22–49; Aamir Mufti, "Reading the Rushdie Affair: Islam, Cultural Politics, Form," in *Critical Essays on Salman Rushdie*, ed. M. Keith Booker (New York: G. K. Hall, 1999), 51–77, and Brennan, "Cultural Politics," 107–28..

47. For an analysis of *Fury* in relation to Rushdie's profile, see Brouillette, *Postcolonial Writers*, 79–111.

48. Anshuman Mondal, "*The Ground beneath Her Feet* and *Fury*: The Reinvention of Location," *The Cambridge Companion to Salman Rushdie*, ed. Abdulrazak Gurnah (Cambridge: Cambridge University Press, 2007), 171.

49. Goldman, *Modernism*, 12, 24–26, 29.

50. Gary Larson, Far Side greeting card (Kansas City: Farworks and Oz-Andrews and McMeel, 1991).

51. Salman Rushdie, *The Ground beneath Her Feet* (New York: Holt-Picador, 1999), 461. Subsequent citations from this source will appear parenthetically in the text.

52. See, for example, Sabina Sawhney and Simona Sawhney, "Reading Rushdie after September 11, 2001," *Twentieth Century Literature* 47 (2001): 31–43; Robert Spencer, "Salman Rushdie and the War on Terror," *Journal of Postcolonial Writing* 46 (2010): 251–65; Rushdie, *Joseph Anton*, 624.

53. For some early arguments about the novel's global politics, see Randy Boyagoda, "Three Kings of Disorient: A Globalized Search for Home in *The Ground beneath Her Feet*," *South Asian Review* 24 (2003): 131–43; and Mariam Pirbhai, "The Paradox of Globalization as 'Untotalizable Totality' in Salman Rushdie's *The Ground beneath Her Feet*," *International Fiction Review* 28 (2001): 54–66.

54. See, for example, Judith Leggatt, "Other Worlds, Other Selves" 105–125; Justyna Deszcz, "Salman Rushdie's Subversive Play with the Diana *Märchen:* The Fairy-tale Construction of a Diana-like Protagonist in *The Ground beneath Her Feet*," in *Representing Gender in Cultures*, ed. Elzbieta Olesky and Joanna Rydzenska (Frankfurt-am-Main and New York: Peter Lang, 2004), 119–27; and Jaina Sanga, *Salman Rushdie's Postcolonial Metaphors: Migration, Translation, Hybridity, Blasphemy, and Globalization* (Westport, CT: Greenwood Press, 2001), 145–48.

55. Randy Boyagoda, *Race, Immigration, and American Identity in the Fiction of Salman Rushdie, Ralph Ellison, and William Faulkner* (London: Routledge, 2008), 38.

56. Boyagoda, "Three Kings," 136. Boyagoda modifies this argument in his treatment of the American immigrant experience and the American South in *Race, Immigration*, 3–49.

Bibliography

Ahmad, Aijaz. *In Theory: Classes, Nations, Literatures.* London: New Left-Verso, 1992.
Ahsan, M. M., and A. R. Kidwai, eds. *Sacrilege versus Civility: Muslim Perspectives on* The Satanic Verses *Affair.* Leicester, Eng.: Islamic Foundation, 1991.
Alloula, Malek. *The Colonial Harem.* Trans. Myrna Godzich and Wald Godzich. Minneapolis: University of Minnesota Press, 1986.
Almond, Ian. *The New Orientalists: Postmodern Representations of Islam from Foucault to Baudrillard.* London: I. B. Tauris, 2007.
Amber, R. B., and M. Babey Brooke. *The Pulse in Occident and Orient: Its Philosophy and Practice in India, China, Iran, and the West.* New York: Santa Barbara Press; London: Dawsons, 1966.
Appignanesi, Lisa, and Sara Maitland, *The Rushdie File.* London: Fourth Estate, 1989.
Appleyard, Brian. "Why Don't We Love Science Fiction?" London *Times*, 2 December 2007, Features 8.
Asad, Talal. *Formations of the Secular: Christianity, Islam, Modernity.* Stanford: Stanford University Press, 2003.
———. *Genealogies of Religion: Discipline and Reasons of Power in Christianity and Islam.* Baltimore: Johns Hopkins University Press, 1993.
———. "Religion, Nation-State, Secularism." In *Nation and Religion: Perspectives on Europe and Asia,* edited by Peter van der Veer and Hartmut Lehman, 178–96. Princeton: Princeton University Press, 1999.
Atherton, James. *The Books at the Wake: A Study of Literary Allusions in James Joyce's* Finnegans Wake. New York: Viking, 1960.
Atkins, Nicholas, and Frank Tallett. *Priest, Prelates and People: A History of European Catholicism since 1750.* Oxford: Oxford University Press, 2003.
Attridge, Derek, and Marjorie Howes, eds. *Semicolonial Joyce.* Cambridge: Cambridge University Press, 2000.
Babb, Lawrence. "Glancing: Visual Interaction in Hinduism." *Journal of Anthropological Research* 37 (1981): 387.

Backus, Margot. *The Gothic Family Romance: Heterosexuality, Child Sacrifice, and the Anglo-Irish Colonial Order*. Durham: Duke University Press, 1999.

Backus, Margot. "Sexual Figures and Historical Repression in 'The Dead.'" In *James Joyce and the Fabrication of an Irish Identity*, edited by Michael Patrick Gillespie, 111–31. European Joyce Studies 11. Amsterdam: Rodopi, 2001.

Balsamo, Gian. *Joyce's Messianism: Dante, Negative Existence, and the Messianic Self*. Columbia: University of South Carolina Press, 2004.

Bassi, Shaul. "Salman Rushdie's Special Effects." In *Co-terminous Worlds: Magical Realism and Contemporary Post-Colonial Literature in English*, edited by Elsa Linguanti et al., 47–60. Amsterdam: Rodopi, 1999.

Batty, Nancy E. "The Art of Suspense: Rushdie's 1,001 (Mid-)Nights," *Ariel* 18.3 (1987): 49–65.

Baucom, Ian. *Out of Place: Englishness, Empire, and the Locations of Identity*. Princeton: Princeton University Press, 1999.

Baudrillard, Jean. *Simulation and Simulacra*. Translated by Sheila Faria Glaser. Ann Arbor: University of Michigan Press, 1994.

Begam, Richard. "Joyce's Trojan Horse: *Ulysses* and the Aesthetics of Decolonization." In *Modernism and Colonialism: British and Irish Literature, 1899–1919*, edited by Michael Valdez Moses and Richard Begam, 185–208. Durham: Duke University Press, 2007.

Benjamin, Walter. "The Work of Art in the Age of Mechanical Reproduction." In *Illuminations*, edited by Hannah Arendt, translated by Harry Zohn, 217–52. New York: Schoken-Random House, 1969.

Bennett, Arnold. "Concerning James Joyce's *Ulysses*." Review of *Ulysses*, by James Joyce. *Bookman* [New York], August 1922, 570.

Bernauer, James. *Michel Foucault's Forces of Flight: Toward an Ethics for Thought*. Atlantic Highlands, NJ and London: Humanities Press, 1990.

Beville, Maria. "The Gothic Postmodernist 'Waste Land' of Ellowen Deeowen: Salman Rushdie's Nightmarish Visions of a Postmodern Metropolis." *Nebula* 4.1 (2007): 1–18.

Bhabha, Homi. *The Location of Culture*. London: Routledge, 1994.

———, ed. *Nation and Narration*. London: Routledge, 1990.

Biernoff, Suzannah. *Sight and Embodiment in the Middle Ages*. Basingstoke, Eng.: Palgrave-Macmillan, 2002.

Bishop, John. *Joyce's Book of the Dark*: Finnegans Wake. Madison: University of Wisconsin Press, 1986.

Bowlby, Rachel. "'But She Would Learn Something from Lady Chatterley': The Obscene Side of the Canon." In *Decolonizing Tradition: New Views of Twentieth-Century 'British' Literary Canons*, edited by Karen Lawrence, 113–35. Urbana: University of Illinois Press, 1992.

Boldrini, Lucia. *The Poetics of Literary Relations: Joyce, Dante, and the Poetics of* Finnegans Wake. Cambridge: Cambridge University Press, 2001.

Boldrini, Lucia, ed. *The Medieval Joyce*. Amsterdam: Rodopi, 2002.

Boone, Joseph. "Staging Sexuality: Repression, Representation, and 'Interior' States in *Ulysses*." In *Joyce: The Return of the Repressed*, edited by Susan Stanford Friedman, 190–221. Ithaca: Cornell University Press, 1993.

Boscagli, Maurizia, and Enda Duffy. "Joyce's Face." In *Marketing Modernisms*, edited by Kevin Dettmar and Steven Watt, 133–59. Ann Arbor: University of Michigan Press, 1996.

Boyagoda, Randy. *Race, Immigration, and American Identity in the Fiction of Salman Rushdie, Ralph Ellison, and William Faulkner*. London: Routledge, 2008.

———. "Three Kings of Disorient: A Globalized Search for Home in *The Ground beneath Her Feet*." *South Asian Review* 24 (2003): 131–43.

Boyd, Ernest. "Concerning James Joyce," *New York World*, 25 January 1925, n.p. In *James Joyce: The Critical Heritage*, edited by Robert Deming, 320–24. 2 vols. New York: Barnes and Noble, 1970.

———. *Ireland's Literary Renaissance*, rev. ed., 1923, 402–3. In *James Joyce: The Critical Heritage*, edited by Robert Deming, 301–5. 2 vols. New York: Barnes and Noble, 1970.

Boyle, Robert. "*Finnegans Wake*, Page 185: An Explication." In *Critical Essays on James Joyce's* Finnegans Wake," edited by Patrick McCarthy, 252–68. New York: G. K. Hall-Macmillan, 1992.

———. *James Joyce's Pauline Vision: A Catholic Exposition*. Carbondale: Southern Illinois University Press, 1978.

Brennan, Timothy. "The Cultural Politics of Rushdie Criticism: All or Nothing." In *Critical Essays on Salman Rushdie*, edited by M. Keith Booker, 107–28. New York: G. K. Hall, 1999.

———. *Salman Rushdie and the Third World: Myths of the Nation*. London: Macmillan, 1989.

Brooker, Joseph. *Joyce's Critics: Transitions in Reading and Culture*. Madison: University of Wisconsin Press, 2004.

Brouillette, Sarah. *Postcolonial Writers and the Global Literary Market*. Basingstoke, Eng.: Palgrave-Macmillan, 2007.

Budgen, Frank. *James Joyce and the Making of* Ulysses. New York: Harrison Smith and Robert Haas, 1934.

Buford, Bill. "Swallowing the Whole World." Review of *Midnight's Children*, by Salman Rushdie. *New Statesman*, 1 May 1981, 22.

Burkhardt, Richard. *The Spirit of the System: Lamarck and Evolutionary Biology*. Cambridge, MA: Harvard University Press, 1977.

Butler, Judith. "Performative Acts and Gender Constitution: An Essay on Embodiment and Feminist Theory." In *Writing on the Body: Female Embodiment and Feminist Theory*, edited by Katie Conboy, Nadia Medina, and Sarah Stanbury, 401–17. New York: Columbia University Press, 1997.

Buzard, James. "'Culture' and the Critics of *Dubliners*," *James Joyce Quarterly* 37 (1999–2000): 47–61.

———. *Disorienting Fiction: The Autoethnographic Work of Nineteenth-Century British Novels*. Princeton: Princeton University Press, 2005.

Bynum, Caroline Walker. *The Resurrection of the Body in Western Christianity, 200–1336*. New York: Columbia University Press, 1995.

Cantwell, Robert. "The Influence of James Joyce," *New Republic*, 27 December 1933, 200–201.

Carpentier, Alejo. "On the Marvellous Real in America." In *Magical Realism, Theory, History, Community*, edited by Lois Parkinson Zamora and Wendy B. Faris, 75–88. Durham: Duke University Press, 1995.

Carrette, Jeremy. *Foucault and Religion: Spiritual Corporality and Political Spirituality*. London: Routledge, 2000.

Castle, Gregory. *Modernism and the Celtic Revival*. Cambridge: Cambridge University Press, 2001.

Certeau, Michel de. *The Practice of Everyday Life*. Translated by Steven Rendell. Berkeley: University of California Press, 1984.

Chakravarty, Sumita. *National Identity in Indian Popular Cinema, 1947–87*. New Delhi: Oxford University Press, 1998.

Chauhan, Pradyumna, ed. *Salman Rushdie Interviews: A Sourcebook of His Ideas*. Westport, CT: Greenwood Press, 2001.

Cheah, Pheng. "Given Culture: Rethinking Cosmopolitical Freedom in Transnationalism." In *Cosmopolitics, Thinking and Feeling beyond the Nation*, 290–328. Minneapolis: University of Minnesota Press, 1998.

Cheah, Pheng, and Bruce Robbins, eds. *Cosmopolitics: Thinking and Feeling beyond the Nation*. Minneapolis: University of Minnesota Press, 1998.

Cheng, Anne Anlin. "The Melancholy of Race." *Kenyon Review* 19 (1998): 49–61.

———. *The Melancholy of Race*. Oxford: Oxford University Press, 2000.

Cheng, Vincent. *Joyce, Race, and Empire*. Cambridge: Cambridge University Press, 1995.

———. "'Terrible Queer Creatures': Joyce, Cosmopolitanism, and the Inauthentic Irishman." In *James Joyce and the Fabrication of an Irish Identity*, edited by Michael Patrick Gillespie, 11–38. European Joyce Studies 11. Amsterdam: Rodopi, 2001.

Cheng, Vincent, Kimberly Devlin, and Margot Norris. *Joycean Cultures/Culturing Joyces*. Newark: University of Delaware Press; London: Associated University Presses, 1998.

Cheyette, Bryan. *Constructions of 'the Jew' in English Literature and Society: Racial Representations 1845–1945*. Cambridge: Cambridge University Press, 1993.

Cheyette, Bryan, ed. *Between "Race" and Culture: Representations of "the Jew" in English and American Literature*. Stanford: Stanford University Press, 1996.

Choitner, Isaac. "How the Mullahs Won: Salman Rushdie's Artistic Decline." Review of *Joseph Anton*, by Salman Rushdie, *Atlantic Monthly*, December 2012, 98–103.

Cixous, Hélène. *The Exile of James Joyce*. Translated by Sally Purcell. New York: David Lewis, 1972.

Colley, Linda. *Britons: Forging the Nation, 1707–1837*. Rev. ed. New Haven: Yale University Press, 2009.

Collins, Joseph. "James Joyce's Amazing Chronicle." Review of *Ulysses*, by James Joyce. *New York Times Book Review*, 28 May 1922, 6.

Colum, Padraic. "James Joyce." *Pearson's Magazine*, May 1918, 38–42.

Connolly, S. J. *Priests and People in Pre-Famine Ireland, 1780–1845*. Dublin: Gill and Macmillan; New York: St. Martin's, 1982.

Corrigan, John. *Business of the Heart: Religion and Emotion in the Nineteenth Century*. Berkeley: University of California Press, 2002.

———, ed. "Emotions Research and the Academic Study of Religion." In *Religion and Emotion: Approaches and Interpretations*, 1–31. Oxford: Oxford University Press, 2004.

Couto, Maria. "*Midnight's Children* and Parents: The Search for Indo-British Identity." *Encounter* 58.2 (1982): 61–66.

Cowley, Malcolm. "Religion of Art," *New Republic*, 10 January 1934, 216–19.

Crary, Jonathan. *Techniques of the Observer: On Vision and Modernity in the Nineteenth Century*. Cambridge, MA: MIT Press, 1990.

Crawford, Robert. *Devolving English Literature*. 2nd ed. Edinburgh: University of Edinburgh Press, 2000.

Cullingford, Elizabeth. "Phoenician Genealogies and Oriental Geographies: Joyce, Language, and Race." In *Semicolonial Joyce*, edited by Derek Attridge and Marjorie Howes, 219–39. Cambridge: Cambridge University Press, 2000.

Cummingham, Valentine. "Nosing Out the Indian Reality." Review of *Midnight's Children*, by Salman Rushdie. London *Times Literary Supplement*, 15 May 1981, 535.

Cundy, Catherine. "Rehearsing Voices: Salman Rushdie's *Grimus*." In *Reading Rushdie: Perspectives on the Fiction of Salman Rushdie*, edited by M. D. Fletcher, 45–54. Amsterdam: Rodopi, 1995.

Daaen, Theo L. "Magical Realism and Postmodernism: Decentering Privileged Centers."

In *Magic Realism, Theory, History, Community*, edited by Lois Parkinson Zamora and Wendy B. Faris, 191–208. Durham: Duke University Press, 1995.

Daly, Nicholas. "Colonialism and Popular Literature at the Fin de Siècle. In *Modernism and Colonialism, British and Irish Literature, 1899–1919*, edited by Michael Valdez Moses and Richard Begam, 19–42. Durham: Duke University Press, 2007.

Danius, Sara. *The Senses of Modernism: Technology, Perception, and Aesthetics*. Ithaca: Cornell University Press, 2002.

Davison, Neil. *James Joyce, Ulysses, and the Construction of Jewish Identity: Culture, Biography and 'the Jew' in Modernist Europe*. Cambridge: Cambridge University Press, 1998.

Dawson, Ashley. *Mongrel Nation: Diasporic Culture and the Making of Postcolonial Britain*. Ann Arbor: University of Michigan Press, 2007.

Deane, Seamus. *Strange Country: Modernity and Nationhood in Irish Writing since 1790*. Oxford: Clarendon, 1997.

Deming, Robert. *James Joyce: The Critical Heritage*. 2 vols. New York: Barnes and Noble, 1970.

Denny, Frederick. *An Introduction to Islam*. 2nd ed. New York: Macmillan, 1994.

Derrida, Jacques. "Plato's Pharmakon." In *Dissemination*, edited and translated by Barbara Johnson, 63–171. Chicago: University of Chicago Press, 1981.

Desai, Anita. "Where Cultures Clash by Night." Review of *Midnight's Children*, by Salman Rushdie. *Washington Post Book World*, 15 March 1981, 1, 13.

Despland, Michel. *Reading an Erased Code: Romantic Religion and Literary Aesthetics in France*. Toronto: University of Toronto Press, 1994.

Deszcz, Justyna. "Salman Rushdie's Subversive Play with the Diana *Märchen*: The Fairy-tale Construction of a Diana-like Protagonist in *The Ground beneath Her Feet*." In *Representing Gender in Cultures*, edited by Elzbieta Olesky and Joanna Rydzenska, 119–27. Frankfurt-am-Main and New York: Peter Lang, 2004.

Dettmar, Kevin. *The Illicit Joyce of Postmodernism: Reading against the Grain*. Madison: University of Wisconsin Press, 1996.

Dettmar, Kevin, and Steven J. Watt, eds. *Marketing Modernisms: Self-Promotion, Canonization, Re-reading*. Ann Arbor: University of Michigan Press, 1996.

Devji, Faisal. "Apologetic Modernity." In *An Intellectual History for India*, edited by Shruti Kapila, 52–67. Cambridge: Cambridge University Press, 2010.

Dissanayake, Wimal. "Towards a Decolonised English: South Asian Creativity in Fiction." *World Englishes* 4.2 (1985): 233–42.

Doheny, Gerald. Dubliners' *Dozen: The Games Narrators Play*. Madison: Farleigh Dickinson University Press, 2004.

Dole, Andrew. *Schleiermacher on Religion and the Natural Order*. Oxford: Oxford University Press, 2010.

Doyle, Laura. *Bordering on the Body: The Racial Matrix of Modern Fiction and Culture*. Oxford: Oxford University Press, 1994.

Dubuisson, Daniel. *The Western Construction of Religion: Myths, Knowledge, and Ideology*. Translated by William Sayers. Baltimore: Johns Hopkins University Press, 2003.

Duffy, Enda. *The Subaltern Ulysses*. Minneapolis: University of Minnesota Press, 1994.

Durix, Jean-Pierre. "Magic Realism in *Midnight's Children*." *Commonwealth Essays and Studies* 8 (1985): 57–63.

Dwyer, Rachel, and Christopher Pinney, eds. *Pleasure in the Nation: The History, Politics, and Consumption of Public Culture in India*. Oxford: Oxford University Press, 2001.

Dwyer, Rachel, and Divia Patel. *Cinema India: The Visual Culture of Hindi Film*. Newark: Rutgers University Press; London: Reaktion Books, 2002.

Earle, David. "'Green Eyes I See You. Fang, I Feel': The Symbol of Absinthe in *Ulysses*." *James Joyce Quarterly* 40 (2003): 691–709.

Eck, Diana. *Darśan: Seeing the Divine Image in India*. Chambersburg, PA: Anima Books, 1981.

Eco, Umberto. *The Aesthetics of Chaosmos: The Middle Ages of James Joyce*. Translated by Ellen Esrock. Cambridge, MA: Harvard University Press, 1989.

Ellmann, Richard. *James Joyce*. Oxford: Oxford University Press, 1959.

———. *James Joyce*. Rev. ed. Oxford: Oxford University Press, 1982.

English, James. *Comic Transactions: Literature, Humor, and the Politics of Community in Twentieth-Century Britain*. Ithaca: Cornell University Press, 1994.

———. *The Economy of Prestige: Prizes, Awards, and the Circulation of Cultural Capital*. Cambridge, MA: Harvard University Press, 2008.

Erikson, John. *Islam and Postcolonial Narrative*. Cambridge: Cambridge University Press, 2009.

Esty, Jed. *A Shrinking Island: Modernism and National Culture in England*. Princeton: Princeton University Press, 2003.

Fairhall, James. *James Joyce and the Question of History*. Cambridge: Cambridge University Press, 1993.

Faris, Wendy B. "Scheherazade's Children: Magical Realism and Postmodern Fiction." In *Magic Realism, Theory, History, Community*, edited by Lois Parkinson Zamora and Wendy B. Faris, 163–90. Durham: Duke University Press, 1995.

Feinstein, Elaine. Review of *Midnight's Children*, by Salman Rushdie. London *Times*, 23 April 1981, 10F.

Ford, Ford Madox. "*Ulysses* and the Handling of Indecencies." *English Review* (December 1922), 538–48.

Fordham, Finn. *Lots of Fun at Finnegans Wake: Unravelling Universals*. Oxford: Oxford University Press, 2007.

Foucault, Michel. *The History of Sexuality*. 3 vols. Vol. 3, *The Care of the Self*. Translated by Robert Hurley. New York: Pantheon-Random House, 1986.

———. *Madness and Civilization*. Translated by Richard Howard. New York: Random House, 1965.

———. *Technologies of the Self: A Seminar with Michel Foucault*. Edited by Luther Martin, Huck Gutman, and Patrick Hutton. Amherst: University of Massachusetts Press, 1988.

Franchot, Jenny. "Unseemly Commemoration: Religion, Fragments, and the Icon." In *Religion and Cultural Studies*, edited by Susan Mizruchi, 37–55. Princeton: Princeton University Press, 2001.

Freitag, Sandria. "Visions of the Nation: Theorizing the Nexus between Creation, Consumption, and Participation in the Public Sphere." In *Pleasure in the Nation: The History, Politics, and Consumption of Public Culture in India*, edited by Rachel Dwyer and Christopher Pinney, 35–75. Oxford: Oxford University Press, 2001.

Friedman, Susan Stanford, ed. *James Joyce and the Return of the Repressed*. Ithaca: Cornell University Press, 1993.

Froula, Christine. *Modernism's Body: Sex, Culture and Joyce*. New York: Columbia University Press, 1996.

Gandhy, Behroze, and Rosie Thomas. "Three Indian Film Stars." In *Stardom: Industry of Desire*, edited by Christine Gledhill, 111–35. London: Routledge, 1991.

Gane, Gillian. "Migrancy, the Cosmopolitan Intellectual, and the Global City in *The Satanic Verses*." *Modern Fiction Studies* 48 (2002): 18–49.

Geertz, Clifford. "Deep Play: Notes on the Balinese Cockfight." In *Interpretive Social Science:*

A Reader, edited by Paul Rabinow and William Sullivan, 181–223. Berkeley: University of California Press, 1979.

Ghiselin, Brewster. "The Unity of Joyce's *Dubliners*." *Accent* 16 (1956): 75–88; 196–231.

Ghosh, Bishnupriya. "An Invitation to Indian Postmodernity: Rushdie's English Vernacular as a Situated Cultural Hybridity." In *Critical Essays on Salman Rushdie*, edited by M. Keith Booker, 129–53. New York: G. K. Hall, 1999.

———. *When Borne Across: Literary Cosmopolitics in the Contemporary Indian Novel.* New Brunswick: Rutgers University Press, 2004.

Gibbons, Luke. "'Have You No Home to Go To?' James Joyce and the Politics of Paralysis." In *Semicolonial Joyce,* edited by Derek Attridge and Marjorie Howes, 150–71. Cambridge: Cambridge University Press, 2000.

Gibson, Andrew. *Joyce's Revenge: History, Politics, and Aesthetics in* Ulysses. Oxford: Oxford University Press, 2002.

Gibson, Andrew, and Len Platt, eds. *Joyce, Ireland, Britain.* Gainesville: University Press of Florida, 2006.

Gifford, Frank. *Joyce Annotated: Notes for* Dubliners *and* A Portrait of the Artist as a Young Man. 2nd ed., rev. Berkeley: University of California Press, 1982.

Gikandi, Simon. *Maps of Englishness: Writing Identity in the Culture of Colonialism.* New York: Columbia University Press, 1996.

Gilbert, Sandra, and Susan Gubar. "Sexual Linguistics: Gender, Language, Sexuality." *New Literary History* 16 (1985): 515–43.

Gilbert, Stuart. *James Joyce's* Ulysses. New York: Vintage, 1955.

———, ed. *The Letters of James Joyce.* Rev. ed. London: Faber and Faber, 1966.

Gillespie, Michael Patrick, ed. *James Joyce and the Fabrication of an Irish Identity.* European Joyce Studies 11. Amsterdam: Rodopi, 2001.

Givens, Seon. *James Joyce: Two Decades of Criticism.* New York: Vanguard, 1948.

Glendinning, Victoria. "A Novelist in the Country of the Mind." In *Salman Rushdie Interviews: A Sourcebook of His Ideas,* edited by Pradyumna Chauhan, 3–6. Westport, CT: Greenwood Press, 2001.

Glover, David. "The 'Spectrality Effect' in Early Modernism." In *Gothic Modernisms,* edited by Andrew Smith and Jeff Wallace, 29–43. Basingstoke, Eng.: Palgrave-Macmillan, 2001.

Goldman, Jonathan. *Modernism Is the Literature of Celebrity.* Austin: University of Texas Press, 2011.

Gorman, Herbert. *James Joyce: The First Forty Years.* New York: Farrar and Rinehart, 1939.

Gottfried, Roy. *Joyce's Misbelief.* Gainesville: University Press of Florida, 2008.

Griffin, Susan. *Anti-Catholicism and Nineteenth-Century Fiction.* Cambridge: Cambridge University Press, 2004.

Hagopian, John. "The Epiphany in Joyce's 'Counterparts.'" *Studies in Short Fiction* 1 (1964): 272–76.

Halberstam, Judith. *Skin Shows: Gothic Horror and the Technology of Monsters.* Durham: Duke University Press, 1995.

Heiland, Donna. *Gothic and Gender: An Introduction.* Oxford: Blackwell, 2004.

Herr, Cheryl. *Joyce's Anatomy of Culture.* Urbana: University of Illinois Press, 1986.

———. "The Erotics of Irishness." *Critical Inquiry* 27 (1990): 1–35.

Herwitz, Daniel, and Ashutosh Varshney, eds. *Midnight's Diaspora: Critical Encounters with Salman Rushdie.* Ann Arbor: University of Michigan Press, 2008.

Hoberman, John. "Otto Weininger and the Critique of Jewish Masculinity." In *Jews and Gender: Responses to Otto Weininger,* edited by Nancy Harrowitz and Barbara Hyams, 141–68. Philadelphia: Temple University Press, 1995.

Hogle, Jerrold. "The Gothic Ghost of the Counterfeit and the Progress of Abjection." In *A Companion to the Gothic*, edited by David Punter, 293–304. Oxford: Blackwell, 2000.
Hone, Joseph. "Letter from Ireland." *London Mercury* 5 (1923), 306–8.
Hoppen, K. Theodore. *Ireland since 1800: Conflict and Conformity*. London: Longman, 1989.
Huggan, Graham. *The Postcolonial Exotic: Marketing the Margins*. London: Routledge, 2001.
Hungerford, Amy. *Postmodern Belief: American Literature since 1960*. Princeton: Princeton University Press, 2010.
Huyssen, Andreas. *After the Great Divide*. Bloomington: Indiana University Press, 1986.
"Is Rushdie Just the Beginning?" London *Times*, 28 May 1989, 22.
Jackson, John Wyse, and Peter Costello. *John Stanislaus Joyce: The Voluminous Life and Genius of James Joyce's Father*. New York: St. Martin's, 1998.
Jaffe, Aaron. *Modernism and the Culture of Celebrity*. Cambridge: Cambridge University Press, 2005.
Jastrebski, Joan. "Pig Dialectics: Women's Bodies as Performed Dialectical Images in the Circe Episode of *Ulysses*." In *James Joyce and the Fabrication of an Irish Identity*, edited by Michael Patrick Gillespie, 151–75. European Joyce Studies 11. Amsterdam: Rodopi, 2001.
Jaurretche, Colleen. *The Sensual Philosophy: Joyce and the Aesthetics of Mysticism*. Madison: University of Wisconsin Press, 1997.
Jay, Martin. *Downcast Eyes: The Denigration of Vision in Twentieth-Century French Thought*. Berkeley: University of California Press, 1993.
Jeffries, Stuart. "'I Am Funny—And So Are My Books.'" London *Guardian*, 11 July 2008, Features 4.
Joshi, B. K., and Victoria Glendinning. "It May Be Long But It's Not Overwritten." *Times of India*, 1 November 1982, 8.
Joyce, James. *The Critical Writings of James Joyce*. Edited by Ellsworth Mason and Richard Ellmann. New York: Viking, 1964.
———. *Dubliners*. Edited by Hans Walter Gabler. New York: Vintage-Random House, 1993.
———. *Finnegans Wake*. New York: Viking, 1939.
———. *Letters of James Joyce*. 2 vols. Volume 1, edited by Stuart Gilbert. New York: Viking, 1957. Volume 2, edited by Richard Ellmann. New York: Viking, 1966.
———. *A Portrait of the Artist as a Young Man*. Edited by Hans Walter Gabler. New York: Vintage-Random House, 1993.
———. *Selected Letters of James Joyce*. Edited by Richard Ellmann. New York: Viking, 1975.
———. *Stephen Hero*. Edited by Theodore Spencer, John J. Slocum, and Herbert Calhoun. New York: New Directions, 1963.
———. *Ulysses*. Edited by Hans Walter Gabler, Wolfhard Steppe, and Claus Melchior. New York: Random House-Vintage, 1986.
Joyce, Stanislaus. *The Complete Dublin Diary*. Edited by George Healey. Ithaca: Cornell University Press, 1971.
Joyce, Stanislaus. *My Brother's Keeper*. Edited by Richard Ellmann. London: Faber & Faber, 1958.
Jussawalla, Feroza. "Rushdie's *Dastan-e-Dilruba*: *The Satanic Verses* as Rushdie's Love Letter to Islam." In *Critical Essays on Salman Rushdie*, edited by M. Keith Booker, 78–106. New York: G. K. Hall, 1999.
Kahane, Claire. "The Gothic Mirror." In *The (M)other Tongue: Essays in Feminist Psychoanalytic Interpretation*, edited by Shirley Nelson Garner, Claire Kahane, and Madelon Sprengnether, 334–51. Ithaca: Cornell University Press, 1985.
Kalupahana, David. *The Principles of Buddhist Psychology*. Albany: State University of New York Press, 1987.

Kanaganayakam, C. "Myth and Fabulousity in *Midnight's Children*." *Dalhousie Review* 67.1 (1987): 86–98.

Kapur, Geeta. "Mythic Material in Indian Cinema." *Journal of Arts and Ideas* 14–15 (1987): 79–108.

———. "Ravi Varma: Representational Dilemmas of a Nineteenth-Century Indian Painter." *Journal of Arts and Ideas* 17–18 (1989): 59–80.

Kaufman, Michael. "Author from Three Countries." *New York Times Book Review*, 13 November 1983, BR 22.

Kaye, Julian. "The Wings of Daedalus: Two Stories in *Dubliners*." *Modern Fiction Studies* 4 (1958): 31–41.

Kelly, Joseph. *Our Joyce: From Outcast to Icon*. Austin: University of Texas Press, 1999.

Kenner, Hugh. *Ulysses*. London: Allen & Unwin, 1980.

Kershner, R. B. *Joyce, Bakhtin, and Popular Literature: Chronicles of Disorder*. Chapel Hill: University of North Carolina Press, 1989.

Kesevan, Mukul. "Urdu, Awadh, and the Tawaif: The Islamicate Roots of Indian Cinema." In *Forging Identities: Gender, Community, and the State in India*, edited by Zoya Hasan, 246–53. Boulder: Westview Press; New Delhi: Kali for Women, 1994.

Kiberd, Delcan. *Inventing Ireland: The Literature of the Modern Nation*. Cambridge, MA: Harvard University Press, 1997.

King, Richard. *Orientalism and Religion: Postcolonial Theory, India, and "the Mystic East."* London: Routledge, 1999.

Kleinman, Arthur. *The Illness Narratives: Suffering, Healing, and the Human Condition*. New York: Basic, 1988.

———. *Social Origins of Distress and Disease: Depression, Neurasthenia, and Pain in Modern China*. New Haven: Yale University Press, 1986.

Kluwick, Ursula. *Exploring Magic Realism in Salman Rushdie's Fiction*. Oxon, Eng.: Routledge, 2011.

Krieger, Martin. "Making Physical Objects: The Law of the Excluded Middle, Dumbing-up the World, & Handles, Tools, and Fetishes." *Configurations* 2.1 (1994): 107–17.

Kristeva, Julia. *Powers of Horror: An Essay on Abjection*. Translated by Leon S. Radios. New York: Columbia University Press, 1982.

Kumar, Amitava. *Bombay London New York*. London: Routledge, 2002.

Kurup, P. N. V., and K. Raghunathan. "Human Physiology and Ayurveda." In *The Science of Medicine and Physiological Concepts in Ancient and Medieval India*, edited by N. H. Keswani, 67–75. New Delhi: All-India Institute of Medical Sciences, 1974.

Lalvani, Suren. *Photography, Vision and the Production of Modern Bodies*. Albany: State University of New York Press, 1996.

Lannoy, Richard. *The Speaking Tree: A Study of Indian Culture and Society*. London: Oxford University Press, 1971.

Larbaud, Valéry. "James Joyce." *Nouvelle revue française* 18 (April 1922): 387–88. Translated as "The *Ulysses* of James Joyce." *Criterion* 1 (October 1922): 94–103. In *James Joyce*, edited by Robert Deming, 252–62. 2 vols. New York: Barnes and Noble, 1970.

Larkin, E. "The Devotional Revolution in Ireland, 1850–75." *American Historical Review* 77 (1972): 625–52.

———. *The Roman Catholic Church in Ireland and the Fall of Parnell, 1888–1891*. Chapel Hill: University of North Carolina Press, 1979.

Larson, Gary. Far Side greeting card. Kansas City: Farworks and Oz-Andrews and McMeel, 1991.

Lawrence, Karen. "Compromising Letters: Joyce and Women." *Western Humanities Review* 42 (1988): 1–17.
Leclerq, Jean. *The Love of Learning and the Desire for God: A Study of Monastic Culture*. Translated by Catharine Misrahi. New York: Fordham University Press, 1961.
Leggatt, Judith. "Other Worlds, Other Selves: Science Fiction in Salman Rushdie's *The Ground beneath Her Feet*." *Ariel* 33.1 (2002): 105–25.
Leonard, Garry. *Advertising and Commmodity Culture in Joyce*. Gainesville: University Press of Florida, 1998.
———. *Reading* Dubliners *Again: A Lacanian Perspective*. Syracuse: University of Syracuse Press, 1993.
Leonard, John. "Books of the Times." Review of *Midnight's Children*, by Salman Rushdie. *New York Times*, 23 April 1981, C21.
Lernout, Geert. *Help My Unbelief: James Joyce and Religion*. New York: Continuum, 2010.
Leslie, Shane [Domini Canis]. Review of *Ulysses*, by James Joyce, *Dublin Review* 171 (July–September 1922): 112–19.
Leslie, Shane. Review of *Ulysses*, by James Joyce. *Quarterly Review* 238 (October 1922): 219–34.
Levin, Harry. *James Joyce: A Critical Introduction*. New York: New Directions, 1941.
Lewis, Pericles. *Modernism, Nationalism, and the Novel*. Cambridge: Cambridge University Press, 2000.
———. *Religious Experience and the Modernist Novel*. Cambridge: Cambridge University Press, 2010.
Lewis, Wyndham. *Time and Western Man*. 1927. Boston: Beacon Press, 1957.
Lilienfeld, Jane. *Reading Alcoholisms: Theorizing Character and Narrative in Selected Novels of Thomas Hardy, James Joyce, and Virginia Woolf*. New York: St. Martin's, 1999.
Lincoln, Bruce. *Theorizing Myth: Narrative, Ideology, and Scholarship*. Chicago: University of Chicago Press, 1999.
Lloyd, David. "'Counterparts': *Dubliners*, Masculinity, and Temperance Nationalism." In *Semicolonial Joyce*, edited by Derek Attridge and Marjorie Howes, 128–49. Cambridge: Cambridge University Press, 2000.
———. "The Memory of Hunger." In *Loss: The Politics of Mourning*, edited by David L. Eng and David Kazanjian, 205–28. Berkeley: University of California Press, 2003.
Lynch, Owen. *Divine Passions: The Social Construction of Emotion in India*. Berkeley: University of California Press, 1990.
Lyotard, Jean-Françoise. *The Postmodern Condition: A Report on Knowledge*. Translated by Geoff Bennington and Brian Massumi. Minneapolis: University of Minnesota Press, 1984.
Maddox, Brenda. *Nora: A Biography of Nora Joyce*. New York: Fawcett-Columbine, 1988.
Mahadevan-Dasgupta, Uma. "Milestone: Midnight Turns 21." *Statesman* (India), 21 October 2002, n.p.
Majid, Anouar. *Unveiling Traditions: Postcolonial Islam in a Polycentric World*. Durham: Duke University Press, 2000.
Malcolm, Elizabeth. *"Ireland Sober, Ireland Free": Drink and Temperance in Nineteenth-Century Ireland*. Dublin: Gill and Macmillan, 1986.
Manganaro, Marvin. *Culture 1922: The Emergence of a Concept*. Princeton: Princeton University Press, 2002.
Marriott, McKim, ed. "Constructing an Indian Ethnosociology." In *India through Hindu Categories*. New Delhi: Sage, 1990.
Marshik, Celia. *British Modernism and Censorship*. Cambridge: Cambridge University Press, 2006.

Marx, John. *The Modernist Novel and the Decline of Empire*. Cambridge: Cambridge University Press, 2005.

Masuzawa, Tomoko. *The Invention of World Religions, Or, How European Universalism Was Preserved in the Language of Pluralism*. Chicago: University of Chicago Press, 2005.

Masuzawa, Tomo. "The Production of Religion and the Task of the Scholar." *Culture and Religion* 1 (2000): 123–30.

Mauss, Marcel. *Sociology and Psychology: Essays*. Translated by Ben Brewster. London: Routledge & Kegan Paul, 1979.

McClintock, Anne. *Imperial Leather: Race, Gender and Sex in the Colonial Contest*. London: Routledge, 1995.

McCole, Camille. *"Ulysses,"* review of *Ulysses*, by James Joyce, *Catholic World*, March 1934, 722–726.

McCourt, John. "Queering the Revivalist's Pitch: Joycean Engagements with Primitivism." In *Irish Modernism and the Global Primitive*, edited by Maria McGarrity and Claire Culleton, 17–39. Basingstoke, Eng.: Palgrave-Macmillan, 2009.

McCutcheon, Russell. *The Discipline of Religion: Structure, Meaning, Rhetoric*. London: Routledge, 2003.

McLeod, Hugh. "Protestantism and British National Identity 1815–1945." In *Nation and Religion: Perspectives on Europe and Asia*, edited by Peter van der Veer and Hartmut Lehman, 44–70. Princeton: Princeton University Press, 1999.

McNamer, Sarah. *Affective Meditation and the Invention of Medieval Compassion*. Philadelphia: University of Pennsylvania Press, 2010.

Mendes, Ana Cristina. "Salman Rushdie's 'Epico-Mythico-Tragico-Comico-Super-Sexy-High-Masala Art' or Considerations on Undisciplining the Boundaries." In *Salman Rushdie and Visual Culture: Celebrating Impurity, Disrupting Borders*, 1–11. Oxon, Eng.: Routledge 2011.

——, ed. *Salman Rushdie and Visual Culture: Celebrating Impurity, Disrupting Borders*. Oxon, Eng.: Routledge, 2011.

Michener, Charles. "A Burst of New Fiction." Review of *Midnight's Children*, by Salman Rushdie. *Newsweek*, 20 April 1981, 89.

Miles, Robert. *Gothic Writing, 1750–1820*. London: Routledge, 1993.

Miller, D. W. "Irish Catholicism and the Great Famine." *Journal of Social History* 9 (1975): 81–98.

Mishra, Vijay. *Bollywood Cinema: Temples of Desire*. London: Routledge, 2002.

——. *The Literature of the Indian Diaspora: Theorizing the Diasporic Imaginary*. London: Routledge, 2008.

——. "Rushdie-Wushdie: Salman Rushdie's Hobson-Jobson." *New Literary History* 40 (2009): 385–410.

Mishra, Vijay, Peter Jeffery, and Brian Shoesmith. "The Actor as Parallel Text in Bombay Cinema." *Quarterly Review of Film and Video* 11 (1989): 49–67.

Mizruchi, Susan. Introduction to *Religion and Cultural Studies*, ix–xxv. Princeton: Princeton University Press, 2001.

Moglen, Helene. *The Trauma of Gender: A Feminist Theory of the English Novel*. Berkeley: University of California Press, 2001.

Mondal, Anshuman. "*The Ground beneath Her Feet* and *Fury*: The Reinvention of Location." In *The Cambridge Companion to Salman Rushdie*, edited by Abdulrazak Gurnah, 169–84. Cambridge: Cambridge University Press, 2007.

Morrisson, Mark S. *The Public Face of Modernism*. Madison: University of Wisconsin Press, 2001.

Morse, J. Mitchell. *The Sympathetic Alien: James Joyce and Catholicism*. New York: New York University Press, 1959.

Morton, Stephen. "Metaphors of the Secular in the Fiction of Salman Rushdie." In *Metaphor and Diaspora in Contemporary Writing*, edited by Jonathan P. A. Sell, 151–69. Basingstoke, Eng.: Palgrave-Macmillan, 2012.

———. *Salman Rushdie: Fictions of Postcolonial Modernity*. Basingstoke, Eng.: Palgrave-Macmillan, 2008.

Moses, Michael Valdez, and Richard Begam, eds. *Modernism and Colonialism: British and Irish Literature, 1899–1919*. Durham: Duke University Press, 2007.

Mufti, Aamir. "Reading the Rushdie Affair: Islam, Cultural Politics, Form." In *Critical Essays on Salman Rushdie*, edited by M. Keith Booker, 51–77. New York: G. K. Hall, 1999.

Mukherjee, Anki. "Fissured Skin, Inner Ear Radio, and a Telepathic Nose: The Senses of Media in Salman Rushdie's *Midnight's Children*." *Paragraph* 29.3 (2003): 55–76.

Mukherjee, Bonny. "A Big City Novel." *India Today*, 16 May 1981, 126.

Mukherjee, Meenakshi. "The Anxiety of Indianness: Our Novels in English." *Economic and Political Weekly*, 27 November 1993, 2608.

———, ed. *Rushdie's Midnight's Children: A Book of Readings*. Delhi: Pencraft International, 1999.

Mullin, Katherine. "English Vice and Irish Vigilance: The Nationality of Obscenity in *Ulysses*." In *Joyce, Ireland, Britain*, edited by Andrew Gibson and Len Platt, 68–82. Gainesville: University Press of Florida, 2006.

———. *James Joyce, Sexuality, and Social Purity*. Cambridge: Cambridge University Press, 2003.

Murphy, J. H. *Catholic Fiction and Social Reality 1973–1922*. Westport, CT: Greenwood Press, 1997.

Murry, John. "Mr. Joyce's *Ulysses*. Review of *Ulysses*, *Nation & Athenaeum*, 22 April 1922, 124–25.

Nadel, Ira. "The Incomplete Joyce." *Joyce Studies Annual* 2.1 (1991): 86–100.

———. *Joyce and the Jews: Culture and Texts*. Iowa City: University of Iowa Press, 1989.

Nanporia, N. J. "I Have Always Been a Public Property." *Times of India*, 3 July 1982, 8F.

Nash, John. "'In the Heart of the Hibernian Metropolis'?: Joyce's Reception in Ireland, 1900–40." In *A Companion to James Joyce*, edited by Richard Brown, 108–22. Oxford: Blackwell, 2011.

———. "Irish Audiences and English Readers: The Cultural Politics of Shane Leslie's *Ulysses* Reviews." In *Joyce, Ireland, Britain*, edited by Andrew Gibson and Len Platt, 126–66. Gainesville: University Press of Florida, 2006.

———. *James Joyce and the Act of Reception: Reading, Ireland, Modernism*. Cambridge: Cambridge University Press, 2006.

———, ed. *Joyce's Audiences*. Amsterdam: Rodopi, 2002.

Nasta, Susheila. *Home Truths: Fictions of the South Asian Diaspora in Britain*. Basingstoke, Eng.: Palgrave-Macmillan, 2002.

Neville, Robert Cummings. *Religion in Late Modernity*. Albany: State University of New York Press, 2002.

Niemeyer, Carl. "'Grace' and Joyce's Method of Parody." *College English* 27 (1965): 196–201.

Nolan, Emer. *James Joyce and Nationalism*. London: Routledge, 1994.

Noon, William T. *Joyce and Aquinas*. New Haven: Yale University Press, 1963.

Norris, Margot. *Suspicious Readings of Joyce's Dubliners*. Philadelphia: University of Pennsylvania Press, 2003.
Osteen, Mark. *The Economy of* Ulysses: *Making Both Ends Meet*. Syracuse: Syracuse University Press, 1995.
Parameswaran, Uma. "Handcuffed to History: Salman Rushdie's Art." *Ariel* 14.4 (1983): 34–45.
Parkes, Adam. *Modernism and the Theater of Censorship*. Oxford: Oxford University Press, 1996.
Pearce, Richard. "Simon's Wild Irish Rose: Famine Songs, Blackfaced Minstrels, and Women's Repression in *A Portrait*." In *Joyce and the Return of the Repressed*, edited by Susan Stanford Friedman, 128–46. Ithaca: Cornell University Press, 1993.
Pickering, Michael. "White Skin, Black Masks: 'Nigger' Minstrelsy." In *Music Hall: Performance and Style*, edited by J. S. Bratton, 70–91. Philadelphia: Milton Keynes-Open University Press, 1986.
Pierce, David. *Joyce and Company*. New York: Continuum, 2006.
Pinney, Christopher. *Camera Indica: The Social Life of Indian Photographs*. Chicago: University of Chicago Press, 1997.
———. "Public, Popular, and Other Cultures." In *Pleasure in the Nation: The History, Politics, and Consumption of Public Culture in India*, edited by Rachel Dwyer and Christopher Pinney, 1–34. Oxford: Oxford University Press, 2001.
Pirbhai, Mariam. "The Paradox of Globalization as 'Untotalizable Totality' in Salman Rushdie's *The Ground beneath Her Feet*." *International Fiction Review* 28 (2001): 54–66.
Platt, Len. "The Buckeen and the Dogsbody: Aspects of History and Culture in 'Telemachus.'" *James Joyce Quarterly* 27 (1988):77–87.
———. *Joyce and the Anglo-Irish: A Study of Joyce and the Literary Revival*. Amsterdam: Rodopi, 1998.
"Portrait." *Newsweek*, 10 November 1941, 76.
Pritchett, V. S. "Two Novels." Review of *Midnight's Children*, by Salman Rushdie. *New Yorker*, 27 July 1981, 84–86.
Proudfoot, Wayne. *Religious Experience*. Berkeley: University of California Press, 1985.
Pugh, Judy F. "Person and Situation in North Indian Counseling: The Case of Astrology." In *South Asian Systems of Healing*, edited by E. Valentine Daniel and Judy Pugh, 85–105. Leiden, Neth.: E. J. Brill, 1984.
Rainey, Lawrence. *The Institutions of Modernism*. New Haven: Yale University Press, 1998.
Rajadhyaksha, Ashish. "The Phalke Era: Conflict of Traditional Form and Modern Technology." *Journal of Arts and Ideas* 14-15 (1989): 47–78.
Ramachandran, Hema. "Salman Rushdie's *The Satanic Verses*: Hearing the Postcolonial Cinematic Novel." *Journal of Commonwealth Literature* 40.3 (2005): 102–17.
Reder, Michael, ed. *Conversations with Salman Rushdie*. Jackson: University Press of Mississippi, 2000.
Rege, Josna. "Victim into Protagonist? *Midnight's Children* and the Post-Rushdie National Narratives of the Eighties." *Studies in the Novel* 29 (1997): 342–75.
Reizbaum, Marilyn. *James Joyce's Judaic Other*. Stanford: Stanford University Press, 1999.
Reynolds, Mary T. *Joyce and Dante: The Shaping of Imagination*. Princeton: Princeton University Press, 1981.
Riemenschneider, Dieter. "History and the Individual in Anita Desai's *Clear Light of Day* and Salman Rushdie's *Midnight's Children*." In *The New Indian Novel in English: A Study of the 1980s*, edited by Viney Kirpal, 187–200. New Delhi: Allied, 1990.
Rody, Caroline. *The Interethnic Imagination: Roots and Passages in Contemporary Asian-American Fiction*. Oxford: Oxford University Press, 2009.

Roh, Francis. "Magic Realism: Post-Expressionism." Reprinted in *Magical Realism: Theory, History, Community*, edited by Lois Parkinson Zamora and Wendy B. Faris, 15–31. Durham: Duke University Press, 1995.

Rose, Nikolas. *Inventing Ourselves: Psychology, Power, and Personhood*. Cambridge: Cambridge University Press, 1998.

Roy, Parama. *Indian Traffic: Identities in Question in Colonial and Postcolonial India*. Berkeley: University of California Press, 1998.

"The Rushdie Affair: A Muslim's Perspective." *Index on Censorship*, April 1990, 13.

Rushdie, Salman. "Damme, This Is the Oriental Scene for You!" *New Yorker*, 23 & 27 July 1997, 50–61.

———. *East, West: Stories*. New York: Pantheon, 1994.

———. "The Empire Writes Back with a Vengeance." London *Times*, 3 July 1982, 8F.

———. *The Enchantress of Florence*. New York: Random House, 2008.

———. *Fury*. New York: Random House, 2001.

———. *Grimus*. 1975. New York: Random House, 2003.

———. *The Ground beneath Her Feet*. New York: Holt-Picador, 1999.

———. *Haroun and the Sea of Stories*. London: Granta; New York: Viking-Penguin, 1991.

———. *Imaginary Homelands: Essays and Criticism, 1981–91*. London: Granta; New York: Viking-Penguin, 1991.

———. Interview, "Charlie Rose Show." Public Broadcasting System, 30 June 2008.

———. *Joseph Anton: A Memoir*. New York: Random House, 2012.

———. *Luka and the Fire of Life*. New York: Random House, 2010.

———. *Midnight's Children*, 1981. New York: Penguin, 1991.

———. *The Moor's Last Sigh*. New York: Pantheon, 1995.

———. *The Satanic Verses*. 1988. New York, Viking, 1989.

———. *Shalimar the Clown*. New York: Random House, 2005.

———. *Shame*. New York: Knopf, 1983.

———. *Step across this Line: Collected Nonfiction, 1992–2002*. New York: Random House, 2002.

———. *The Wizard of Oz*. London: BFI, 1992.

"Rushdie's Parallel View of India through a Brilliant Novel." Review of *Midnight's Children*, by Salman Rushdie. *India West*, 12 June 1981, 7.

Ruthven, Malise. *A Satanic Affair: Salman Rushdie and the Wrath of Islam*. Rev. ed. London: Hogarth-Chatto & Windus, 1991.

Sandru, Cristina. "Visual Technolgies in Rushdie's Fiction: Envisioning the Present in the Imagological Age." In *Salman Rushdie and Visual Culture: Celebrating Impurity, Disrupting Borders*, edited by Ana Cristina Mendes, 137–57. Oxon, Eng.: Routledge 2011.

Sanga, Jaina. *Salman Rushdie's Postcolonial Metaphors: Migration, Translation, Hybridity, Blasphemy, and Globalization*. Westport, CT: Greenwood Press, 2001.

Sangari, Kumkum. "Interview with Salman Rushdie," *The Book Review* 8.5 (1984), 247–53. In *Salman Rushdie Interviews: A Sourcebook of His Ideas*, edited by Pradyumna Chauhan, 63–74. Westport, CT: Greenwood Press, 2001.

———. *Politics of the Possible: Essays on Gender, History, Narratives, Colonial English*. London: Anthem South Asian Studies-Wimbledon, 2002.

Sardar, Ziauddin, and Merryl Wyn Davies. *Distorted Imagination: Lessons from the Rushdie Affair*. London: Grey Seal; Kuala Lumpur: Berita, 1990.

Sawhney, Sabina, and Simona Sawhney. "Reading Rushdie after September 11, 2001." *Twentieth Century Literature* 47 (2001): 31–43.

Sayyid, Bobby. *A Fundamental Fear: Eurocentrism and the Emergence of Islam*. London: Zed; New York: St. Martin's, 1997.

Schimmel, Annamarie. *And Muhammad Is His Messenger: The Veneration of the Prophet in Islamic Piety.* Chapel Hill: University of North Carolina Press, 1985.

Schleiermacher, Friedrich. *On Religion: Speeches to Its Cultured Despisers.* Translated by Richard Crouter. Cambridge: Cambridge University Press, 1988.

Schloss, Carol Loeb. *Lucia Joyce: To Dance in the Wake.* New York: Farrar, Straus and Giroux, 2003.

Schlossman, Beryl. *Joyce's Catholic Comedy of Language.* Madison: University of Wisconsin Press, 1985.

Schoene, Berthold. *The Cosmopolitan Novel.* Edinburgh: Edinburgh University Press, 2009.

Scholes, Robert. "'Counterparts' and the Method of *Dubliners.*" In *Dubliners: Text and Criticism,* by James Joyce, edited by Robert Scholes and A. Walton Litz, 339–47. New York: Viking-Penguin, 1996.

Schwarze, Tracey Teets. *Joyce and the Victorians.* Gainesville: University Press of Florida, 2002.

Scott, David, and Charles Hirschkind, eds. *Powers of the Secular Modern: Talal Asad and His Interlocutors.* Stanford: Stanford University Press, 2006.

Segall, Jeffrey. *Joyce in America: Cultural Politics, and the Trials of* Ulysses. Berkeley: University of California Press, 1993.

Seldes, Gilbert. Review of *Ulysses,* by James Joyce. *Nation,* 30 August 1922, 211–12.

Sethi, Sunil. "An Indian Scheherazade." Review of *Midnight's Children,* by Salman Rushdie. *India Today,* 16 May 1981, 126–27.

Sharma, Shailja. "'Precious Gift/Piece of Shit': Salman Rushdie's *The Satanic Verses* and the Revenge of History." In *Scandalous Fictions: The Twentieth-Century Novel in the Public Sphere,* edited by Jago Morrison and Susan Watkins, 136–49. Hampshire, Eng.: Palgrave-Macmillan, 2006.

Sicari, Stephen. *Joyce's Modernist Allegory.* Columbia: University of South Carolina Press, 2001.

"Silence, Exile, and Death." *Time,* 10 February 1941, 72.

Slemon, Stephen. "Magic Realism as Post-colonial Discourse." *Canadian Literature* 116 (1988): 9–24.

Slote, Sam. *The Silence in Progress of Dante, Mallarmé, and Joyce.* New York: Peter Lang, 1999.

Smith, Jonathan Z. *Relating Religion: Essays in the Study of Religion.* Chicago: University of Chicago Press, 2004.

Sournia, John-Charles. *A History of Alcoholism.* Translated by Nick Hindley and Gareth Stanton. Oxford: Basil Blackwell, 1990.

Spencer, Robert. "Salman Rushdie and the War on Terror." *Journal of Postcolonial Writing* 46 (2010): 251–65.

Spiegel, Alix. "One Man Tackles Psychotherapy for the Amish." *All Things Considered,* National Public Radio, 18 March 2009, http://www.npr.org/templates/story/story.php?storyId=102053475

Spivak, Gayatri Chakravorty. "Reading *The Satanic Verses.*" *Public Culture* 2 (1989): 79–99.

Spurr, David. *Joyce and the Scene of Modernity.* Gainesville: University Press of Florida, 2002.

Stadtler, Florian. "Nobody from Bombay Should Be without a Basic Film Vocabulary: *Midnight's Children* and the Visual Culture of Popular Cinema." In *Salman Rushdie and Visual Culture: Celebrating Impurity, Disrupting Borders,* edited by Ana Cristina Mendes, 123–23. Oxon, Eng.: Routledge 2011.

Stephens, John. "*Midnight's Children:* The Parody of an Indian Novel." *Journal of the South Pacific Association for Commonwealth Literature and Language Studies* 81 (1985): 184–208.

Suleri, Sara. "Contraband Histories: Salman Rushdie and the Embodiment of Blasphemy." *Yale Review* 78 (1989): 604–24.
———. *The Rhetoric of English India.* Chicago: University of Chicago Press, 1992.
Sullivan, Kevin. *Joyce among the Jesuits.* New York: Columbia University Press, 1958.
Syed, Mujeebuddin. "Warped Mythologies: Salman Rushdie's *Grimus.*" *Ariel* 25.4 (1994): 135–51.
Taylor, Lawrence J. *Occasions of Faith: An Anthropology of Irish Catholics.* Philadelphia: University of Pennsylvania Press, 1995.
ten Kortenaar, Neil. *Self, Nation, and Text in Salman Rushdie's* Midnight's Children. Montreal and Kingston: McGill-Queen's University Press, 2004.
Teverson, Andrew. *Salman Rushdie.* Manchester: Manchester University Press, 2007.
Thayer, Scofield. "James Joyce." *Dial* 773 (September 1918), 202.
Theall, Donald. *James Joyce's Techno-Poetics.* Toronto: University of Toronto Press, 1997.
Thiara, Nicole Weickgennant. *Salman Rushdie and Indian Historiography: Writing the Nation into Being.* Basingstoke, Eng.: Palgrave-Macmillan, 2009.
Thomas, Rosie. "Sanctity and Scandal: The Mythologization of Mother India." *Quarterly Review of Film and Video* 11 (1989): 11–30.
Tinniswood, Peter. Review of *Grimus,* by Salman Rushdie. London *Times,* 21 February 1975, 8D.
Torchiana, Donald. *Backgrounds for Joyce's* Dubliners. Boston: Allen and Unwin, 1986.
Towers, Robert. "On the Indian World Mountain." Review of *Midnight's Children,* by Salman Rushdie. *New York Review of Books,* 24 September 1981, 28–30.
Townsend, Paul. *Father Mathew, Temperance, and Irish Identity.* Dublin: Irish Academic Press, 2002.
"Traveling Joyce." *Time,* 17 February 1947, 109.
Tripathi, Salil. "The Last—and the Best—Salman Rushdie Interview in India!" *Celebrity* (May 1983): n.p. Reprinted in *Conversations with Salman Rushdie,* edited by Michael Reder, 20–29. Jackson: University Press of Mississippi, 2000.
Trivedi, Harish. "Salman the Funtoosh: Magic Bilingualism in *Midnight's Children.*" In *Rushdie's* Midnight's Children, edited by Meenakasi Mukherjee, 69–94. Delhi: Pencraft International, 1999.
Updike, John. "Paradises Lost." Review of *Shalimar the Clown,* by Salman Rushdie, *New Yorker,* 9 September 2005, http://www.newyorker.com/archive/2005/09/05/050905crbo
Vanderham, Paul. *Joyce and Censorship.* New York: New York University Press, 1988.
Valente, Joseph. "James Joyce and the Cosmopolitan Sublime." In *Joyce and the Subject of History,* edited by Mark Wollaeger, Victor Luftig, and Robert Spoo, 59–80. Ann Arbor: University of Michigan Press, 1996.
———. *James Joyce and the Problem of Justice: Negotiating Sexual and Colonial Difference.* Cambridge: Cambridge University Press, 1995.
———. *The Myth of Manliness in Irish National Culture, 1880–1922.* Urbana: University of Illinois Press, 2011.
———. "Neither Fish nor Flesh; or How 'Cyclops' Stages the Double-Bind of Irish Manhood." In *Semicolonial Joyce,* edited by Derek Attridge and Marjorie Howes, 96–127. Cambridge: Cambridge University Press, 2000.
van Boheemen, Christine. "Joyce's Sublime Body: Trauma, Textuality, and Subjectivity." In *Joycean Cultures/Culturing Joyces,* edited by Vincent Cheng, Kimberly Devlin, and Margot Norris, 23–43. Newark: University of Delaware Press; London: Associated University Presses, 1998.

van der Veer, Peter. *Imperial Encounters: Religion and Modernity in India and Britain*. Princeton: Princeton University Press, 2001.
van der Veer, Peter, and Hartmut Lehman, eds. *Nation and Religion: Perspectives on Europe and Asia*. Princeton: Princeton University Press, 1999.
Vasudevan, Ravi. "Addressing the Spectator of a 'Third World' National Cinema: The Bombay 'Social Film' of the 1940s and 1950s." *Screen* 36 (1995): 305–24.
———. "The Politics of Cultural Address in a 'Transitional' Cinema: A Case Study of Indian Popular Cinema." In *Reinventing Film Studies*, edited by Christine Gledhill and Linda Williams, 130–64. Oxford: Oxford University Press; London: Arnold, 2000.
Vesala-Varttala, Tanja. *Sympathy and Joyce's Dubliners: Ethical Probing of Reading, Narrative, and Textuality*. Tampere: University of Tampere Press, 1999.
Viswanathan, Gauri. "The Literary Rushdie." In *Midnight's Diaspora: Critical Encounters with Salman Rushdie*, edited by Daniel Herwitz and Ashutosh Varshney, 23–39. Ann Arbor: University of Michigan Press, 2008.
———. *Outside the Fold: Conversion, Modernity, and Belief*. Princeton: Princeton University Press, 1998.
Wachtel, Eleanor. "Salman Rushdie." Reprinted in *Salman Rushdie Interviews: A Sourcebook of His Ideas*, edited by Pradyumna Chauhan, 121–35. Westport, CT: Greenwood Press, 2001.
Waldmeir, John. *Cathedrals of Bone: The Role of the Body in Contemporary Catholic Literature*. New York: Fordham University Press, 2009.
Walkowitz, Rebecca. *Cosmopolitan Style: Modernism beyond the Nation*. New York: Columbia University Press, 2006.
Welch, Claude. *Protestant Thought in the Nineteenth Century*. 2 vols. Vol. 2, 1870–1914. New Haven: Yale University Press, 1985.
Werbner, Pnina. "Stamping the Earth with the Name of Allah: *Zikr* and the Sacralizing of Space among British Muslims." In *Making Muslim Space in North America and Europe*, edited by Barbara Daly Metcalf, 167–85. Berkeley: University of California Press, 1996.
Wexler, Joyce Piell. *Who Paid for Modernism*. Fayetteville: University of Arkansas Press, 1997.
Wicke, Jennifer. *Advertising Fictions*. New York: Columbia University Press, 1998.
Wilson, David. "Fable-minded." Review of *Grimus*, by Salman Rushdie. London *Times Literary Supplement*, 21 February 1975, 185.
Wilson, Edmund. "*Ulysses*." Review of *Ulysses*, by James Joyce. *New Republic*, 5 July 1922, 164–66.
Wilson, Jon E. "Subjects and Agents in the History of Imperialism and Resistance." In *Powers of the Secular Modern: Talal Asad and His Interlocutors*, edited by David Scott and Charles Hirschkind, 180–205. Stanford: Stanford University Press, 2006.
Wilt, Judith. "The Imperial Mouth: Imperialism, the Gothic, and Science Fiction." *Journal of Popular Culture* 14 (1981): 618–28.
Wood, James. *The Broken Estate: Essays on Literature and Belief*. New York: Picador-St. Martin's, 1999.
Yacoubi, Youssef. *The Play of Reasons: The Sacred and the Profane in Salman Rushdie's Fiction*. New York: Peter Lang, 2002.
Zamora, Lois Parkinson, and Wendy B. Faris, eds. *Magical Realism: Theory, History, Community*. Durham: Duke University Press, 1995.
Žižek, Slavoj. "Cyberspace, or, How to Traverse the Fantasy in the Age of the Retreat of the Big Other." *Public Culture* 10 (1998): 483–513.
———. *The Sublime Object of Ideology*. London: Verso, 1989.

Index

Ahmad, Aijaz, 53
alcohol, drink, and drunkenness: in *Dubliners* (See *Dubliners*); in *Finnegans Wake*, 143–44; Joyce's drinking habits, 149–50; in *Midnight's Children*, 60; in *Ulysses*, 88–93
Aldiss, Brian, 46
Ali, Monica, 157
Almond, Ian, 117
Amis, Martin, 66
anarchy, Joyce and, 147
Angeli, Diego, 22–23, 25, 165n81
anonymity: communal illness in *Dubliners* and, 34; drunkard as anonymous type, 26; of drunkard in *Dubliners*, 16, 31–32; notorious-anonymous person in *Finnegans Wake*, 143
anthropological religion, 4, 8, 15, 24
antiquarianism in *Ulysses*, 77
Aquinas, Thomas, St., 148
Aramis, 125–26, 129
Aristotle, 84
"The Art of Suspense" (Batty), 51
art-religion binary, 120–23, 157
Asad, Talal, 4, 10, 42, 72, 82, 136, 160n19
Ashraf, Syed Ali, 137
audience as body divided, in Joyce, 14
Augustine of Hippo, St., 147

authenticity: belief as pastness and, 3; "Counterparts" (*Dubliners*) and, 28; gothic and, 100, 101; impersonation and, 99; in *Midnight's Children*, 43, 53, 66–67, 104; racial, 112; Rushdie on, 45; in *Satanic Verses*, 111–12, 119
Āyurvedic medicine, 5, 56–60

Babb, Lawrence, 105
Bachchan, Ambitabh, 103
Backus, Margot, 76, 77, 82
Bakhtin, Mikhail, 32
Barth, John, 51
Bassi, Shaul, 64
Batty, Nancy E., 51
Baudrillard, Jean, 100, 112, 115, 153
Begam, Richard, 161n6
belief: anthropological understanding of, 24; Christian orthodoxy and, 10; Irish Catholicism and, 131, 146; Joyce and disciplinary belief, 156; in *Midnight's Children*, 56, 114, 116–17; orthodoxy and, 3–4; "rational religion" and, 42; Rushdie on India and, 42–43; *Satanic Verses* and, 123, 138; secularization and privatization of, 11; in *Ulysses*, 69–73, 81, 82, 94–96; *Ulysses* and *Satanic*

Verses controversies and, 121; Wells on worldly vs. private, 130–31. *See also* orthodoxy; orthopraxy
Benedictine "active reading," 81, 85
Benjamin, Walter, 108
Bennett, Arnold, 125–26, 129
Berkeley, George, 84
Bhabha, Homi, 163n51
Biernoff, Suzannah, 85
Bishop, John, 143
blood: in *Dubliners*, 33–34; in *Midnight's Children*, 58, 60, 62, 105; in *Portrait of the Artist as a Young Man*, 75; in *Satanic Verses*, 119; in *Ulysses*, 71, 88–89, 95, 125–26
bodies and embodiment: audience as divided body in Joyce, 14; "being" vs. "having" a body, 127, 131; Certeau's strategic embodiment, 101, 106, 123, 127; Irish Catholicism and bodily control, 12; minority religious practices and spiritually disciplined bodies, 2–3; modernist substitution of text for bodies, 6; provincial, 4, 5, 15. *See also* senses; somatopsychic model; *specific works*
Boscagli, Maurizia, 146
Bowlby, Rachel, 133
Boyagoda, Randy, 152, 155, 183n56
Boyd, Ernest, 14, 15, 132, 163n47
Boyle, Robert, 70
Brennan, Timothy, 53, 170n71
Brock, A. Clutton, 21
Brooker, Joseph, 124, 172n2, 178n7
Brooks, Van Wyck, 22, 147
Buchan, John, 78
Buford, Bill, 47
Butler, Judith, 4, 11
Buzard, James, 9, 24
Bynum, Caroline Walker, 85

Carpentier, Alejo, 68
Carrette, Jeremy, 160n19
Castle of Otranto (Walpole), 100
Cates, Jim, 1
celebrity and public persona: defined, 141; godlike stars in Indian film, 102–4; Joyce and, 141–50; Rushdie and, 141–42, 150–57
Certeau, Michel de, 2, 101, 106, 123, 127
Chakravarty, Sumita, 99
Chamber Music (Joyce), 17
Cheah, Pheng, 163n51
Cheng, Anne, 112
Cheyette, Bryan, 70
Choitner, Isaac, 142
Christianity: Bynum on body and, 85; Islam and Judaism contrasted with, 11, 81, 135; liberal Christianity and personhood, 1–2; modern, secular "self" and, 42; orthodoxy and, 3, 10–11, 81; temperance movement and, 27. *See also* Irish Catholicism; orthodoxy
Colum, Padraic, 23, 25, 165n81
communal identity, communal body, and communal illness: British imperialism and, 11; in *Dubliners*, 16, 26, 28, 30–31, 34–35; individualism vs., 5; in *Midnight's Children*, 56, 62; orthopraxy vs. orthodoxy and, 11, 81; in *Satanic Verses*, 99, 113–14, 123, 136, 137; in *Ulysses*, 71, 89–90
compulsive practice in *Dubliners*, 16, 26, 28, 34, 35–36, 39
Connolly, Cyril, 147
Connolly, S. J., 12
conversion in *Dubliners*, 16, 27–30, 34–35, 37, 38
Corrigan, John, 3, 10
cosmopolitanism: *Finnegans Wake* and, 143, 146–47; Joyce and, 5, 14–15, 148; *Midnight's Children* and, 41, 44–45, 51, 52–53, 66–67; modernism and, 4; Rushdie and, 5; *Satanic Verses* and, 98–99, 116; *Ulysses* and, 126, 131–33; *Ulysses* controversy and, 132–33
"Counterparts" (Joyce), 25, 27–30
Couto, Maria, 49
Cowley, Malcolm, 146
Crary, Jonathan, 82–83, 109, 127–28
Crawford, Robert, 9
Cullen, Paul, 82
culture and religion, 9–10
Cunningham, Valerie, 48

Danius, Sara, 83
darsanic gaze, 104–5, 108, 114–15, 117–18
Darwin, Charles, 110–11
Davison, Neil, 70
Dawson, Ashley, 105–6
Deane, Seamus, 81
death: in *Dubliners*, 37–38; in *Finnegans Wake*, 147; in *Ground beneath Her Feet*, 152–53; Rushdie and Elvis in Far Side cartoon, 150–51; in *Ulysses*, 75–76, 87, 89, 144. *See also* ghosts
degeneration and degeneracy: in *Dubliners*, 26; in *Satanic Verses*, 99–100, 106, 109–10, 115; in *Ulysses*, 71, 78–80, 88, 91, 93
Deming, Robert, 23, 165n81
Denny, Frederick, 135–36
Derrida, Jacques, 34–35, 74
Desai, Anita, 48–49, 50
Desani, G. V., 44, 49
Despland, Michel, 10
Devji, Faisal, 113
disciplinary religion and belief: archaism and, 3; in *Ground beneath Her Feet*, 155–56; Irish Catholicism and, 4–5, 11–12; as productive, 2; in *Ulysses*, 69–72, 82–83, 88, 93–95. *See also* orthopraxy
disciplined bodies: alcohol and, in *Dubliners*, 5, 13–17, 25–35, 30–31; Hinduism and, 42; Indian Muslims and, 6; Irish Catholicism and, 12–13; in *Portrait of the Artist as a Young Man*, 12–13; in *Satanic Verses*, 104, 105; in *Ulysses*, 122–23, 131
Dissanayake, Wimal, 51
Dole, Andrew, 10
Doyle, Laura, 70, 88
Dracula (Stoker), 75, 78
drunkenness. *See* alcohol, drink, and drunkenness; *Dubliners*
Dubliners (Joyce): alcohol as counterdisciplinary agency in, 5, 13–17; alcohol as surrogate for spiritual discipline in, 25–26; bodily visual inspection and detached narrative stance in, 17, 32–33, 39–40; complaints against, 124; "Counterparts," 25, 27–30; divided audience and, 14; early reviews and reception of, 17–23; "Grace," 25, 28, 30–35; Irish-Catholic orthopraxy and, 5; New Criticism on, 18, 24–25; orthopraxy and, 40; "A Painful Case," 17, 35–39, 89, 144; provincial-cosmopolitan binary and, 14–15; Rushdie's *Midnight's Children* and, 43; spiritual-medical nexus of, 26; temperance movements and, 26–27; themes in, 15–17
Dubuisson, Daniel, 8
Duffy, Enda, 79, 146
Durix, Jean-Pierre, 52

Eco, Umberto, 70
Eglinton, John, 133
Ellmann, Richard, 148–49, 182n37, 182n42
The Enchantress of Florence (Rushdie), 150
English, James, 111–12, 142

fable, modernist vs. "Indian," 49
Farrell, J. G., 49
Faruqi, M. H., 137
Feinstein, Elaine, 47
femininity and female bodies: female sympathies in *Dubliners*, 36–37, 38, 144; in *Finnegan's Wake*, 144; Irish-Catholic mother and ghost in *Ulysses*, 71, 75–76, 93–94; in *Midnight's Children*, 62; in *Ulysses*, 77, 95; *Ulysses* controversy and, 126
fetish structure, 134–35
film, Indian, 99–106
Finnegans Wake (Joyce), 141, 142–47
Ford, Ford Madox, 132
Fordham, Finn, 143, 144–45
Forster, E. M., 48
Foucault, Michel, 26, 36, 101, 160n19
Franchot, Jenny, 3
Freud, Sigmund, 143
Freund, Gisèle, 146
Froula, Christine, 74, 75
Fury (Rushdie), 150

Gandhi, Mohandas, 42

Gandhy, Behroze, 102
Gargi, Balwant, 50, 169n53
gaze, darsanic, 104–5, 108, 114–15, 117–18
gaze, detached: in *Midnight's Children*, 54; narrative stance in *Dubliners* and, 17, 32–33, 39–40; in *Satanic Verses*, 108–10; in *Ulysses*, 83–84, 128–29
Geertz, Clifford, 53, 121
genealogy, in *Ulysses*, 74
Ghiselin, Brewster, 24
Ghosh, Bishnupriya, 53
ghosts: gothic signification of, 100; in *Satanic Verses*, 108; in *Ulysses*, 75–76, 93–94. *See also* gothic tropes
Gibson, Andrew, 72, 74, 77
Gikandi, Simon, 116
Givens, Seon, 148
Glover, David, 75
Goldman, Jonathan, 145, 148, 150
Gorman, Herbert, 131–32, 146
gothic tropes: "imperial" gothic, 78, 109; in *Satanic Verses*, 100–102; in *Ulysses*, 73–80, 93–94
Gottfried, Roy, 70
"Grace" (Joyce), 25, 28, 30–35
Grass, Günter, 47
Griffin, Susan, 74
Grimus (Rushdie), 43, 45–46, 66, 155
The Ground beneath Her Feet (Rushdie), 5, 141–43, 150–57

Haggard, H. Rider, 78
Hagopian, John, 25
Halberstam, Judith, 101
Heap, Jane, 14, 25
hearing, agency of, 84
Heiland, Donna, 76
Herderian romanticism, 42
Herr, Cheryl, 39, 93
Hinduism: Āyurvedic medicine, 56–60; darsanic gaze, 104–5, 108, 114–15, 117–18; Indian nationalism and, 42; *Midnight's Children* and, 49, 55–60, 63, 68; *Satanic Verses* and, 97–104; somatization and, 55
Hoberman, John, 79

Hogle, Jerrold, 100
"The Holy Office" (Joyce), 148
Hone, Joseph, 132–33
Huddleston, Sisley, 124
Hungerford, Amy, 161n2
Hussain, Mushahid, 138

Ibsen, Henrik, 149
"Ibsen's New Drama" (Joyce), 149
identificatory assimilation, 112
"Imaginary Homelands" (Rushdie), 64–65
immunity in *Midnight's Children*, 62–63
"impersonation," 99–100, 116
Indian film, popular, 99–106
Indian myth, 41–43
Indian provincialism and Indianness in *Midnight's Children*, 44–49, 53, 61
individual subjectivity, self, and the person: Amish adolescents and, 1; anonymity and, 32; art-religion binary and, 120–21, 122–23; assumption of, 1; Certeau's strategic embodiment, 101, 106, 123, 127; fetish structure and, 134–35; Joyce's reformulation of, 13; liberal Christianity and personhood, 1–2; *Midnight's Children* and, 53–54, 57–59, 67–68; *Satanic Verses* and, 101–2, 106; *Ulysses* and, 72, 88, 95–96; *Ulysses* controversy and, 126–27
injury: divine injury from *Satanic Verses*, 124; in *Dubliners*, 26, 31–34; in *Midnight's Children*, 59–60
insider-outsider position: clinical gaze in *Dubliners* and, 39; *Midnight's Children* and, 41, 43, 53, 66–67, 167n12; provincial spiritual body and, 4, 9; religion and, 2; *Ulysses* and, 71, 84
interiority: belief and, 3, 10; in *Dubliners*, 16; in *Midnight's Children*, 68; in *Satanic Verses*, 100–101, 106, 110, 114–15; in *Ulysses*, 71, 72, 76, 78, 89, 121, 128; Wilde and, 150
invasion, reverse, 78–79, 114–15
Irish Catholicism: blamed for Joyce's defects, 146; as defensive strategy, 81–82; doctrine and sensual repression

equated with, 70–71; *Dubliners* and, 21–23, 39–40; Joyce's renunciation of, 148; Judaism as disciplinary orientation of, 71; orthopraxy and, 4–5, 11–13; *Portrait of the Artist as a Young Man* and, 22–23; strategic embodiment and, 123; temperance and, 27; as ultimate Protestant Other, 71; *Ulysses* and, 71–75, 88–93, 95, 130–32

Irish provincialism and Irishness: cosmopolitanism vs., 14–15; *Dubliners* and, 19–20, 21; Joyce's renunciation of Ireland, 148; *Ulysses* and, 132–33, 163n48

Irving, John, 50

Islam and Muslims: as category of identity, 113–14; Christianity contrasted with Judaism and, 11, 81, 135; *Midnight's Children* and, 58–59; orthopraxy and, 3–4, 11, 135–36; Qu'ran, 97–98, 104–5, 112–13, 115, 137–38; strategic embodiment and, 123. See also *The Satanic Verses*

Jaffe, Aaron, 6, 24, 141
Jay, Martin, 82–83, 127–28
Jewish male, in *Ulysses*, 79–80, 82
Jhabvala, Ruth Prawer, 49, 50
Joseph Anton (Rushdie), 43, 142
Joyce, James: archaism and, 4; *Chamber Music*, 17; clinical-ethnographical detachment of, 17, 39–40; cosmopolitanism and, 5, 14–15; death of, 147; drinking habits of, 149–50; *Finnegans Wake*, 141, 142–47; "The Holy Office," 148; "Ibsen's New Drama," 149; provincialism and, 4–5, 9, 14–15. See also *Dubliners*; *A Portrait of the Artist as a Young Man*; *Ulysses*
Joyce, John, 149
Joyce, Lucia, 149, 182n42
Joyce, Stanislaus, 149, 182n37
"Joyce's Dublin" (Colum), 23
Judaism: Christianity contrasted with Islam and, 11, 81, 135; Irish Catholicism, relation to disciplinary orientation of, 70–71; orthopraxy and, 3–4, 5; in *Satanic Verses*, 100; in *Ulysses*, 82, 84, 95

Jung, Carl, 149
Jussawalla, Feroza, 117

Kahane, Clare, 76
Kain, Richard M., 147
Kanaganayakam, C., 51–52
Kapur, Geeta, 106
Kaufman, Michael T., 45
Kaye, Julian, 24
Kelly, Richard, 20, 163n45, 163n49
Kenner, Hugh, 172n2
Kershner, R. B., 13, 31
Khomeini, Ayatollah, 139, 142, 150
King, Richard, 10
King Solomon's Mines (Haggard), 78, 154
Kleinman, Arthur, 16, 28, 56, 57–58
Krieger, Martin, 135
Kristeva, Julia, 75
Kumar, Amitava, 45
Kundera, Milan, 47–48

labor and drinking in *Dubliners*, 27, 28, 30
Lalvani, Suren, 85
Lamarck, Jean-Baptiste, 110–11
Larbaud, Valéry, 14, 15, 132–33, 163n48
Larson, Gary, 150–51, 152
Lawrence, T. H., 133
Leclerq, Jean, 81, 85
Leggatt, Judith, 168n32
Lehmann, Hartmut, 9
Leonard, Garry, 13
Leonard, John, 47, 48
Lernout, Geert, 5, 70
Leslie, Shane, 125, 133, 178n12
Levin, Harry, 24, 147, 148
Lewis, Pericles, 70
Lewis, Wyndham, 128
Lilienfeld, Jane, 149, 182n37
Lincoln, Bruce, 42
liquor. See alcohol, drink, and drunkenness; *Dubliners*
Lloyd, David, 12, 27, 28, 29, 30, 31, 166n108
Loyola, Ignatius, St., 84

Lynch, Owen, 170n79
Lyotard, Jean-François, 118–19

Macy, John, 22
magic realism, 47, 52, 64, 168n32
Mahadevan-Dasgupta, Uma, 66–67
Mailer, Norman, 139
Mais, S. P. B., 128
Maitland, Cecil, 130, 131–32, 133, 146
Malcolm, Elizabeth, 27
Manganaro, Marvin, 25
Mann, Thomas, 51
Manto, Sadaat Hasan, 67
Markandaya, Kamal, 50
Marquez, Gabriel Garcia, 47
Marriott, McKim, 57
masculinity and male bodies: in *Dubliners*, 28–30; in *Finnegans Wake*, 144; in *Midnight's Children*, 62; in *Satanic Verses*, 117–18; in *Ulysses*, 71, 77–78, 88–93, 126
Masuzawa, Tomoko, 10
Mathew, Theobald, 27
Mauss, Marcel, 12
Mazrui, Ali, 137, 138
McCarthy, Michael J. F., 12
McClintock, Anne, 78
McCole, Camille, 125, 129
McCutcheon, Russell, 10, 161n1
McLeod, Hugh, 71
McNamer, Sarah, 81
medical-clinical paradigms: in *Dubliners*, 13, 16, 26, 34, 36–38, 73; in *Midnight's Children*, 5, 54–55, 60; in *Portrait of the Artist*, 73; in *Ulysses*, 91–92. *See also* gaze, detached; Vedic medicine and philosophy
memory: Benedictine "active reading" and, 81; *Ground beneath Her Feet* and, 153; *Midnight's Children* and, 63, 65
metonymic production in *Midnight's Children*, 63–66
metrocolonials, 15–17, 150, 161n5
Midnight's Children (Rushdie): criticism on, 51–53; *Dubliners* and, 43; "God-shaped hole" in, 138; "Indian myth" and, 41–43; Indianness, genre classification, and early reception of, 44–51; 66–67; metonymic production and mythic authority in, 61–66; orthopraxy and, 5; Rushdie's insider-outsider position and, 41, 43, 53, 66–67, 167n12; *Satanic Verses* and, 98, 102, 104, 119; somatopsychic corpus and Āyurvedic medicine in, 52–60
migrancy and migrant identity: in *Midnight's Children*, 43, 64–65; Rushdie on, 61; in *Satanic Verses*, 99, 116–17
Miles, Robert, 74, 76
mimicry, 92–93, 107
Mishra, Vijay, 102, 140
Mizruchi, Susan, 9
modernism and modernity: archaism and, 3–4; cosmopolitanism and, 15; disciplinary belief and, 2; *Dubliners* and, 22, 25; fable and, 49; gothic monstrosity and, 101; *The Ground beneath Her Feet* and, 141; Joyce's celebrity and, 46, 47; Lyotard on, 118; *Midnight's Children* and, 41–42, 48; panics over *Ulysses* and *Satanic Verses* and, 120, 121–22, 127–28, 131, 140; provincialism and, 9; religion, countermodernity, and, 7, 9–10; reverse invasion and, 78; *Satanic Verses* and, 118–19; temperance movements and, 27; texts substituted for bodies and, 6; *Ulysses* and, 69, 82–83, 86, 94–95; Weber's rationalization and, 57. *See also* cosmopolitanism; postmodernism
Moglen, Helene, 76
Mondal, Anshuman, 150
The Moor's Last Sigh (Rushdie), 150
Morton, Stephen, 177n49
Mother India (film), 104
Mukherjee, Anki, 171n89
Mukherjee, Meenakshi, 45, 61, 66
Mullin, Katherine, 12, 26, 126
Murry, John, 147
Muslims. *See* Islam and Muslims
"Myth and Fabulosity in Midnight's Children" (Kanaganayakam), 51–52
myth and *Midnight's Children*, 41–43, 61

Nadel, Ira, 70

Naipaul, V. S., 47–48
Nanporia, N. J., 49–50
Nargis, 104
Nash, John, 14, 26, 39, 74–75, 77, 125, 126, 163n47
Noon, William T., 70
Norris, Margot, 28, 166n113
nostalgia, in *Satanic Verses*, 118–19

Orientalism, 79–80
orthodoxy: Christianity and, 3, 10–11; defined, 3; *Finnegans Wake* and, 144–45; modal difference between orthopraxy and, 11–12, 81; reading bodies through, 40. See also Christianity; religion
orthopraxy: defined, 3–4, 81; Irish Catholicism and, 4–5, 11–13; Islam and, 135–36; Joyce's and Rushdie's use of, 5–6; modal difference between orthodoxy and, 11–12; Muslim, 5, 157; reading bodies through orthodoxy and, 40; women's praxis, 157. See also disciplinary religion and belief; *specific works*

pain: in *Dubliners*, 26, 28–29; in *Midnight's Children*, 54, 55; Vedic vs. Western epistemology of, 57–58
"A Painful Case" (Joyce), 17, 35–39, 89, 144
parallel texts, in *Satanic Verses*, 97–98, 102–5, 102–7
Parameswaran, Uma, 51
Parekh, Bhikhu, 136
Parsipur, Shahrnush, 157
personhood. See individual subjectivity, self, and the person
Phalke, D. G., 102
phallic and phallogocentric reproduction: in *Midnight's Children*, 63–64, 65; in *Ulysses*, 91, 174n72
Pinney, Christopher, 59, 106
"Plato's Pharmakon" (Derrida), 34–35
A Portrait of the Artist as a Young Man (Joyce): Catholic foundation of, 22–23; complaints against, 124; *Dubliners* reception and, 17–18; medical paradigms in, 73; self-discipline as spiritual praxis in, 12–13; teleology of departure in, 75; *Ulysses* and, 85, 90–91
portraiture, 59, 106
postmodernism: Kundera and, 48; Lyotard on, 118; Rushdie and, 53; *Satanic Verses* and, 5, 98, 109, 115–16, 118–19
Pound, Ezra, 14, 18–24, 163n49
Prester John (Buchan), 78, 154
primitivism and *Ulysses*, 79–80
Proust, Marcel, 147
provincialism: audience and, 14; celebrity and, 141; death and, 143; *Dubliners* and, 13, 14–15, 19; in *Ground beneath Her Feet*, 154, 155; Joyce's and Rushdie's literary terrain of, 4; *Midnight's Children* and, 44–49, 52, 53, 61, 67, 68; modernism and, 9; Rushdie and, 41; *Ulysses* and, 73, 95, 98–99, 122; visibility and the provincial spiritual body, 148–49. See also Irish provincialism and Irishness
psychosomatic illness, in *Midnight's Children*, 54

Quinn, John, 22
Qu'ran, 97–98, 104–5, 112–13, 115, 137–38

racial and ethnic typologies in *Ulysses*, 84
Ramachandran, M. G., 103
Rao, M. T., 103
realism and naturalism, *Dubliners* and, 18–19, 20
redemption in *Dubliners*, 34
Rege, Josna, 66
Reizbaum, Marilyn, 70
religion: anthropological, 4, 8, 15; art-religion binary, 120–23, 157; culture and, 9–10; emotion/knowledge split in, 10–11; Joyce's universalized conception of, 73; New Criticism and, 25; "rational," 42. See also belief; disciplinary religion and belief; orthodoxy; orthopraxy; *specific religions and works*
"Religion of Art" (Cowley), 146
reverse invasion, 78–79, 114–15

Riemenschneider, Dieter, 63
Roh, Francis, 52
Roy, Parama, 100, 106
Rushdie, Salman: archaism and, 4; Booker Prize address (1982), 44; celebrity and, 141–42, 150–57; cosmopolitanism and, 5; *The Enchantress of Florence*, 150; on English vs. Indian vernacular languages, 67; *Fury*, 150; *Grimus*, 43, 45–46, 66, 155; *The Ground beneath Her Feet*, 5, 141–43, 150–57; "Imaginary Homelands," 64–65; *Joseph Anton*, 43, 142; Khomeini's death threat against, 139, 142, 150; *The Moor's Last Sigh*, 150; myth and mysticism, use of, 42–43; provincialism and, 4–5, 9; rootlessness of, 61; *Shalimar the Clown*, 150; *Shame*, 43, 45, 47. See also *Midnight's Children*; *The Satanic Verses*

salat, 135–36
Sangari, Kumkum, 53, 170n75
The Satanic Verses (Rushdie): celebrity and, 142; controversy and protests over, 67, 120–23, 134–40; gothic-religious embodiment, monstrosity, and Indian popular film in, 99–102; *Ground beneath Her Feet* and, 150, 153, 156; Indian film and Qu'ran as parallel texts in, 97–98, 102–7; Islam and reverse invasion in, 110–16; London media and monstrous simulacra in, 107–10; migrant return as vampiric in conclusion of, 116–18; Muslim orthopraxy and, 5; orthopraxy and, 5–6; *Ulysses* and *Midnight's Children* compared to, 97–98, 100, 102, 104, 119
Sayyid, Bobby, 136
Schleiermacher, Friedrich, 10
Schwarze, Tracey Teets, 165n89
Scott, Paul, 48, 49
secularization and secularism: Ireland and, 12; Irish Catholicism as strategy against, 81–82; Morton on, 177n49; split identity and, 11. See also orthodoxy

self. See individual subjectivity, self, and the person
self-discipline in *Portrait of the Artist as a Young Man*, 12–13. See also disciplined bodies
senses: attention to, in *Dubliners*, 20–21; in *Finnegans Wake*, 143, 145; integrated sensorium in *Ulysses*, 71–72, 80–88, 127–29; self-discipline in *Portrait* and, 12–13
Sethi, Sunil, 50
Shalimar the Clown (Rushdie), 150
Shame (Rushdie), 43, 45, 47
Sharma, Shailja, 139, 167n12
Shattuck, Charles, 24
Slemon, Stephen, 52
Smith, Jonathan Z., 10
Smith, Zadie, 157
somatopsychic model: in *Dubliners*, 16, 38; Kleinman on, 16; in *Midnight's Children*, 52–60, 63, 65; in *Satanic Verses*, 99, 110; in *Ulysses*, 35, 72–73, 82, 88, 94–95
soul: body and, 3, 85; Pinney on photography and, 59; *Satanic Verses* and, 101, 106, 110, 153; *Ulysses* and, 128
Spivak, Gayatri Chakravorty, 116
Squire, J. C., 21
Stephens, John, 51
strategic embodiment of agency, 101, 106, 123, 127
Suleri, Sara, 103, 113, 116
Sullivan, Kevin, 13, 70

Taylor, Lawrence, 12
temperance movements, 26–27. See also *Dubliners*
Thayer, Scofield, 20
Theall, Donald, 73, 143–44, 145
Thomas, Rosie, 102
Thomas Aquinas, St., 148
A Thousand and One Nights, 51
Tindall, William York, 147
Tinniswood, Peter, 46
Torchiana, Donald, 28
Towers, Robert, 49
transcendence: *Dubliners* and, 15; fetish

structure and, 134; *Ground beneath Her Feet* and, 155; Joyce and, 146, 149; Rushdie and, 5, 153; *Satanic Verses* and, 98, 100, 103, 112, 117–18, 153; simulacrum and, 115; *Ulysses* and, 129, 130, 132–33
Trivedi, Harish, 66

Ulysses (Joyce): alcohol and the Irish-Catholic father in, 88–93; as banned or censored, 124; "Calypso," 79, 87; celebrity and, 145–46; "Circe," 84, 89, 93–94; criticism on, 69–70, 122–23; *Dubliners* reception and, 17–18; "Eumaeus," 94; gothic tropes and reverse invasion in, 73–80; "Hades," 87; Irish-Catholic orthopraxy and, 5, 13; "Ithaca," 93–94; Larbaud on Ireland and, 163n48; "Lotos Eaters," 79–80, 89; "Nestor," 78, 84; orthopraxy and, 5–6, 82, 94–95; orthopraxy's production and integrated sensorium in, 71–72, 80–88, 127–29; "Oxen in the Sun," 89–90, 91–92; "Proteus," 75–76, 84–86, 143; religious practice and orthopraxy in, 70–73; *Satanic Verses* compared to, 97–99, 100; "Sirens," 71, 89–90; "Telemachus," 74–78, 86, 93, 100
Ulysses controversy: art-religion binary and, 120–23; Catholic discipline and, 25; responses and defenses, 131–34; themes of complaint, 124–31

Updike, John, 142

Valente, Joseph, 16, 17, 27, 29, 30, 31, 126, 161n5
van Boheemen, Christine, 12–13
van der Veer, Peter, 9
Vasudevan, Ravi, 104–5, 106, 115
Vedic medicine and philosophy, 5, 56–60
vision: *Satanic Verses* and, 104–5; *Ulysses* and, 72, 83–84, 128–29
Viswanathan, Gauri, 7, 9, 11
voice and voicelessness: in *Dubliners*, 32, 36; in *Midnight's Children*, 43, 44; in *Satanic Verses*, 102, 105, 107, 109, 113, 115; in *Ulysses*, 90, 92

Walkowitz, Rebecca, 126
Walpole, Horace, 100
War of the Worlds (Wells), 78, 109
Weber, Max, 57
Welch, Claude, 3, 10
Wells, H. G., 21, 109, 130–31, 134, 146
Wilde, Oscar, 150, 155
Wilson, David, 46
Wilt, Judith, 78
Woolsey, John, 124

Žižek, Slavoj, 16, 115, 134–35

LITERATURE, RELIGION, AND POSTSECULAR STUDIES
Lori Branch, Series Editor

Literature, Religion, and Postsecular Studies publishes scholarship on the influence of religion on literature and of literature on religion from the sixteenth century onward. Books in the series include studies of religious rhetoric or allegory; of the secularization of religion, ritual, and religious life; and of the emerging identity of postsecular studies and literary criticism.

Conspicuous Bodies: Provincial Belief and the Making of Joyce and Rushdie
    Jean Kane

Victorian Sacrifice: Ethics and Economics in Mid-Century Novels
    Ilana M. Blumberg

Lake Methodism: Polite Literature and Popular Religion in England, 1780–1830
    Jasper Cragwall

Hard Sayings: The Rhetoric of Christian Orthodoxy in Late Modern Fiction
    Thomas F. Haddox

Preaching and the Rise of the American Novel
    Dawn Coleman

Victorian Women Writers, Radical Grandmothers, and the Gendering of God
    Gail Turley Houston

Apocalypse South: Judgment, Cataclysm, and Resistance in the Regional Imaginary
    Anthony Dyer Hoefer

www.ingramcontent.com/pod-product-compliance
Lightning Source LLC
Chambersburg PA
CBHW020124240426
43673CB00038B/583